George Washington

George Washington

Ordinary Man,
    Extraordinary Leader

by ROBERT F. JONES

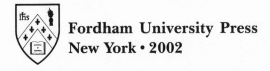 Fordham University Press
New York • 2002

Library of Congress Cataloging-in-Publication Data

Jones, Robert Francis, 1935–
    George Washington : ordinary man, extraordinary leader / Robert
F. Jones.—Rev. ed.
        p.   cm.
    Includes bibliographical references and index.
    ISBN 0-8232-2186-5—ISBN 0-8232-2187-3 (pbk.)
    1. Washington, George, 1732–1799.   2. Presidents—United
States—Biography.   I. Title.
E312 .J79   2002
973.4′1′092—dc21   2002000525

Printed in the United States of America
02   03   04   05   06   5   4   3   2   1
Revised Edition

VXORI PVLCHRISSIMAE ET SERENAE

CONTENTS

PREFACE

THIS WORK IS AN extensive revision and enlargement of my book *George Washington, A Biography,* originally published in 1979. Since 1986, Fordham University Press has published it, largely unaltered, in a paperback version. I am grateful to that press for keeping the book in print and for giving me this opportunity to incorporate in a new edition the scholarly work done on Washington and his times since the book was originally written. As with that book, what I have aimed at doing here is to synthesize the best of contemporary scholarship into a relatively brief and readable biography for the general reader and student. John Adams once predicted that the view the future would take of the American Revolution was "one continued lye from one end to the other," that "Dr. Franklin's electrified Rod smote the Earth and out sprung General Washington. . . . That Franklin electrified him with his rod—and thence forward these two conducted all the Policy, Negotiations, Legislatures and War." It has not been quite that bad, but most Americans do know only a few things about George Washington, general and president—some false, practically all distorted. I hope this book, while setting the record straight on a few of the more notable "lyes" Mr. Adams predicted, will help readers gain a proper understanding of Washington's character and of his contribution to the securing of American independence.

When I began work on this revision, I was pleasantly surprised at not only the quantity but also the quality of the scholarship that has appeared about the "Father of His Country" since 1979. A first-rate, one-volume general biography by John Ferling and special studies by Glenn Phelps, Paul Longmore, Robert Dalzelle and Lee Dalzelle, and Don Higginbotham stand out from a list too long to be given here. Perhaps the single greatest advantage a writer on Washington has today, an advantage that will increase in the future, is the editorial and publishing project *The Papers of*

George Washington, begun in the 1970s under the overall direction of William W. Abbot and continued under Dorothy Twohig and, most recently, Philander D. Chase. To date, forty-four volumes with many previously unpublished items have appeared in a text as close as possible to the original manuscripts and accompanied by extensive notes. A student of the period, at whatever level, owes a considerable debt to all those associated with this project. Finally, I want to restate my own debt to the labors of Douglas Southall Freeman and James Thomas Flexner.

In my original preface, I thanked the staffs of the Fordham University Library, the New-York Historical Society, and The New York Public Library, and I am again in their debt for the assistance I was given for this revision. Ellen Clark of the Society of the Cincinnati Library helped with illustrations. They demonstrate why the word *service* appears in librarians' job descriptions. My graduate assistants, Michael Vargas and Elizabeth Hardman, were efficient and speedy in their work. Fordham University awarded me a faculty fellowship that afforded free time to begin the serious rewriting and expansion of the biography. A series of five annual symposia on George Washington, sponsored by the Ladies of Mount Vernon and the Barra Foundation, 1995 to 1999, afforded me the opportunity to hear current scholarship and to talk informally with most of the scholars interested in Washington and his times. My original inspiration to go back to the biography came as a result of the first of these meetings. Mary V. Thompson, curatorial registrar at Mount Vernon, shared with me some of her research on slave life on the Washington estate.

As customary (and necessary), I take responsibility for any errors of fact in the text or in the attributions. As before, the dedication is an attempt to say the unsayable and to pay an unpayable debt.

RFJ
July 2001

LIST OF ILLUSTRATIONS AND MAPS

CHRONOLOGY

1732   Feb. 22 (11 O.S.), born at Wakefield, Westmoreland County, Virginia.

1733   April 12, death of father, Augustine Washington

1743   Oct. 31–Jan. 16, 1754, delivery of Governor Dinwiddie's ultimatum to the French

1754   Mar.–Oct., first campaign against the French

1755   Apr.–July, aide-de-camp to General Braddock; Aug., appointment as Colonel of the Virginia Regiment

1758   June–Nov., Forbes expedition against Fort Duquesne. July 24, elected Burgess for Frederick County (served until July 1765, then elected for Fairfax County, in which he served until 1775); Dec., resignation of commission

1759   Jan. 6, marriage to Martha Dandridge Custis

1774   Sep.–Oct., Virginia delegate to the First Continental Congress

1775   May–June, Virginia delegate to the Second Continental Congress; June 16, elected General and Commander in Chief of the Army of the Continental Congress; July 3, took command of the troops at Cambridge, Massachusetts

1776   Mar. 17, occupied Boston; Aug. 26, Battle of Long Island; Oct. 28, Battle of White Plains; Dec. 25–Jan. 3, 1777, Trenton-Princeton campaign

1777   Sep. 11, Battle of Brandywine; Oct. 4, Battle of Germantown

1778   June 28, Battle of Monmouth

1781   Aug.–Oct., Yorktown campaign, ending in the surrender of Cornwallis on Oct. 19

1783   Mar. 15, reply to Newburgh Address by mutinous officers; Dec. 23, resignation of commission before Congress at Annapolis, Maryland.

1787   May 25, elected president of the Constitutional

Convention; Sep. 17, draft of the Constitution signed and convention adjourned

1789 Feb. 4, unanimously elected President of the United States; Apr. 30, inaugurated at New York

1790 Sep., took up residence in Philadelphia, temporary capital

1792 Dec. 5, unanimously reelected president

1793 Mar. 5, inaugurated president for second term at Philadelphia; Apr. 22, Neutrality Proclamation; Dec. 18, laid cornerstone of the Capitol at Washington, D.C.

1796 Sep. 19, publication of Farewell Address (dated Sep. 17) in Philadelphia *Daily American Advertiser*

1797 Mar. 4, retirement following John Adams's inauguration as president

1798 July 4, appointment as Lieutenant General and Commander in Chief of the Armies of the United States

1799 Dec. 14, death at Mount Vernon; Dec. 18, buried in family vault

LIST OF ABBREVIATIONS

Carroll and Ashworth: John Alexander Carroll and Mary Wells Ashworth, *George Washington, A Biography* (New York: Scribner Bros., 1957). Completes the biography by Douglas Southall Freeman.

Diaries: Donald Jackson, ed., Dorothy Twohig, assoc. ed., *The Diaries of George Washington,* 6 vols. (Charlottesville: University Press of Virginia, 1975–79).

Flexner: James Thomas Flexner, *George Washington,* 4 vols. (Boston: Little, Brown, 1965–72).

Freeman: Douglas Southall Freeman, *George Washington, A Biography,* 6 vols. (New York: Scribner Bros., 1948–57).

GW Reconsidered: Don Higginbotham, ed., *George Washington Reconsidered* (Charlottesville: University Press of Virginia, 2001).

Jefferson Papers: Julian P. Boyd et al., eds. *The Papers of Thomas Jefferson,* 28 vols., to February 1796 (Princeton: Princeton University Press, 1950–2000).

Papers/Col: W. W. Abbot, ed., Dorothy Twohig, assoc. ed., *The Papers of George Washington, Colonial Series, 1748–June 1775,* 10 vols. (Charlottesville: University Press of Virginia, 1985–95).

Papers/Conf: W. W. Abbot, ed., Dorothy Twohig, assoc. ed., *The Papers of George Washington: Confederation Series, January 1784 to September 1788,* 6 vols. (Charlottesville: University Press of Virginia, 1992–97).

Papers/P: Dorothy Twohig, ed., *The Papers of George Washington: Presidential Series, September 1788–March 1797,* 9 vols. to date, to February 1792 (Charlottesville: University Press of Virginia, 1987–2000).

Papers/Ret: Dorothy Twohig and Philander D. Chase, eds., *The Papers of George Washington: Retirement Series, March 1797–December 1799,* 4 vols. (Charlottesville: University Press of Virginia, 1998–99).

Papers/Rev: Philander D. Chase, ed., *The Papers of George Wash-*

ington: Revolutionary War Series, June 1775–December 1783, 10 vols. to date, to August 1777 (Charlottesville: University Press of Virginia, 1985–2000).

Writings: John C. Fitzpatrick, ed., *The Writings of George Washington, 1745–1799,* 36 vols. (Washington, D.C.: Government Printing Office, 1931–40).

George Washington

1

In the Service of Virginia, 1732–1758

> If I shall find it worthwhile to push my Fortune in the military Line.
>
> GW to John Augustine Washington, May 14, 1755

It is a penetrating glimpse of the obvious to say that the event was not the least unusual, and there was no reason to suspect that anyone who noted it realized it was the start of a life that would help to revolutionize the English-speaking world: a Virginia planter and his second wife were blessed with their first child. On February 22, 1732, Mary Ball Washington gave birth to a baby boy who, some weeks later, was christened "George" after his mother's guardian and other family friends. The birth took place at a plantation on Pope's Creek, one of several belonging to Augustine Washington, a third-generation Virginian. Since the 1650s, the Washingtons had been active in Virginia affairs and had firmly established themselves in the middle rank of the colony's gentry. Augustine Washington did not rest content with what he inherited from his acquisitive ancestors, but enlarged his holdings, purchasing a tract on Little Hunting Creek, near the Potomac, in 1726, which became the nucleus of the future Mount Vernon. He was astute enough to see that wealth lay not only with the land and so invested in the Principio Iron Company, a venture mounted mainly by English Quakers.[1]

The Virginia into which George had been born was a little more than a century old and still showed its youth; the frontier began within a day's ride of his birthplace. The West, the frontier,

---

[1] Martin H. Quitt's "The English Cleric and the Virginia Adventurer: The Washingtons, Father and Son," in *GW Reconsidered*, 15–37, gives sketches of GW's great-grandfather and grandfather.

and the limitless challenge and opportunity that these words suggest to Americans were not abstractions but reality to the young
man, and he spent much of his early life testing himself at the
edge of settlement and beyond. But colonial Virginia was also
the home of great plantations owned by an upper class who lived,
as much as their circumstances permitted, in the style of the British gentry. A conspicuous difference, which anyone from the old
country noted at once, was the presence of slaves as field hands
and servants. Thus, the Virginia of George's youth was a land of
sharp contrasts: cultivated fields and rough wilderness, polished
gentry and ignorant bondsmen. It was an economy that, necessarily, lived off the land, cultivating the tobacco that had given it
its first taste of prosperity and was still its most important product. But in the mid–eighteenth century, the price of tobacco had
dropped to the point where it was only marginally profitable for
many planters, and the more enterprising had started to diver-
sify their interests, as witness Augustine's investment in the Principio. The pattern of Virginia's trade, however, held most
planters to tobacco. Trading directly with English or Scottish
mercantile houses, they had incurred or inherited debts that had
gradually converted them into "a species of property annexed to
certain English mercantile houses," in Thomas Jefferson's succinct phrase. Faced with large debts, most planters stayed with
the one cash crop they knew, tobacco, while some of them looked
to speculation in western lands for economic salvation, an unful-
filled hope for most of them. Virginia's tobacco economy had
passed its peak, and, in the future, prosperity would go to only
the most enterprising and diligent planters.[2]

Young George naturally knew little of this as he played about
the acres of the Little Hunting Creek plantation where the family
had moved shortly after his birth. In 1739, Augustine gave the
tract to a son of his first marriage, Lawrence, and moved the
family (a sister and three brothers had followed George) to another plantation near Fredericksburg. After Augustine died in
1743, George divided his time between home and his half-

---

[2] Bruce Ragsdale, *A Planters' Republic: The Search for Economic Independence in
Revolutionary Virginia* (Madison, Wis., 1996), 21–36; hereafter, Ragsdale, *Planters' Republic.*

brother Augustine Jr.'s home on Pope's Creek. There, either from tutors or an infant school in the neighborhood, he learned to write in a clear hand and became, for someone who probably lacked the instinct of a good speller, reasonably adept in that arcane art. He also studied composition, geography, and deportment. Only in mathematics did his schooling go beyond the elementary level, and most of that seems to have been in the practical discipline of surveying. Little more than this can be said of his childhood, possibly the period most worked on by the mythmakers because there is so little evidence to go on.[3]

His study of deportment was based on the work *Rules of Civility and Decent Behaviour*, originally compiled as a guide to young sixteenth-century Italian aristocrats serving as pages at court. Because its primary aim was to develop a consciousness of the effect one's behavior had on others, it could easily be used in the education of any youngster. Some of the more pertinent rules (there were 110) were: number 17, "Be no Flatterer"; number 25, "Superfluous Compliments and all Affectations of Ceremonie are to be avoided, yet where due they are not to be Neglected"; and number 82, "Undertake not what you cannot perform but be Carefull to keep your Promise." No biographer can resist the temptation to trace out the adult character from such juvenile influences, but any such conclusions are obviously tentative. It is my opinion that the mature Washington generally kept to the letter and spirit of these rules, but the young adult violated several of them in his ambition to get ahead; once he had attained an assured position as a Virginia planter and, perhaps, a measure of self-confidence, his conduct toward others was almost always considerate and generous.[4]

However incomplete George's education and happy his childhood, the death of his father seriously affected his present situation and future prospects. Although Augustine's estate was large, it had to be divided among seven children and his widow.

---

[3] Freeman, 1: chap. 3.

[4] Charles Moore, ed., *George Washington's Rules of Civility and Decent Behaviour in Company and Conversation* (Boston, 1936), and numerous other editions. Guthrie Sayen's "George Washington's 'Unmannerly' Behavior: The Clash between Civility and Honor," *Virginia Magazine of History and Biography* 107 (1999): 5–36, analyzes GW's success in following these guides and others.

George's share proved to be modest: Ferry Farm, near Fredericksburg, 260 acres and ten slaves, one-half of the Deep Run tract (in all, almost 2,200 acres in an area known for its poor soil), three town lots in Fredericksburg, and one-fifth of his father's residual personal property. All in all, not a splendid inheritance, it was just large enough to serve as a springboard for future advancement, but it was also large enough to support George as a planter of modest fortune.

George's relationship with his mother is something of a puzzle; Mary Washington was a strong woman, extraordinarily self-reliant. Freed by widowhood from immediate male direction, she henceforth sought advice from her brother Joseph Ball in London, far enough away to be ignored if necessary. George spent a good bit of time with his half-brothers, especially Lawrence. Mary's concern for her son was not selfish; the famous incident in which she refused to allow him to accept a proffered midshipman's post on a visiting Royal Navy vessel is a case in point. As Joseph Ball retroactively but correctly pointed out, young George lacked the "interest" needed to win advancement in the navy and fully approved of his sister's refusal. "Interest" was shorthand for the system of influence and preference by which English aristocrats pushed their chosen into positions of honor and profit. In England and throughout the British Empire generally, merit had little and who your friends were much to do with advancement under the Crown. Thus, George's career would almost certainly have been difficult and undistinguished. It is not known whether or not he appreciated how correct his mother was on this occasion, but he did submit to her decision. His attitude toward her combined, as one writer has suggested, distance and deference. Throughout her long life (she died in 1789), he made certain she lacked nothing and often corresponded with her but visited infrequently and never encouraged her to visit or live at Mount Vernon.[5]

---

[5] Freeman, 1: xix, 192–95, 198–99; however, see Don Higginbotham's "George Washington and Three Women," in *George Washington and Conceptions of the Eighteenth Century South* (Gainsville, Fl., forthcoming), in which the author acquits both GW and his mother of a lack of feeling toward each other and argues that the relationship was a strong and loving one. He also credits her with GW's independence and determination. See also his comments on George's relationship with Sally Fairfax and the Fairfax family; hereafter, Higginbotham, "Three Women."

Although "interest" in England was beyond George, its Virginia equivalent was readily available. Lawrence, a kind of surrogate father, had married Anne Fairfax, the daughter of Colonel William Fairfax, agent and cousin of the proprietor of the Fairfax Grant, initially practically all of northern Virginia. In 1747, the proprietor himself, Thomas, Lord Fairfax, chose to live on his lands and moved to a hunting lodge, Greenway Court, in the Shenandoah Valley. Thus, through Lawrence, George was well connected with the Fairfaxes and became acquainted with a genuine English lord, albeit one who preferred foxhounds to ladies and the Shenandoah to Sussex.

More important than the lord in introducing Washington to the adult world were his brother Lawrence and Colonel Fairfax. Both were well educated and had wide experience outside Virginia; when they spoke of their adventures, they may have set the boy to dreaming of similar glory. And both moved in a polished and glittering social circle, much different from the comfortable but crude circumstances of Ferry Farm or even of Greenway Court. If George developed his inclination to a military career and his refined tastes from anything other than his own innate character, then a strong influence would be the society in which he took a youthful part at Mount Vernon, the name that Lawrence gave the Hunting Creek acres, and at the adjacent Fairfax plantation, Belvoir. The Fairfaxes gave the young Virginian a taste and desire for quite a different level of Virginia society than the one into which he had been born. Belvoir probably seemed to him another and very desirable world.

His association with the Fairfaxes may have given him something far more valuable than an inclination to arms and a familiarity with genteel society. Samuel Eliot Morison has suggested that Colonel Fairfax acquainted George with Stoic philosophy, a philosophy of life that stressed the attainment of *virtus*, inadequately translated as virtue, a combination of wisdom, courage, self-control, and justice. In striving for this goal, one would put oneself beyond the touch of a rude and capricious fortune, becoming as self-sufficient as possible. The goal of this approach was not a removal from society, but rather a life of service and responsibility. As Seneca, the most useful of the Stoics, wrote: "plunge into the midst of public life . . . to try to gain office . . .

attracted . . . by the desire to be more serviceable and useful to
my friends and relatives and all my countrymen and then to all
mankind." This commitment to public service, so prominent in
George's adult life, was reinforced for him by the example of
those around him, all of whom were busy not only tending their
own plantations but also assisting in the political life of the colony. One may infer this same exemplification of the Stoic ideal
from Marcus Cunliffe's comment that there was much in Washington's career and in the Virginia society of his youth that was
Roman. Virtue was a goal, an end that would never be reached,
but in the attempt to achieve it one might acquire two priceless
gifts: an inner serenity and the well-merited applause of one's
fellow citizens. It is difficult to think of a better model or set of
precepts for someone whose life contained the trials and opportunities Washington's did.[6]

These trials and opportunities were in the future, for now
George certainly saw as more pressing the usual problems of adolescence. He was a big boy, somewhat gawky until he gained
control of his body, and was blessed with a naturally strong constitution supplemented by the rude good health of youth. He
seems to have had a natural aptitude for mathematics and somewhere learned the rudiments of surveying, not only useful for a
landowner but also a skill much in demand in the constantly
growing colony. He began to earn small sums running off simple
assignments for neighbors before he was sixteen. He went along
with his friend George William Fairfax, the colonel's son, on a
surveying party in the Shenandoah in 1748, where he sampled a
firsthand taste of the frontier. George William and he did not
find it especially to their liking, so they broke off and came home
early, but George was careful to keep a detailed journal of the
trip, soberly entering his judgment on some German squatters
the party encountered: "as ignorant a set of people as the Indians," they could not even speak English! Despite the premature
end to the trip, he had seen what the frontier required and, for

---

[6] Samuel Eliot Morison, "Young Man Washington," in *By Land and by Sea*
(New York, 1953), 168–72. Marcus Cunliffe, *George Washington: Man and Monument* (1958, repr., New York, n.d.),162–63; hereafter, Cunliffe, *Man and Monument*.

a sixteen-year-old boy from comfortable circumstances, dealt satisfactorily with it.[7]

In 1749, George qualified as the official surveyor for Culpeper County and could now sign surveys and work anywhere within the province. This occupation gave him an assured income, and within a year he had saved enough to buy almost 1,500 acres on Bullskin Creek in the Shenandoah. In colonial Virginia, surveyors were in a particularly advantageous position to pick up attractive tracts of land at low prices. They were also well paid for their labors, as befitted their status as members of a respected profession. In 1751, George interrupted his surveying to accompany Lawrence, who had contracted tuberculosis, on a trip to Barbados. Surveyors could work conveniently only in the fall and the spring, when the bare trees gave them clear sight lines. George sacrificed the fall season for the trip. Not only did Lawrence not improve, but George came down with smallpox and fought off the disease only with difficulty. Lawrence decided to go on to Bermuda and sent George home before he lost another season. He was back in Virginia before the end of January 1752, thus ending the only trip he would ever make outside the continental limits of the future United States. He immediately resumed his surveying and within two months was able to add another 500 acres to the Bullskin tract.[8]

Despite his steady employment and land purchasing, he also had the usual concerns of any twenty-year-old young man and in the spring of 1752 gave fair warning to William Fauntleroy that he would presently visit his plantation to secure "a revocation of the former cruel sentence" that Fauntleroy's fifteen-year-old daughter Betsy had imposed; like some of his later campaigns, this one was a failure. This incident was not his first disappointment in romance; earlier he had been taken with an unnamed "lowland beauty" and sometime around 1748 had started an

---

[7] "A Journal of my Journey over the Mountains," Mar. 11–Apr. 13, 1748, *Diaries*, 1: 6–23.

[8] Philander D. Chase, "A Stake in the West: George Washington as Backcountry Surveyor and Landholder," in Warren R. Hofstra, ed., *George Washington and the Virginia Backcountry*, 159–94 (Madison, Wis., 1998); hereafter, Hofstra, *Backcountry*. See also Sarah S. Hughes, *Surveyors and Statesmen: Land Measuring in Colonial Virginia* (Richmond, Va., 1979), 92, 93, 125, 156 ff. "Voyage to Barbados, 1751–52," *Diaries*, 1: 24–117, editorial note and facsimile.

acrostic poem to Frances Alexander. Although he managed to get past the X with "Xerxes that great, was't free from Cupid's dart," the poem was never finished. Probably, as in most such efforts, Frances or George or Cupid, or possibly all three, lost interest.[9]

This busy, happy life was marred by Lawrence's death in July 1752, a loss that deprived George of the person to whom he had looked the most often for guidance. He had lost more than a mentor and a brother; he had lost a friend. His regard for Lawrence was seen in his refusal to rename Mount Vernon when he rented it from Lawrence's widow, Anne Lee, in 1754. When she died in 1761, the estate became his according to the terms of Augustine's will. Another kind of bequest came in George's appointment as adjutant of the Northern Neck District, in charge of militia training, a post Lawrence had formerly held and carrying with it a provincial commission as a major and a salary of one hundred pounds a year. Because this commission came, as it did, almost on his twenty-first birthday, Major Washington may have regarded it as a kind of birthday gift and reflected that for a younger son of small fortune and uncertain prospects he had not done badly since his father's death ten years earlier. He now had assured employment as a surveyor; owned almost 5,000 acres of land in various parcels; had a strong constitution, having already survived malaria, smallpox, and pleurisy; could travel and survive in the wild; and, for someone with limited formal education, could write a reasonably good letter. He was well equipped to open a new act in his life; he would now try, as he later put it, "to push my Fortune in the military Line."

Washington's opportunity came because of a worldwide contest for empire and profit between England and France that had been going on since the end of the seventeenth century. Since 1748 there had been a truce in the struggle. Although the truce could have been broken at any one of a dozen places around the globe, the break happened to come on the American frontier. In 1753, the French had begun to push south from Lake Erie toward the Forks of the Ohio (the confluence of the Allegheny, Monongahela, and Ohio Rivers and the site of present-day Pitts-

---

[9] "Poetry," GW to William Fauntleroy Sr., May 20, 1752, *Papers/Col*, 1: 47, 49.

burgh), an area that both Virginia and Pennsylvania claimed. Robert Dinwiddie, Virginia's lieutenant governor since 1751, regarded the American colonies as one of the richest assets of the British Empire and did all he could to convince Virginia's penurious and unwilling legislature, the House of Burgesses, to head off French occupation of what was obviously the key to the Ohio Valley. Boosting Governor Dinwiddie's interest was a share in the Anglo-American Ohio Company, which had received a contingent land grant in the area. Into this tangle of imperial, colonial, and private selfishness, with implications reaching far beyond even the vast area immediately concerned, George Washington was sent, hardly conscious of the consequences of his actions.

Governor Dinwiddie, a Scot who was an energetic and reasonably effective administrator, had a charge from the king to secure the Forks against the French. The first step was to be a formal warning, for which he needed a messenger. Possibly tipped off by Colonel Fairfax, Washington went to Williamsburg and secured the charge. He was directed to deliver the warning to the French commander and to return with a reply and whatever knowledge he could gather of the strength and intentions of the French. Although the mission had its dangers, its successful fulfillment could bring the young man future preferment. By November 14, 1753, he had reached Wills Creek (later Cumberland, Maryland), where he convinced Christopher Gist, an experienced frontiersman, to accompany him. When he reached the Forks, he discovered the French were still in the north, but before he moved, he gathered members of the friendly local Delaware tribe for a conference. Here he showed his greenness in dealing with them. When the leader, Tanachariston, the "Half-King" (so called because the Delaware were vassals of the Iroquois), regaled him with the ferocious speech that he, Tanachariston, had delivered to the French commander, Major Washington only soberly asked the best way to French headquarters instead of replying in kind by describing the immense power and implacable will of the British king. But he learned quickly and consented readily to wait while some ceremonial wampum belts, to be returned to the French as indicators of the Half-King's anger, were brought from another village. Fort LeBouef and the French commander were finally reached on December 11, and

Washington delivered Dinwiddie's formal notice to the French that they were trespassing on the lands of the king of England. While waiting for the reply, the major determined that the French were going to move south with the spring floods. He was also given some anxious moments by French attempts to seduce the natives, confiding to his journal: "I can't say that ever in my Life I suffered so much Anxiety as I did in this Affair." Despite the adolescent hyperbole, the comment showed he appreciated the importance of the natives to the success of either side.

Washington managed to get both the Indians and himself away on December 16, and after an eventful and difficult trip (he was shot at by a native whom he and Gist encountered, and he fell into the icy Allegheny), he reached Wills Creek on January 2. Leaving Gist, he rode alone to Williamsburg and delivered the French reply to Dinwiddie on January 16: it was a polite but firm refusal to move until ordered by their king. Along with the reply, Washington gave the governor valuable information on the strength and intentions of the French and the solidity of the native tribes' attachment to the British. All in all, a creditable performance by an inexperienced twenty-one-year-old militia officer. To Washington's surprise, Dinwiddie asked for a formal report, and the major sat up half the night throwing together a narrative from his rough notes. Pleased with the report, the governor ordered it printed and distributed throughout the colonies and that copies be sent to London, so that before Washington was twenty-two, his name had spread well beyond his own colony, even to London and to George III.[10]

Now that the aggressive intentions of the French in the area of the Forks were known, Dinwiddie moved to place an English presence there and bent all his efforts to convince the burgesses to raise and support a regiment of soldiers. After they had complied, the governor added a land bounty of 200,000 acres on the Ohio to supplement the enlisted men's pay of eight pennies a day. Washington's interest was not strong enough to secure him command of the force—which went to Joshua Fry, a man with

---

[10] "Journey to the French Commandant, Oct. 31, 1753–Jan. 16, 1754," *Diaries,* 1: 118–61; "Instructions from Robert Dinwiddie, Oct. 30, 1753," *Papers/ Col,* 1: 60–61.

wide public experience who had lately moved to the frontier—
but he was given the lieutenant colonelcy. Despite his openly expressed disappointment at finding his salary much below that of
an officer on royal service, he accepted and, at Dinwiddie's order,
took the men already enlisted toward the Ohio. An independent
command, at least until Colonel Fry caught up, was some compensation. Although Washington was ordered to act defensively,
he was also to "restrain" any trespassers and "in Case of resistance to make Prisoners of or kill and destroy them." If Dinwiddie wanted to put the onus for starting any hostilities on the
French, and such was the clear intention of the Crown's orders
to him, he did not make this plan clear to his subordinate.[11]

Arriving at Wills Creek with 159 ill-trained, ill-supplied men,
Washington learned that the French had pushed some men employed by the Ohio Company away from the Forks and had
begun a fort. He decided to move on toward the Forks, building
a road as he went so that an attack might be more easily mounted
once Fry arrived and also to reassure the Half-King, who was
increasingly anxious about his alliance with the British. The hard
work of road building added to Washington's and, according to
him, his officers' discontent over their inferior pay. News that
two independent companies, with officers on royal service, were
on their way only increased the young officer's anxiety because
those officers might also claim the superior authority their royal
commissions gave them, regardless of rank. This situation
aroused all Washington's ire about his low pay, and he angrily
threatened Dinwiddie with his resignation if his pay were not
raised to the royal standard; rather than dishonor himself by
serving for a pittance, he would serve as an unpaid volunteer.

In late May 1754, the force reached the Great Meadows, approximately fifty miles southeast of the Forks, where Washington
was told of a large French scouting party nearby. On the morning of May 28, the Virginians and some Indian allies surrounded
the French and attacked them. In the brief skirmish that followed, several Frenchmen, including their commander, the Sieur

[11] Robert Dinwiddie to GW, [Jan. 1754], *Papers/Col*, 1: 65. GW's reconstructed
diary entries for the period Mar.–June 1754 are in "Expedition to the Ohio,
Mar. 31–Jun. 27,1754," *Diaries*, 1: 162–210; the events are fully described in
Freeman, 1: chaps. 10–12.

de Jumonville, were killed. Only then did the French, who had been camped in a well-hidden glade, produce documents supporting their claim that their mission was peaceful: to deliver an order from their commander that the British leave their lands. Washington rejected their claim; he reasoned that a peaceful party would not have hidden themselves away, nor were thirty men needed to deliver such a message. Implicitly he was using his own conduct the previous winter as a standard. Although the French claim was dubious, it sufficed to give them propaganda when Washington later inadvertently reinforced it.

In reporting to the governor, the young officer clearly showed what was most on his mind. Only after repeating most of his complaints about pay and conditions of service did he tell Dinwiddie about the skirmish and its results. He described the encounter more vividly to his brother, concluding with the self-confident observation: "I heard the bullets whistle, and, believe me, there is something charming in the sound." Realizing that the French were probably in force in the area, Washington pulled up short at the Meadows and began to build a small post, Fort Necessity. Presently he learned of Fry's death and of his own appointment as colonel, but neither this news nor the arrival of additional Virginians along with an independent company of South Carolinians commanded by a cooperative Captain James Mackay cheered him. Supplies were always uncertain, and his Delaware allies were becoming more and more fainthearted. The Iroquois Council had ordered their dependent tribes to be neutral, and the Half-King was understandably concerned about defying his overlords by staying with a loser. Assessing the situation of the British in the area, a council of officers on June 28 advised the colonel to pull back to Wills Creek. Low supplies, inadequate transport, and the exhaustion of the men meant that even this move could not be done quickly, and while Washington prepared for the withdrawal, the Half-King considered his alternatives and left some time during the night of July 2. The young commander was not worried about the delay in his own departure because he was quite proud of his fort. Actually, it was poorly sited, within musket shot of the woods, and too small for the force he had; it well deserved the Half-King's derisive description as "that little thing upon the Meadow."[12]

The Delawares had not gotten away a moment too soon. As the morning of July 3 came, gray with the promise of rain, French scouts were seen in the neighborhood. By noon, the fort was surrounded and under fire from the forest. The rain and the gunfire continued through the day, with the defenders being able to make little reply. By nightfall, with the powder wet and the men weary and disorderly, having broken into the rum supply, resistance was almost at an end. From the darkness, a shouted "*Voulez-vous parler?*" was heard and refused, but a second offer to treat outside the fort was accepted. There the Virginians' interpreter, Adam VanBraam, working from a smudged copy by a guttering candle in the rainy night, explained the surprisingly moderate French terms. The enemy commander was having trouble with his own native allies and with supplies, and feared the imminent arrival of enemy reinforcements; thus, a quick surrender was as advantageous for the French as it was necessary for Washington. But hidden in the capitulation agreement was a statement that Washington's party was responsible for Jumonville's "assassination"; VanBraam mistranslated this word as "death." The colonel's signature on the agreement was a virtual admission that he was a murderer, and the French later made much of this admission when they issued a statement justifying the resumption of hostilities.[13]

Washington managed to bring approximately 165 of his force of 400 back to Wills Creek, most of the losses being caused by desertion. Although the first verdict on Washington's command was favorable and sympathetic, it was soon qualified, and he was accused of impetuosity and disobedience to orders, among other things. Few of the charges had much substance; his orders, for

[12] GW to Robert Dinwiddie, May 29, 1754, to John Augustine Washington, May 31, 1754, to Robert Dinwiddie, June 10, 1754, *Papers/Col*, 1: 107–13, 118, 129–38. "George Washington's Account of the Capitulation of Fort Necessity," [1786], *Papers/Col*, 1: 172–73; Frederick Tilberg, "Washington's Stockade at Fort Necessity," *Pennsylvania History* 20 (1953): 240–57.

[13] Freeman, 1: 402–12, treats this episode fully; see also his "The Capitulation at Fort Necessity," appendix I–10.

example, were vague and left much to his judgment; whether or not he disobeyed them is a moot point. Impetuosity was a fair enough charge, but what should Dinwiddie have expected from an inexperienced officer eager to prove himself in his first command? Caution and circumspection developed slowly in Washington, as a person and as an officer, and only as the result of strenuous self-discipline. The basic problem in the Fort Necessity campaign was the lack of men and supplies. Virginia alone could not throw back the French, as attempted in 1754; in some respects, the campaign was a miniature rehearsal of what Washington would have to endure later during the War for Independence. On his return to Williamsburg, the colonel discovered that Dinwiddie had decided to break up the regiment into ten companies, with no officer higher than a captain. Washington angrily refused the offer of one of the captaincies and resigned his commission in October. His first attempt to push his "Fortune in the military Line" had come to an end.[14]

But he had not given up, and while he rested at Belvoir, interesting rumors were circulating around the colony, rumors that were soon confirmed. A new expedition was to be sent against the Forks, organized around a nucleus of British regulars commanded by General James Braddock. The general arrived at Alexandria in February 1755, and Washington lost no time in making himself known, sending a rather unctuous congratulatory note assuring Braddock that the French would presently be pushed out of the Ohio Valley. In part because of this note but probably more because of Dinwiddie's recommendation, Washington was invited to go along as a volunteer aide on Braddock's staff. He hesitated, balancing the costs of his neglect of Mount Vernon against the benefits of a possible royal commission issued on the recommendation of a successful general. Hope won out over practical considerations, and he accepted. Washington left Mount Vernon in the care of his younger brother John Augustine ("Jack"), and he joined Braddock at Frederick, Maryland, early in May.

---

[14] This episode was actually the opening of the French and Indian War; its American phase is narrated in Fred Anderson, *Crucible of War: The Seven Years War and the Fate of Empire in British North America* (New York, 2000).

Braddock was already experiencing the frustration that his new aide had experienced the previous year. The truth seems to have been that, even with all the guineas in the world, Virginia's economy was too oriented toward the production of tobacco and its settlement too dispersed to serve as a supply base for a large military force. The wild, mountainous terrain between Frederick and the Forks only magnified the supply problem. After leaving Wills Creek on May 7, Braddock could cover only a little more than two miles a day and consulted with Washington on how things might be speeded up. The Virginian suggested splitting the force in two; one unit with most of the infantry would move ahead, relieved of the baggage and heavy artillery, which would come on behind. Braddock accepted the advice in the hope of blocking the advance of French reinforcements to the Forks. Unfortunately, Washington was sick with typhoid and had to stay with the second unit until he recovered.

By July 8, Washington had joined the first unit, which was only twelve miles from the Forks. Early the next morning the men set out on what they expected to be their last day of marching; for too many of them it was their last day. A tricky double crossing of the winding Monongahela was pulled off successfully, and the way seemed clear to the Forks. Braddock ordered the band to play "The Grenadier's March," and the redcoats moved through the forest almost as if it were Hyde Park. But the general was no fool, so flankers and an advance party guarded the main force. All this preparation meant nothing when, shortly before noon, the advance party was surprised by a mixed force of French and Iroquois, who themselves had not expected to find the British so close to the Forks. The hurried retreat of the advance men threw the main body into confusion, and they were unable to prevent themselves from being surrounded by the more adaptable enemy. The British were now on a sunken pathway through a thick forest and receiving heavy fire from the hidden enemy. The men began to bunch up in the center of the path and to fire their muskets indiscriminately; when the officers tried to form them into lines and start them toward the enemy, they refused to leave the specious safety of the open area. Trained for an entirely different kind of fighting, the redcoats were at a serious disadvantage and soon panicked. Washington and the other officers were prime targets; near the end of the battle, Braddock took a ball through his lungs, but the Virginian was luckier. Although he lost two horses and several shots went through his clothes, he survived the day unscathed—either the purest luck or perhaps Providence, for he behaved with "the greatest courage and resolution," according to Robert Orme, one of Braddock's aides.

More than courage was needed as the retreat degenerated into a rout. After discipline was restored, Washington was sent to get help from the second unit. All night he moved slowly through the almost impenetrable darkness, occasionally falling over wounded men who had fled the action, to find Colonel Thomas Dunbar already aware of the defeat and ready to move forward. The division of the force had been especially fortunate because it gave the remnants of the first unit a nearby refuge, albeit a temporary one. Reforming his units, Braddock discovered he had lost 977 of the 1,459 men he had taken forward with him. Late on the night of July 13, another figure was added to the casualty list when the general himself died. Courageous but obstinate, a solid, conventional tactician, he was the wrong man in a task for which there was, quite possibly, no right man. Three days after his general's death, Colonel Dunbar brought the survivors into Fort Cumberland and prepared them for the march to Philadelphia and winter quarters.

They had made a good many mistakes in the expedition, but Washington fastened on the unexpected time and place of the battle. Braddock had expected trouble at the Monongahela fords; once past them he had assumed the expedition would not be molested until it reached the Forks. For their part, the French had wanted to hit the British at the fords but had been delayed by trouble with the Iroquois; they were hurrying toward the fords when they encountered the redcoats. When the shooting began, "Victory was their [the French company's] smallest expectation," as Washington put it. The quick flexibility of the French and Iroquois as well as the unfamiliarity of the British with the forest setting and proper tactics almost dictated the outcome of the battle. Washington had been taught a valuable lesson on the virtues of adaptability. Before the end of July, he was convalescing at Mount Vernon from both typhoid and the exertions of the campaign.[15]

Dunbar's withdrawal left Virginia defenseless, and Governor Dinwiddie had no alternative but to ask the burgesses once again to tap the colony's resources. They responded quickly and, for the time being, generously with forty thousand pounds to support a regiment of 1,000 soldiers and several companies of rangers. Although Washington had come to regret the cost of his earlier service to Virginia, he could not refuse the colonelcy of the new regiment if it were offered because it was equivalent to his old position. The Stoic concept of duty dictated that if the post were "offer'd upon such terms as can't be objected against, it wou'd reflect eternal dishonor upon me to refuse it." For all his sincere concern about duty and honor, Washington nevertheless made certain the terms could not be "objected against" before he accepted Dinwiddie's offer of a provincial colonelcy in August 1755, securing increased pay and control of the selection of officers.[16]

The colonel began his duties with a flurry of activity that reflected the urgency of his task and the accuracy of Dinwiddie's description of him as "a man of great merit and resolution." But more than good character was going to be needed to defend a frontier several hundred miles long against roving bands of natives. Soon, as Washington remembered it in 1786, "the frontiers were continually harassed, but not having enough force to carry the war [to the Forks], he could do no more than distribute the Troops along the Frontiers in the Stockaded Forts; more with a

---

[15] The campaign is described in Freeman, 2: chaps. 2–4. See also *Papers/Col*, 1: 241–364, for GW's letters. See "Biographical Memoranda" (1786) for Washington's later description of the action, in Rosemary Zagarri, ed., *David Humphreys' "Life of General Washington" with George Washington's "Remarks"* (Athens, Ga., 1991), 10–22; hereafter, Zagarri, *Humphreys' "Life."* Documents can be found in Carson I. A. Ritchie, ed., *General Braddock's Expedition* (London, 1962), and in Charles Hamilton, ed., *Braddock's Defeat* (Norman, Okla., 1959). Robert Orme's comment is in William M. Darlington, ed., *Christopher Gist's Journals* (Pittsburgh, 1893), 268. Don Higginbotham analyzes GW's experience with Braddock in *George Washington and the American Military Tradition* (Athens, Ga., 1985), part 1; hereafter Higginbotham, *Tradition.*

[16] GW to Mary Washington, Aug. 15, 1755, "Commission," "Instructions" from Robert Dinwiddie, Aug. 15, 1755, *Papers/Col*, 1: 359–60, 2: 3–7.

view to quiet the fears of the Inhabitants than from any expectation of giving securities in so extensive a line to the settlements."

The only false note here is Washington's apparent acquies-
cence; he acquiesced in nothing and worked almost without rest
to deploy the inadequate resources he had for his task. The fron-
tiersmen tended to panic at the least sign of natives; the militia
were reluctant to turn out, even when their families were safe in
protected settlements; impressment of men and supplies
brought threats of violence against the colonel; and few of his
subordinates performed satisfactorily, throwing an even heavier
burden on him. The regiment's soldiers had been conscripted
into service in order to fill out quotas imposed on the counties
and came mainly from the lowest ranks of Virginia society. Discipline, especially for desertion, was severe and readily meted out.
The colonel was not able to see the humor of a panic in Winches-
ter caused, as his own personal investigation disclosed, by "3
drunken Soldiers of the Light-Horse" firing their muskets in a
clearing near the town. The "raiding party" was marched off to
the guardhouse to sober up, helped along by a number of lashes
on their bare backs. Dinwiddie responded to the colonel's endless requests for more support with endless requests to the burgesses, even while he counseled the younger man to be patient
and to persist. Unfortunately for both the governor and the colonel, the burgesses supported the regiment only grudgingly after
their initial appropriation, making a difficult task practically impossible. To Washington, acutely eager for public esteem and
anxious about the effect of the unit's poor performance on his
reputation, the frustrations of command were severe, causing
him to be unreasonably demanding of—at times, downright in-
subordinate to—the governor, whose situation was almost as
frustrating as his own, and to grasp eagerly at a royal commission
as if it were a magic talisman that would instantly cure all his
problems.[17]

---

[17] Higginbotham, *Tradition*, 16–33. Hofstra, *Backcountry*, has several relevant
essays, especially those by Robert D. Mitchell, Warren D. Hofstra, and John E.
Ferling. James Titus's *The Old Dominion at War: Society, Politics, and Warfare in
Late Colonial Virginia* (Columbia, S.C., 1991) is a detailed and perceptive analysis of its topic, especially the Virginia Regiment. Freeman, 2: chaps. 6–16, gives
a detailed description of events.

The young officer's pride and insecurity were clearly seen when he encountered Captain John Dagworthy, who had once possessed a royal commission, in command of a Maryland force at Fort Cumberland. Dagworthy claimed precedence over Washington because of his royal commission, and when unable to talk Dagworthy out of the claim, Washington simply stayed away from Cumberland, even recommending to Dinwiddie that Virginia abandon the fort despite its obvious value. Throughout the quarrel, Dinwiddie loyally supported Washington, even permitting him to go to Boston in February and March 1756 to get a ruling on the matter from Governor William Shirley, the commander in chief of His Majesty's forces in North America at the time. Shirley's decision did not settle the matter, and Washington continued to avoid the fort, even disobeying a direct order from Dinwiddie. The governor forgave this disobedience and again permitted Washington a furlough, this time to carry his case to New York and Lord Loudoun, the new commander in chief. In presenting his position to Loudoun in the spring of 1757, the colonel styled himself "free from guile," but he nevertheless accompanied a request for royal commissions for himself and his officers with a description of Dinwiddie as obstructive and interfering, hardly a fair verdict. Washington was so anxious about his own reputation and eager for a royal commission that he could not see the situation clearly enough to do justice to his immediate superior. Loudoun ignored the petition. Fortunately, Dinwiddie returned to Britain in 1757, leaving Washington to work things out with his successor.[18]

Almost coincidental with Dinwiddie's retirement, the king's new chief minister, William Pitt, ordered an offensive in North America in 1758 that aimed at several strategic points, including the Forks of the Ohio, where the French had built Fort Duquesne. Hoping to ensure a full-strength colonial effort, Pitt opened wide the royal purse, offering to subsidize liberally the colonies' forces. Using Philadelphia as his base, Brigadier General John Forbes commanded the effort against the Forks. Vir-

---

[18] GW to Robert Dinwiddie, Jan. 14, 1756, Robert Dinwiddie to GW, Jan. 22, 1756, GW to John Campbell, Earl of Loudoun, Jan. 10, 1757, *Papers/Col*, 2: 283–85, 290–93, 4: 79–90.

ginia's new governor, Francis Fauquier, received authorization for a second regiment from the burgesses along with permission for both regiments to go outside the colony. Assisted by British funds, things went smoothly, and Washington and his colleague Colonel William Byrd III took almost 2,000 men into the field with Washington as a courtesy "brigadier" at their head. Washington's desire to "be distinguished in some measure from the *common run* of provincial officers" (emphasis in original) seemed about to be satisfied: he was now to be adequately supported, with a reasonable number of men who had freely enlisted for a ten-pound bounty, was to be given increased pay, and was working under a skilled and successful commander.

The expedition began well, with Forbes and his subordinate, Colonel Henry Bouquet, consulting the provincial officers and adopting some of their suggestions, including Washington's idea of hunting shirts and leggings as a suitable uniform for the wild. But the possibility of dissension was there from the beginning. Forbes was to cut a road as he went. Expecting peacetime civilian traffic to follow it, both Pennsylvania and Virginia wanted the road inside their borders. Starting from Philadelphia, Forbes was predisposed to push straight across Pennsylvania, but the Virginians argued strongly to bend the road south at Raystown so that it would meet Braddock's old road at Cumberland. Although this route was longer, they argued that taking it would go more quickly than building a new road. Forbes was no fool; he was well aware of the provincial rivalry and discounted both sides' arguments. Delay did not frighten him because the British were already working on the native tribes elsewhere with diplomacy (and gifts), and the coming of winter always made the "savages" eager to return to their villages and prepare for cold weather. Time only improved the effectiveness of both these factors. Finally, other British forces were moving against other French posts; the success of any of them would weaken the French position at Duquesne. None of these points seemed significant to Washington as he persistently advocated Braddock's road as the only reasonable choice. Even after Forbes had decided to push straight across from Raystown, Washington hinted darkly that he and Bouquet were the "d[u]pes, or something worse to P[enn]-s[yl]v[ania]n Artifice." And his prophecy of disaster should the force not use Braddock's road seemed about to come true as the expedition apparently bogged down in mid-November, still approximately fifty miles from Duquesne. But intelligence came, via a French deserter, that Duquesne was weakly manned and that the French had been abandoned by their native allies. Twenty-five hundred men, Washington's regiment among them, were sent forward on a reconnaissance; they found the fort burned and deserted. By the end of November, the Forks were in British hands. Washington did not understand how Forbes had succeeded where Braddock had failed and claimed that the "possession of this fort has been a matter of great surprise to the whole army," a statement Forbes would have resented had he seen it. The British general's slow, steady advance while the factors mentioned above were working had pushed the French away from the Forks with no more luck than is commonly found in human affairs.[19]

The colonial troops were sent back to their respective colonies, except for a small unit of Virginians assigned to garrison Fort Pitt over the winter while Forbes took his Scottish Highlanders, the only regulars in the expedition, back to Philadelphia. While riding through the now familiar country between Fort Pitt and Williamsburg, Washington must frequently have mulled over his recent experiences and reaffirmed the decision he had made unconsciously before the campaign had begun. As his imprudent support of Braddock's road had shown, he was now putting provincial concerns ahead of his desire for a royal commission. Why else would he antagonize Forbes by so assiduously pushing Virginia's interest? He was going to resign his commission, return to Mount Vernon, and tend to his lands. The attempt to push his "Fortune in the military Line" was at an end.

Unbeknownst to him, Washington had learned much that would help him get through his next effort "in the military Line." Many of the problems he encountered in commanding

---

[19] Freeman, 2: chaps.18, 20. Niles Anderson's "The General Chooses a Road—The Forbes Campaign of 1758 to Capture Fort Duquesne," *Western Pennsylvania Historical Magazine* 42 (1959): 109–38, 241–58, 383–401, has much of the relevant correspondence. GW to John Stanwix, Apr. 10, 1758, to John Robinson, Sep. 1, 1758, to Francis Fauquier, Nov. 28, 1758, *Papers/Col,* 5: 117–18, 432–33, 6: 158–60.

the Continental forces during the War for Independence had been present with the Virginia Regiment: poor and sometimes grudging support by a suspicious legislature, recalcitrant militia and local authorities, and an enemy who seemed to have all the advantages. This experience had taught him more than he knew. His officers wrote a "Humble Address" on the occasion of his resignation. It was unstinting in its praise and affection for a commander who, they insisted, had schooled them thoroughly in command; it speaks volumes for Washington's ability to inspire and gain the affection of those who served immediately under him. He had learned his military science in the same school all officers, provincial and royal, did—the field—and had gained the respect not only of his own officers but of most of the British officers with whom he had served. Ironically, one of his major shortcomings, a lack of respect for civilian authority or, as Don Higginbotham has put it, for "civil control of the military *and all that it meant*" (emphasis in original) would somehow be turned into one of his most admirable and valuable traits during the War for American Independence.[20]

---

[20] Higginbotham, *Tradition*, 38.

2

Gentleman, Planter, Rebel, 1759–1775

> I am now, I believe, fixed at this Seat with an agreable
> Consort for Life, and hope to find more happiness in
> retirement than I ever experienced amidst a wide and
> bustling World.
>
> GW to Richard Washington, September 20, 1759

THE COLONEL had not returned to Mount Vernon to sulk; there
was far too much to do. He had proposed to Martha Dandridge
Custis sometime in the spring of 1758, and now the wedding was
scheduled for early in 1759. The couple began their union with
a high regard for one another that matured into a quiet and
deep love, a love that calmed and nourished both. Mrs. Custis
was a widow with a large estate to administer and two children to
raise; she was probably as glad to hand the properties over to her
new husband as he was pleased to have a wife to grace—and to
run—the house at Mount Vernon. The marriage certainly had
elements of convenience for both parties. At their marriage on
January 6, 1759, at the Custis home, the White House, on the
Pamunkey River in New Kent County, the colonel and his lady
made a contrasting couple. Washington was more than six feet
tall, reasonably slim at 175 pounds, whereas Martha was just over
five feet tall and amiably described herself as plump. Whereas
his general build was large-boned, she was petite; and whereas
his demeanor was "at all times composed and dignified," she
was smiling and chatty. It was more a study in complementary
attributes than in opposites.[1]

---

[1] George Washington's description is by George Mercer in W. S. Baker, ed.,
Early Sketches of George Washington (Philadelphia, 1894), 13–14. In "Three
Women," Higginbotham describes the relationship and also treats sensibly
GW's association with the Fairfax family, especially Sally.

Washington's lands had been neglected despite his brother's stewardship, neglect for which he did not blame him, but which nevertheless was real. He described his situation when he later asked a friend to "consider under what terrible management and disadvantages I found my Estate when I retired from the Public Service of this Colony; and that besides some purchases of Land and Negroes I was necessitated to make . . . I had provisions of all kinds to buy for the first two or three years; and my Plantation to stock in short with everything; buildings to make, and other matters, which swallowed up, well before I knew where I was, all the money got by Marriage, nay more, brought me into debt."

Washington would remain in debt until 1773, when his step-daughter died and he inherited the child's estate, more than enough to balance the debit owed the London firm with which he corresponded. This would be the culmination of a process he had begun in 1759 with the improvements made to Mount Vernon. The property then consisted of 5,518 acres; further purchases would increase it to 8,000 acres. He also owned Ferry Farm, but his mother lived there and took its income, and some 7,000 acres in the Piedmont and the Shenandoah Valley, none of it especially valuable then. All in all, it was a slim enough base, but with hard work and systematic management it would do.[2]

Although Martha had brought with her a substantial fortune, much of it was dowered to her when Daniel Custis died without a will; her "widow's third" was hers only for life. The children's thirds were held in trust until their majority. As noted, when the little girl, Martha, died in 1773, her property became Washington's. During the War for Independence, Washington deputed his friend George Mason to act as trustee for John Parke Custis, noting that he had taken none of his personal expenses in administering the estate. The income of the estate had doubled during Washington's trusteeship, abundant evidence of the intelligence and integrity with which he had discharged the trust.[3]

The charges for improving the plantation seemed all the more onerous when placed against the obvious need to enlarge the

[2] GW to Robert Stuart, Apr. 27, 1763, *Papers/Col,* 7: 205–7; Flexner, 1: 286.

[3] H. T. Louthan, "The Estate of J. P. Custis," *William and Mary Quarterly,* 2d series, 23, no. 2 (April 1943): 209–11; GW to George Mason, May 10, 1776, *Papers/Rev,* 4: 262–63.

mansion house. The house into which Martha moved in 1759 was a cramped one-and-half-story farmhouse. For now, Washington simply added a second story to this structure. Later, as his finances improved and entertaining increased, he added a three-story wing on the west end of the original building. This addition gave him a library on the first floor, a bedroom and dressing rooms for Martha and him on the second, and a third-floor bedroom, probably used by John Parke Custis. An east wing, consisting of a formal dining room on the first floor with a ceiling so high that it took up almost two of the projected three floors was being planned when the war broke out in 1775. It would be completed shortly after the war, construction having proceeded fitfully while it lasted. To get the effect of stone without its expense, the exterior boards were grooved to resemble blocks and sand added to give a rough texture to the surface. The piazza on the river side was also added after the war, giving the house its best-known appearance. This piazza was Washington's personal innovation, designed to give him a place to exercise in bad weather and to take tea and enjoy the view in good weather. Washington designed these additions and also took charge of the interior decoration. He relied on buildings he knew and on some architectural manuals, along with the advice of craftsmen. The result was original, combining both a grand appearance with a comfortable interior.[4]

Perhaps in compensation for the lonely evenings he spent during his military service, Washington entertained frequently. Some of this socializing was imposed by necessity from the distances to be traveled and the absence of comfortable inns, and some by tradition. Washington was true to the tradition; between 1768 and 1775, he and Martha had approximately two thousand dinner guests, most of them staying on for at least one night. Most of the guests were friends and neighbors—George Mason of Gunston Hall, just the other side of Belvoir, and of course the Fairfaxes, along with some of Martha's family. Conventional in

---

[4] Robert Dalzell and Lee Dalzell's *George Washington's Mount Vernon: At Home in Revolutionary America* (New York, 1998) deals with all aspects of the estate; chapters 3, 4, and 5 discuss the architecture and construction of the building; hereafter, Dalzells, *Mount Vernon*. Allan Greenberg's *George Washington, Architect* (London, 1999) is an architect's study of the building and its grounds.

his entertaining, Washington was also conventional in his sports, riding to the hounds, duck shooting, and card playing. But here his urge to keep records surfaced, and in January 1775 he carefully calculated his winnings and losses for the last three years and soberly entered a debit of £6.3.3, "By. Balc.ᵉ against Play"; indulge himself he would, but not to the point of extravagance.[5]

Nor would he be extravagant in the objects with which he surrounded himself; in his orders to Robert Cary and Company, his London consignees, he constantly emphasized three qualities: good, neat, and, where applicable, fashionable but not ostentatious. Like many Virginians he was frequently disappointed by what he received and often complained that the goods were "mean in quality but not in price, for in this they excel." Despite the usual difficulties, the appurtenances of a gentleman's house were gradually accumulated, including a library of several hundred books, strong in history and geography, along with the customary agricultural and legal manuals. In 1772, the noted portraitist Charles Willson Peale painted him and Martha. Clad in his Virginia Regiment uniform, Washington looks out with a grave, studied, and unrevealing expression, fulfilling the subject's prophecy that "the skill of this Gentleman's Pencil, will be put to it in describing to the World what manner of Man I am." Peale did not succeed, and few who followed him did much better.[6]

Himself personally abstemious, Washington nevertheless took people pretty much as he found them. In 1787, he hired a gardener, obviously a heavy drinker, and provided in the contract that the man, in return for daily sobriety, would receive so many dollars to be drunk for a specified number of days at each holiday. When he headed the regiment, his instructions to his officers were often filled with injunctions against excessive drinking and sexual indulgence, but these injunctions were always linked

---

[5] Paul Wilstach, *Mount Vernon: Washington's Home and the Nation's Shrine* (Garden City, N.Y., 1925), 134; hereafter, Wilstach, *Mount Vernon*. Card Playing Expenses, 1772–1774 [c. Jan. 1775], *Papers/Col,* 10: 222–23.

[6] GW to Robert Cary & Co., Aug. 10, 1760, to Jonathan Boucher, May 21, 1772, *Papers/Col,* 6: 448–51, 9: 49. Paul K. Longmore's *The Invention of George Washington* (Berkeley, Calif., 1988), 119–21, describes GW's library and analyzes his reading, and its appendix, "The Foundations of Useful Knowledge," 213–26, offers more on the subject; hereafter, Longmore, *Invention.*

with the performance of their duties, not with moral strictures. He seems to have lacked a personal religious faith; when he referred to a force that initiated and controlled life, he always vaguely called it Providence or another unrevealing term. The Anglican Church of colonial Virginia had almost entirely lost sight of its religious goals and become simply one of the institutions that helped to govern the colony. Washington's membership in the local parish and its vestry was another of the duties expected of a planter and not necessarily a sign of a religious faith. He was much more constant in his attendance at vestry meetings, which had secular duties in addition to running the parish, than he was at Sunday services; it is easy to see which form of service had priority in his mind.[7]

"Everywhere order, method, punctuality, economy reigned." Thus runs the remembrance by George Washington Parke Custis, Martha's grandson, of his idyllic boyhood at Mount Vernon in the 1780s. However true this description might have been then, it can be taken only as a goal for the Mount Vernon of the 1760s. Although its owner entered into his command of his "people" and into his cultivation of his acres in the same systematic, conscientious manner with which he had run the regiment, slaves and tobacco proved to be as uncooperative as enlisted men, the French, and natives had been. But ingenuity and a willingness to experiment enabled him to make Mount Vernon profitable.

Washington began by vowing to grow the best Virginia tobacco possible, premium leaf for which he would receive premium prices, but he soon realized his soil would not permit this crop. He did increase substantially the quantity, but the quality was always poor. The soil of the Northern Neck (between the Potomac and Rappahannock Rivers) was not suitable for the favored sweet-scented tobacco, and distance from the James River increased shipping costs. Area planters led in developing new crops and in creating different marketing methods. In debt as Washington was, he needed a cash crop; as early as 1760 he was

---

[7] Paul F. Boller Jr., *George Washington and Religion* (Dallas, 1963), 27; hereafter, Boller, *GW and Religion*. Mary Thompson, "George Washington and Religion" (unpublished essay); Ms. Thompson is a staff member at Mount Vernon and has placed GW firmly within the Anglican communion.

experimenting with different grasses and grains, some unknown to local planters. Easing a transition to other crops and markets was a steady income from the tobacco grown on more fortunately situated Custis lands on the York River. By 1763, he was ready to sign a contract with an Alexandria firm to take all his wheat at three shillings and nine pence a bushel; within seven years, the company was receiving more than six thousand bushels a year from him. In 1770, his own mill began to turn his wheat into flour, and he could export directly from his wharf on the Potomac, which was also the source of fish, dried and packed for additional income and fed to the slaves. Yields from livestock, especially sheep for wool, helped to increase his income further. Painstaking attention to his fields, a willingness to try unusual crops, a conscious attempt to cut down purchases from London, and a resolve to purchase no more slaves combined to decrease substantially his debt and to increase the value of Mount Vernon. Still and all, it was only the inheritance from his stepdaughter, Martha Custis, that wiped out the debt in London. Despite this qualification, the steady decrease in debt and the increase in marketable produce make his achievement creditable when contrasted with the growth in debt and the decrease in cash crops owing to poor cultivation and soil exhaustion common to most other Virginia planters. Further, the problems of supply, inadequate resources, supervision of unwilling slaves, incompetent or irresponsible overseers, and connection of all aspects of the plantation's operation to the twin goals of supporting his family and getting himself out of debt—all were a suitable, albeit unconscious, preparation for the problems of command he would encounter during the War for American Independence. Just as the command of the Virginia Regiment had helped to prepare him for the challenge of turning Mount Vernon into a profitable enterprise, so too the plantation's demands were equipping him for that greater public task.[8]

Although Washington was certainly gratified at the steady

---

[8] Ragsdale, *Planters' Republic*, 21–22, 34–36, 68, 80–81; see the same author's "George Washington, the British Tobacco Trade, and Economic Opportunity in Prerevolutionary Virginia," *Virginia Magazine of History and Biography* 97, no. 2 (Apr. 1989): 133–62, for how this plantation trade affected Washington in particular.

gains realized at Mount Vernon, his hopes for gaining a fortune were not based on it. He once observed to a ne'er-do-well neighbor, John Posey, that all the great fortunes in the province had been obtained by securing large tracts of land on the fringes of settlement and beyond, and then waiting for it to appreciate. That he practiced what he preached to Captain Posey could be seen with his first purchase in the Shenandoah. Now he proposed to begin gathering in western acres in earnest. Even before the end of the war, he inquired of Virginia's governor about the honoring of the 1754 land bounty Governor Dinwiddie had proclaimed. However, the Proclamation of 1763 embodied the Crown's decision to postpone western settlement until it could puzzle out a policy for the West. This postponement did not lessen Washington's interest, and he took advantage of the enforced delay to spy out choice tracts, but he had to do it quietly lest "it might give the alarm to others and, by putting them upon a plan of the same nature . . . set the different Interests aclashing, and probably in the end overturn the whole; all which may be avoided by a Silent management."

Washington's expectation of a quick reopening of the West was correct; treaties with native tribes in 1767 cleared an extensive area. The colonel now took advantage of three opportunities to gather in western land: (1) the 1754 Dinwiddie bounty; (2) a 1763 royal bounty to all those who served until the end of the war with the French; (3) land vouchers purchased from fur traders indemnified for losses in Pontiac's Rebellion. Of the three, the Dinwiddie bounty could be handled within the colony, and Washington organized a committee in 1769 to secure its redemption. A trip west in the fall of 1770 permitted him to select a peninsula formed by the Ohio and Great Kanawha Rivers as the most suitable site, and surveying began. At the end of the process, Washington had received 20,147 of the 200,000 acres of the bounty, but his land was concentrated along the river bottoms, the most accessible and the most fertile portion of the tract, "the cream of the Country," as he later described it. Considering that the language of the original proclamation strongly suggested that it was confined to the enlisted men and that Virginia law forbade engrossing the bottom lands to the extent Washington had, his conduct verged on, if it did not move into, the unethical. And every acre he took meant one less for the enlisted men, who received 400 acres each.[9]

Although Washington was ineligible for the 1763 bounty, his participation hurt no one else because the land was taken from the almost illimitable Crown lands, a cow already well milked by many others who had much less justification than Washington, with the losses he had suffered because of his military service. He received a colonel's share, 5,000 acres, and purchased—secretly, to keep the price low—the shares of others who did not care to redeem them. Several thousand more acres in western Pennsylvania were secured with the traders' vouchers. All in all, he secured 33,000 acres, not always by creditable means, but all at minimum or no cost.[10]

Curiously, although Washington recognized both the economic and political importance of the West, his vision of the future development of his lands was backward looking, not forward. He was so concerned with providing a sure income that he thought only of settling his lands with leaseholders or indentured servants, not with freeholders; the land was to stay with Washington and not to be sold. While waiting for willing tenants, he began a farm on the Great Kanawha, to be worked by indentured servants, but this work was interrupted by the War for Independence and never resumed. The war also interrupted another project Washington recognized as important to the development of the country. In 1770, he responded eagerly to a proposal by Thomas Johnson of Maryland that Virginia cooperate in improving the navigation of the Potomac. The modest plan soon developed into a project to improve the river up to Cumberland, where land transport would have to take over. Although Maryland did not act, Virginia did charter a company in 1772, and some work was done before the war began. Washington also interested himself in a plan advanced by William Byrd to develop a large tract of cedar and cypress swamp on the Virginia–North

---

[9] GW to John Posey, June 24, 1767, to William Crawford, Sep. [17], 1767, *Papers/Col,* 8: 1–4, 26–32; GW to Presley Neville, June 16, 1796, *Writings,* 33: 407.

[10] Ray B. Cook, *Washington's Western Lands* (Strasburg, Va., 1930), 2. Bernhard Knollenberg, *George Washington: The Virginia Period, 1732–1775* (Durham, N.C., 1964), 91–100; hereafter, Knollenberg, *Virginia Period.*

Carolina border. As with many such plans, profits were elusive and problems immense; although Byrd's plan eventually paid dividends, they came only after Washington and most of the other investors had died.[11]

Washington never received the great riches he hoped for from his western lands, but in a sense the United States did. His acres on the Ohio reinforced his already strong interest in the West and in the creation of effective ties of commerce and economic interest across the mountains. In 1772, these ties were meant to bind Virginia together and to make the Potomac the principal commercial artery of the region; later they helped to bind together a nation. That Washington evolved from a Virginia provincial into an American nationalist was owing, to an extent, to the bounty lands.

Although Mount Vernon provided full-time occupation, Washington's membership in the Virginia gentry meant that he had to take up other unofficial—and unpaid—duties. County government was conducted almost entirely by planters through their membership on vestries and service as justices of the peace, to which position Washington was appointed in 1770. The gentry also looked after the poor of the neighborhood within and without the system of the poor laws, lent money, and cosigned each other's notes. One of the most burdensome duties that fell unofficially to them was executing wills for friends' widows and orphans; although Washington tried to avoid this obligation, he never could bring himself to refuse flatly and at one point was the executor for five separate estates. Time-consuming as such duties were, they were still welcome signs of his membership in the gentry and of his reputation for integrity and trustworthiness among his peers.

The political system within which Washington worked, although not democratic in the modern definition, did reflect the popular will to a substantial degree and depended on popular support that was invited, not coerced. There were both built-in and customary advantages for the wealthy in the system, but or-

---

[11] Charles Royster, *The Fabulous History of the Dismal Swamp Company: A Story of George Washington's Times* (New York, 1999). Kenneth R. Bowling, *The Creation of Washington, D.C.* (Fairfax, Va., 1991), 111–12; hereafter, Bowling, *Creation*.

dinary men could and did vote in burgess elections, which were social occasions as well as exercises of the franchise. The fact that planters held a near monopoly of government positions reflected both the deference that the middling and lower orders paid their superiors and the concentration in the gentry of those whose native talents were sufficiently developed to make them effective legislators. Although Washington thought of seeking election to the House of Burgesses as early as 1755, it was not until December 1756 that his name was put forward, at the last minute, at the Frederick County election; he finished third in a field of three. With more planning and a sounding out of the local notables, all of whom supported him, he secured election in July 1758 for Frederick County (where he owned land). In 1765, a vacancy opened in Fairfax County, where Mount Vernon was, and he transferred his political base to that county. Among the burgesses, the colonel was not one of the leaders. His distaste for public speaking and a habit of thinking long and hard before coming to a decision, a sign of his success in disciplining the strong feelings he had too often vented on Dinwiddie, kept him from speaking casually and quickly. As Jefferson later noted, Washington shared with Benjamin Franklin a habit of speaking briefly and only to "the main point which was to decide the question." During his burgess terms, he was content to be an inconspicuous though useful member, and one has to look elsewhere to see how he felt about the developing crisis in imperial relations between Britain and the North American colonies.[12]

Washington's first reaction to this crisis centered on the Stamp Act, which Parliament passed in March 1765, levying a tax, to be paid in scarce coin, on practically every kind of printed document used in the colonies. The act inspired the first intercolonial meeting held under American auspices, the Stamp Act Congress, which met in New York in October. Virginia was not represented there because the burgesses were not in session to appoint a delegation. Washington's attention was focused on the nonimportation schemes that several colonies had already adopted. He felt

---

[12] Charles S. Sydnor, *Gentlemen Freeholders: Political Practices in Washington's Virginia* (Chapel Hill, N.C., 1952), 68–79; see also John G. Kolp, *Gentlemen and Freeholders: Electoral Politics in Colonial Virginia* (Baltimore, 1998), 20–21, 79–80, 133.

that whereas such schemes could hurt Britain, they could benefit the colonies by encouraging self-sufficiency; "this consequently will introduce frugality and be a necessary stimulation to industry." His strongest reference to the act was to call it "an Act of Oppression," as anyone who viewed it properly could see. However, throughout the crisis, which ended with the repeal of the act in March 1766, Washington saw it also as a goad to local self-sufficiency, a goal he was ready to abandon if Parliament would act justly toward the colonies. At this time, he apparently was not overly concerned with the constitutional aspect of the controversy, being content to view it within the parochial framework of his own and Virginia's interests.[13]

Nor did the next round of contention with Britain shake him quickly from his apparent unconcern. In 1767, when Parliament levied the Townshend Duties on certain goods imported into the colonies, he skipped the session of the burgesses that passed a vigorous protest. Even his involvement in Virginia's overall resistance shows him to be unfamiliar with Virginia's specific resistance to the levies. When a friend sent him the text of a proposed anti-importation agreement, he copied it and sent it to his neighbor George Mason, the author of the agreement. However belated, his feelings were strong once aroused, and he quickly surpassed most Americans in his objections to the new imperial policies. To him, the only question was how to stop "our lordly masters" from subverting Virginia's liberty. He would not "scruple or hesitate to use a[r]ms in defense of so valuable a blessing," but that would have to be a last resort. Even in his anger he went out of his way to point out the economic advantages to Virginia in cutting down the debt owed to British merchants and in encouraging local manufactures. In May 1769, he took a copy of the agreement to the burgesses' session; before it could be adopted, however, Governor Botetourt dissolved the House for considering anti-Crown resolutions. This action did not stop the burgesses from meeting elsewhere as "the principal Gentlemen of the Colony" or from adopting the report of a committee (of which Washington was a member) that incorporated the main features of the agreement. Washington had obviously set aside

---

[13] GW to Robert Cary & Company, Sep. 20, 1765, *Papers/Col,* 7: 398–401.

his usual posture of passive involvement. The informal meeting adjourned on May 18, and he headed home to muster Fairfax County behind the "Association," as the agreement had been named. Although he claimed that the agreement worked well in Fairfax, this was not true of Virginia (nor Maryland) in general, and the nonimportation movement petered out after Parliament repealed all the Townshend Duties except one on tea in 1770. Despite his active support of the Association, Washington was not yet a rebel. His objections were to specific acts; he would have to see evidence of a consistent plan to subvert Virginia's liberties before he would support anything more drastic than the nonimportation agreements. Such evidence was soon forthcoming.[14]

Ironically, the act that provided the "evidence" was not intended to change the imperial relationship but rather to aid the perennially ailing East India Company by giving it a monopoly on the lucrative American tea market and by remitting all the duties paid on its tea except the Townshend Duty, kept specifically as an assertion of Parliament's right to tax the colonies. The legislation was passed with little thought as to its effect in America, but that effect was immediate and vigorous. Up and down the coast, merchants and people cooperated in refusing the dutied tea; faced with the strong reaction, royal governors usually capitulated. Only in Boston did push come to shove when Governor Thomas Hutchinson insisted in enforcing the act against the obdurate resistance of the local Sons of Liberty. The Boston Tea Party, December 16, 1773, in which a valuable cargo of tea was dumped into the town's harbor, resolved the conflict, but only at the cost of punitive legislation from an angry Parliament. The Intolerable or Coercive Acts, passed in the spring of 1774, unilaterally changed the form of Massachusetts government, closed the port of Boston, strengthened the authority of Crown officials throughout the colonies, and required a closer compliance with the Quartering Act. Parliament's expectation that Massachusetts would find itself isolated and be forced to ac-

---

[14] GW to George Mason, Apr. 5, 1769, to Jonathan Boucher, July 30, 1770, *Papers/Col*, 8: 177–81, 361.

cept the punishment meekly was sorely disappointed. The other colonies immediately supported the Bay Colony.[15]

Washington cooperated fully with Virginia's condemnation of the Coercive Acts and the call for a general meeting of the colonies. Although he disapproved of the destruction of the tea, he affirmed to George William Fairfax (now in Britain) that "the cause of Boston . . . now is and ever will be considered as the cause of America," and he regretted that Virginia, on top of a possible war with native tribes, should find the British government trying "by every piece of Art and despotism to fix the Shackles of Slavery upon us." Cooperating with Mason in a local call for nonimportation, he put forth the idea that the people could be bound only by the actions of their own representatives, a right of all British. The call was adopted at county meetings in July 1774, which also reelected Washington one of the Fairfax County burgesses. By now he had all the proof he needed to see "a fixed and uniform plan to tax us." To the assertion that more petitions to the Crown should be sent, he exploded that Britain had already been told Americans would not accept their taxes: "what reason is there to expect anything from their justice?" The Americans were contending for the right of self-taxation, and, "as Englishmen, we could not be deprived of this essential and valuable part of a constitution." "An innate spirit of freedom" had first told him that Britain's policy was contrary to "natural justice." Others had shown him that it was also contrary to the British constitution and to Virginia's charter. A line had to be drawn between Britain's power and Virginia's rights, although he wished the time for drawing it had not come during his lifetime: "the crisis is arrived when we must assert our rights, or submit to every imposition that can be heaped upon us, till custom and use shall make us as tame and abject slaves, as the blacks we rule over with such arbitrary sway."

Clearly, Washington had reached a point from which there

---

[15] R. L. Scribner, ed., *Revolutionary Virginia: The Road to Independence*, vol. 1 (Charlottesville, Va., 1973), for the relevant documents; hereafter Scribner, *Revolutionary Virginia*. A. M. Schlesinger, *The Colonial Merchants and the American Revolution* (1917, repr., New York, 1957), 135–38, 197–99, 236. Benjamin W. Labaree, *The Boston Tea Party* (New York, 1964), chaps. 4 and 5.

could be no return. Unless Britain changed its colonial policy, steps more drastic and far-reaching than nonimportation would have to be taken. Although independence had not yet occurred to him, it was a logical conclusion to what he had already written.[16]

In August, an extralegal meeting of burgesses convened in Williamsburg and called for a general meeting of the colonies, suggesting that the meeting urge a nonimportation/nonexportation agreement similar to Virginia's, and counseling the diversification of the colony's agriculture and the encouragement of manufacturing (old ideas of Washington's), as well as the easing of trade regulations. Seven burgesses, including Washington, were chosen to represent Virginia at the general meeting, scheduled for Philadelphia in September. Washington had come to his present position entirely out of concern for Virginia; now, meeting and talking with men from other colonies, he would begin to appreciate their differing desires and needs.[17]

By September 5, Washington and a sufficient number of other delegates were in Philadelphia to convene what was soon formally titled the Continental Congress. In the organization and deliberations of the Congress, Washington presumably took a part, but that part is not known. He kept only a bare-bones diary of where and with whom he ate, served on no committees, and was mentioned only glancingly by those who noticed him. Silas Deane of Connecticut approved Washington's "easy, soldier like air and gesture" and was surprised at his youthful appearance, but he also repeated the apocryphal story of the Virginian's offer to raise and support a regiment, commenting cautiously, "His fortune is said to be equal to such an undertaking." Getting back to safer ground, he noted that Washington spoke "very modestly and in a cool but determined style and accent." Another Yankee, Rhode Islander Solomon Drowne, went beyond fair taste when he sent home a verse that concluded: "With manly gait / His

---

[16] GW to George William Fairfax, June 10, 1774, and July 20, 1774, *Papers/ Col*, 10: 95–101, 128–31. GW to Bryan Fairfax, July 4, 1774, and Aug. 24, 1774, *Papers/Col*, 10: 154–56.

[17] Scribner, *Revolutionary Virginia*, 1: 223–39, for the 1774 Association and the instructions to the delegates. Glenn A. Phelps, *George Washington and American Constitutionalism* (Lawrence, Kans., 1993), chap. 1, esp. 17–22 for GW's position at this time; hereafter, Phelps, *GW and Constitutionalism*.

faithful steel suspended by his side, / Pass'd W-shi-gt-n along, Virginia's hero," adding a daydream in which George III and George of Mount Vernon settled the imperial quarrel in personal combat! More accurately, Washington described himself at the Congress as "an attentive observer and witness."[18]

While the Congress debated—and rejected—a plan of union with Britain and approved a firm and spirited defense of colonial rights, Washington's perception of the situation deepened and, to an extent, changed. After a dinner with the leading men of New England, he denied that they or any American wanted independence, his first recorded mention of that definitive step, but he did assert that no Yankee or American would "ever submit to the loss of those valuable rights and privileges, which are essential to the happiness of every free state, and without which life, liberty, and property are rendered totally insecure." No one wanted war, but if Britain refused to back down, "more blood will be spilt on this occasion . . . than history has yet furnished instances of in North America." The congressional delegates' position, gleaned from their statements, was moderate enough. They would not accept English taxation or interference with their internal government, especially interference with personal rights long thought guaranteed by the English Constitution, but they would accept legitimate regulation of their trade for imperial interests. No mention was made of armed resistance, but such thoughts must have occurred to the delegates, as Deane and Drowne's comments attest. They also occurred to Washington, for among his purchases in Philadelphia was a work on military discipline. Perhaps a new opportunity to "push my Fortune in a military Line" was in the future?[19]

Washington returned to Mount Vernon at the end of October. His five weeks in Philadelphia had enlarged his acquaintances, giving him his first glimpse of several of those men with whom his future career would be inextricably bound—John Adams,

---

[18] *Diaries*, 3: 274–88. Silas Deane to Mrs. Deane, Sep. 10, 1774, in Edmund C. Burnett, ed., *Letters of Members of the Continental Congress* (1921, repr., Gloucester, Mass., 1963), 1: 28; hereafter, Burnett, *Letters*. Flexner, 1: 328. Edmund C. Burnett, *The Continental Congress* (1941, repr., New York, 1965), chaps. 2 and 3; hereafter, Burnett, *Congress*.

[19] GW to Robert Mackenzie, Oct. 9, 1774, *Papers/Col*, 10: 171–72.

John Jay, Joseph Reed, and Thomas Mifflin, to name only a few of the famous and not so famous who would figure in the struggle for independence. Although he had played a passive and obscure role in the Congress, he had certainly been observed. Had he gone to the colonial metropolis for the first time in 1775, when the second Congress convened, with many of the same men who had been there seven months earlier, would the opportunity given to him then been given at all?

3

In the Service of Congress, 1775–1783

> The sword was to be forged upon the anvil of necessity.
>
> Proposed address to Congress, April 1789

AFTER WASHINGTON'S SERVICE in the first Continental Congress, his life in Virginia never returned to what he considered normal. Added to his already busy life was service on several committees whose task was to improve Virginia's military defenses. Although these preparations were disguised in the language of loyal submission, they made clear that many felt a resort to "a[r]ms" was becoming more and more likely. The reorganized Fairfax County militia, for example, was partially justified on the ground "that such militia will relieve the mother country from any expense in our protection," thus removing any necessity for a tax on that account and for stationing "standing armies among us—ever dangerous to liberty." Some Virginians felt no need for such disingenuous excuses. Among them was Patrick Henry, who represented a western county at the second Virginia convention in March 1775 and who stirred the delegates with his famous rejection of additional conciliatory petitions, concluding with: "I know not what course others may take; but as for me, give me liberty or give me death!" Descending from the grandiloquent level of Henry's oration, Washington received several more committee assignments at the meeting, and, most important, he was again selected to represent his colony at the second Congress, to be held in Philadelphia in May. He traveled north in a mood of sober resolution, having confided to his brother that it was his "full intention to devote my life and fortune in the cause we are engaged in, if need be." Virginia expected that his contribution would be military; as one anonymous rhymester put it, "In spite of Gage's flaming sword / And Carleton's Canadian troop / Brave Washington will give the word, / And we'll make them howl and whoop." Fortunately, "Brave Washington" did not share the verse's mindless bravado.[1]

The trip to Philadelphia was filled with sober discussions of the repercussions of the military encounters at Lexington and Concord the previous month. Once there, the delegates, a good many of whom had attended the previous meeting, got down to business quickly. All seemed to be "directed by the same firmness of union and determination to resist [British exactions] by all ways and to every extremity." A Massachusetts delegate saw the same feeling in Washington—that conciliation and compromise had been tried and found wanting, now the choice was between fighting or slavery: "Sad alternative! But can a virtuous man hesitate in the choice?" Implicitly, no.[2]

While Congress puzzled out what to do about the New England militia army that was besieging the British in Boston, Washington found himself on several military committees, but their work was aimless until Congress came to a decision. There was only one decision they could make: New England had to be helped. All that could be sent quickly to the aid of the Yankees was the symbol of a commander who would embody the decision of Congress that this cause was not only New England's, but America's. Washington was certainly aware that eyes were turning to him; his suitability was obvious on several counts. As a Virginian, he reassured the Yankees that they were not alone; further, his military experience and reputation made him a plausible candidate, and his age—forty-three—and good health would help him bear the rigors of the position. Wearing the uniform of the Virginia Regiment was not an unsubtle piece of lobbying for the position he would receive; rather, it was a sign that he had made his choice between submission or, if necessary, armed resistance.

---

[1] Resolutions of Fairfax County Committee, [Jan. 17, 1775], *Papers/Col,* 10: 236–37. Freeman, 3: 401–7; Flexner, 1: 328 n, for the verse; GW to John Augustine Washington, Mar. 25, 1775, *Papers/Col,* 10: 308.

[2] R. H. Lee to William Lee, May 10, 1775, in Burnett, *Letters,* 1: 90; Samuel Curwen, Journal, in Burnett, *Letters,* 1: 90 n; GW to George William Fairfax, May 31, 1775, *Papers/Col,* 10: 367. Burnett, *Congress,* remains useful for that body's deliberations.

On June 15, after a two-day debate, Congress formally resolved that "a General be appointed to command all the continental forces, raised, or to be raised, for the defence of American liberty." Immediately, Thomas Johnson of Maryland placed Washington's name formally in nomination; no other nominations were made, and the election was unanimous. The colonel of the Virginia Regiment had embarked "on a tempestuous ocean, from whence, perhaps, no friendly harbor is to be found."[3]

What manner of man had Congress chosen to carry its standard against the "ministerial army"? The younger Washington had a complex character; a combination of pride, ambition, and concern about his present and future status had pushed him forward into tasks from which less-thrusting persons would have turned away. The mission to Fort LeBouef and the Fort Necessity expedition were successful enough to bring him public acclaim, but they also brought on the quarrel with Dinwiddie when the governor reduced him in rank. Too young and insecure to tolerate setbacks, he resigned. The Braddock expedition served admirably to bring him back into the public notice and once again raised the possibility of a royal commission. But neither could he cut himself off from his Virginia roots, and he took on Mount Vernon even as he was resuming his military career with the Virginia Regiment. It was essentially in Virginia's service that he spent three thankless years trying to do the impossible—defend the colony's frontier with always inadequate resources; this task tried both his military ability and his character. He showed himself willing to work to the limit of his health and beyond, but he performed too many of the tasks that should have been left to subordinates. Although he took responsibility for the shortcomings of his officers and men, as was proper, he was also too ready to take offense at slights, both real and imagined, that would have been better left unnoticed, and he often failed to consider the difficulties under which his superiors labored. He could be too conscious of the prerogatives of his rank. By the time of the

---

[3] Knollenberg, *Virginia Period*, chap. 17, and Freeman, 3: 426–37, describe the process by which GW was appointed; GW to Burwell Bassett, June 19, 1775, *Papers/Rev*, 1: 12–13.

Forbes expedition, he had given up trying to secure a royal commission and actively sponsored Virginia's interests in the new military road, to his own detriment. Forbes's success may have helped to bring about Washington's retirement. He did not understand the strategy used, and when it worked, he may have concluded that there was more to military science than he was willing to master.

With the fall of Fort Duquesne, Virginia's frontier was relatively secure, and he could resign with honor. The five years in the colony's service had taught him a good bit about himself, and he brought his slowly and painfully developed self-discipline, his organizational ability, and his capacity for hard work to the task of developing Mount Vernon. Here he also showed a readiness to break from established patterns and to admit failure, even if the admission was unvoiced, as he turned from tobacco to wheat and other crops. His service in the burgesses showed a realization of what he could and could not do, and he willingly took a back seat to his more vocal colleagues. Only in the episode of the 1754 land bounty did his old anxiety about his fortune show itself.

As an adult, Washington was still a person of complex character. The pride, the readiness to take offense, the anxiety about his reputation—"honor," as the eighteenth century would call it—were present and had constantly to be restrained by his hard-bought self-discipline. Here he was helped by the secure place he had earned for himself. Colonel George Washington of Mount Vernon, Fairfax County, Virginia, need apologize to no one. Holder of a commission validated by years of service, he was no "rattlesnake colonel," a term British travelers contemptuously applied to colonial officers. Owner of an extensive and profitable plantation, he was not living off the accumulated capital of his ancestors and pushing his estate deeper into debt by a mindless continuance of a timeworn agriculture on timeworn fields. Had it not been for the revolution and the War for Independence he would have continued the busy, useful life he so enjoyed—respected as a man of prudence, judgment, and integrity in the county and in the colony—and would now forever lose.[4]

---

[4] Longmore, *Invention,* considers how GW was shaped and shaped himself prior to 1775; Higginbotham, *Tradition,* parts 1 and 2, concentrates on the development of GW as a soldier before the war.

When Washington accepted his appointment, he was, literally, *the* Continental army, no men having been enlisted and no other officers appointed. Thus, he became instantly a symbol of the unswerving determination of Congress to resist British policy at any price. As if he already realized this status, he refused any salary for his services, asking only that his expenses, of which he would keep "an exact account," be paid. This refusal was in marked contrast with his attitude in his earlier service, when he was very concerned about compensation. But now he was not one of many officers, nor was he defending only land and people. In resisting British policy, the Americans claimed to be defending eternal principles of liberty. Washington's conduct in his command would, as far as he was able, help to validate that claim. He would be charged with many faults during the war, but avarice would be the least plausible.

Nor could he be plausibly charged with overconfidence. To Congress he confessed that "I, this day, declare with the utmost sincerity, I do not think myself equal to the Command I am honored with." He repeated this sentiment to Martha, adding that he could not have refused "without exposing my character to such censure as would have reflected dishonor upon myself." Thus, he moved to his new post, diffident of his own ability, confident that the cause was just, and not quite understanding how its leadership had fallen to him. But lead he would. Although Congress had more confidence than their general, they did not expect him to fight alone; in addition to providing for the enlistment of troops, they also appointed four major generals: Artemas Ward, then commanding the men around Boston; Charles Lee, an eccentric retired Royal Army officer; Philip Schuyler of New York; and Israel Putnam of Connecticut. Horatio Gates, another retired officer of the king, was appointed adjutant general, and eight brigadiers, all but one from New England, were commissioned. Washington could appoint officers up to colonel for the Continental service, but the colonies would select their own militia officers. It was a less than ideal arrangement, but the parochial jealousies of the colonies and the lack of congressional power made anything better unattainable. After recruiting two personable young Philadelphians as secretaries, Joseph Reed and Thomas Mifflin, Washington left for the camp outside Boston.[5]

Accompanied by Generals Lee and Schuyler and his secretaries, Washington arrived in New York on the same day the colony's royal governor, William Tryon, returned from leave in Britain. Fortunately, the dual reception was carried off with no disturbance to the Continental Congress's general or to the king's governor, but it served to point out the anomalous position of the colonies, who, while claiming to be loyal subjects, were nevertheless resisting what appeared to be the settled policy of king and Parliament. The anomaly was to continue for another year. In welcoming the general, the New York representatives, whose colony enjoyed—if that is the correct verb—a reputation for loyalism, stated that they looked forward to the general's resignation when the disputes with Britain had been resolved. Washington's response was graceful but pointed: "When we assumed the soldier, we did not lay aside the citizen; and we shall sincerely rejoice with you in that happy hour when the establishment of American liberty, upon the most firm and solid foundations, shall enable us to return to our private stations in the bosom of a free, peaceful, and happy country." The New Yorkers certainly noted the qualification in the response. Schuyler was detached after have been given virtually unlimited discretion in his command. Though necessity dictated a loose rein on his detached subordinates, Washington had carelessly given up the right of the commander in chief to make all the truly important decisions; this decision would have important repercussions in the future.[6]

The American headquarters at Cambridge were reached late on July 2, and Washington had his first glimpse of his new command and its possible field of battle. Eighteenth-century Boston (the modern city is much changed in its geography and cannot be used to illustrate the 1775 city) was admirably suited for both the defenders and the besiegers. The British forces were isolated

---

[5] GW to John Hancock, June 16, 1775, to Martha Washington, June 18, 1775, *Papers/Rev,* 1: 1, 3–4.

[6] Address from New York Provincial Congress, Address to New York Provincial Congress, June 26, 1775, Instructions to Philip Schuyler, June 25, 1775, *Papers/Rev,* 1: 40–41, 36–38; Freeman, 3: 305.

on the two peninsulas of Boston and Charlestown, both connected by narrow necks to the mainland. Thus, without using boats, the British could not break out, but, conversely, the Americans would find it all but impossible to break in. The defensive works that the Americans had erected were, with few exceptions, well sited, and the New England militia seemed to be in good spirits. It took more than a week to secure an accurate count of the men—16,000 present, 14,000 fit for duty—but only a few minutes to realize that the army had no cannon or military engineers. One bright spot was the estimated supply of powder, 308 barrels, but even that was illusory, and a month later Washington discovered that only 36 barrels were on hand; the higher amount was the total collected since Concord. The new general immediately began, in the fashion of new commanders, to tighten up his forces. All the militia was taken into the Continental army on July 4, the general order that announced this praying that "all distinctions of Colonies would be laid aside." But distinctions of rank were not, and officers were ordered to wear colored ribbons indicative of their status, and some were separated from the service for various shortcomings. Owing to a basic lack of supplies, there were limits to what could be accomplished with the motley units besieging Boston, but Washington succeeded in bringing in a degree of order and regularity that was a pleasant contrast with what had been. William Emerson, minister of the Concord church, rejoiced at the "New lords, new laws" that had wrought such a surprising change as early as the middle of July.[7]

As the army was brought into a degree of order, Washington began to wonder what to do with it. Congress had ordered him to consult his generals. Although the legislators had meant this consultation to be for his guidance, Washington took it to be for his governance and went along with whatever the council of war

---

[7] General Orders, July 4, 1775, *Papers/Rev*, 1: 54–56. Don Higginbotham's *The War of American Independence: Military Attitudes, Policies, and Practice, 1763–1789* (New York, 1971) is excellent; hereafter, Higginbotham, *War*. Part 3 of Higginbotham's *Tradition* concentrates on its subject's development as a commander during the war. Christopher Ward's *The War of the Revolution*, John R. Alden, ed., 2 vols. (New York, 1952), describes the military actions; hereafter, Ward, *War*. George A. Billias, ed., *George Washington's Generals* (New York, 1964) and *George Washington's Opponents* (New York, 1969) present brief evaluations of the principal commanders on both sides.

decided, no matter how contrary to his own wishes the decision was. In the beginning, this approach was good because the new commander in chief was spoiling for a fight with the enemy that he thought would bring the conflict to a quick end, but at a time when the result would actually have been an American defeat. His first council of war advised simply a continuance of the siege while more troops were enlisted.

Washington was too active to rest content with such a passive attitude and looked for ways to annoy the British. He commissioned some converted merchantmen as privateers and sent them to intercept royal supply ships bound for Boston. He also approved a two-pronged attack on Canada, one force under Brigadier General James Montgomery moving up from New York; the other—under a short, swarthy, energetic officer from Connecticut, Benedict Arnold—would go through Maine. The official reason for this attack by the king's loyal subjects was to forestall a British-Iroquois attack from Canada. This ingenious excuse underlines one of the main difficulties Washington faced at this time. Officially, the war was an effort to prevent the Royal Army from enforcing obnoxious royal policies on otherwise loyal Americans. Invading Canada or taking the king's ships hardly fit in here. Washington and Congress were finding out that there was no such thing as fighting a purely defensive war. Once the fighting had started, it became war, no adjectives. And once that had come about, independence was the next logical step. The siege of Boston, the Canadian expedition, Washington's "navy," advice he gave to New England governors on loyalists and other matters—all together would constitute one of the major influences moving Congress to declare "that these United Colonies are, and of right ought to be, free and independent."[8]

In September, another council of war held Washington back from an attack on the enemy lines; their reasons were both military and political (a conciliatory proposal from Parliament was expected), but the general betrayed his eagerness to take the offensive when he reported the decision to Congress. Later commentators have styled Washington a Fabian in his military

---

[8] See Curtis Nettels's *George Washington and American Independence* (Boston, 1951) for GW's contributions in this area.

strategy; that is, he set out to wear the enemy down in a series of small encounters that, even when they were American defeats, hurt the British sufficiently to take away their desire to continue the war, all with little risk to the Americans in any single encounter. Although it is true that Washington was frequently reduced to this stratagem, he never tired of planning a coup de main that would end the war by a single, overwhelming victory. In 1775–76, that coup would be the taking of Boston; later, after the loss of Manhattan, the retaking of the island would be Washington's objective. Thus, although circumspection, conservation, and caution often characterized his strategy, sometimes he had to be restrained from a daring gamble in which everything could be won—or lost. Fabian by necessity, he was a gambler by instinct.

As the year ended, Washington had to abandon all thought of attack and bend every effort to keeping the army together. Practically all of the men had enlisted only to the year's end, and although Congress had optimistically authorized an army of more than 22,000, everyone soon discovered that authorization was one thing, and enlistment was quite another; with six weeks to go, less than 1,000 men had reenlisted. Further, the reduction in the number of regiments meant some officers had to go, and this had to be done without breaking provincial lines and without putting, for example, a Rhode Islander in command of Connecticut troops. Washington almost despaired at the "dearth of public spirit, and want of virtue," and marveled at the "fertility in all the low arts" while the new officers were being chosen. The only real reinforcement he received while the new army was being formed was Martha's arrival on December 11; the sustenance of her quiet, pleasant presence certainly meant much as her husband wrestled with his apparently insoluble problems. This winter was the first of six she spent by the general's side during the war. By one expedient or another, the staffing problems were solved, and early in January, while the returns disclosed only 5,582 men present and fit for duty, there were 8,212 enlisted for the new year. Although there was a troublesome shortage of muskets, and powder remained in short supply, the lines were again manned. Washington could untypically but pardonably boast: "Search the vast volumes of history through, and I much question whether a case similar to ours is to be found; to wit, to maintain a post against the flower of the British troops for six months together, without [powder], and at the end of them to have one army disbanded and another to raise within the same distance of a reinforced enemy." One wonders if he would have exulted quite so much if he had known that he would have to do the same thing for all but the last year of the war and that there were seven more years to go.[9]

The remanning of the lines was the only bright spot. From Britain came news of the king's speech to Parliament in October in which he called for an all-out effort to crush the rebellion. From Canada, Washington learned of the failure of Arnold and Montgomery to take Quebec, with the latter's death; the situation there was not lost, but it was in grave peril. Obviously the war had turned into a long-term effort. Charles Lee was sent to New York City, a likely British target, to improve its defenses, and Washington dropped his resistance to long-term enlistments and bounties, which he had opposed as wasteful.[10]

He was beginning to understand and accept some of the peculiarities of a citizen army; the men needed the bounties to help their families subsist while they were serving, not to profit from the public's necessity. Washington's progress in this area was uneven; he implicitly relied on the standard European military treatises for advice on discipline, but these treatises were based on the aristocratic European armies. They disregarded the motive force of patriotism and the personal stake that all Americans who opposed British policy had in the struggle. However, even a superficial reading of his general orders shows the value he placed on these feelings. In a sense, he operated on two levels as commander in chief: when dealing with Congress, he constantly tried to get them to form a "real" army—that is, on the model he had observed when serving with Braddock and Forbes—but when he had to work with the daily problems of keeping his army in being, he accommodated himself to the realities of his rag-tag forces and bent his ingenuity to keeping them together as best

---

[9] GW to Joseph Reed, Nov. 28, 1775, Jan. 4, 1776, *Papers/Rev*, 2: 449, 4: 23–25.

[10] Bernhard Knollenberg's *George Washington and the Revolution, A Reappraisal* (1940, repr., Hamden, Conn., 1968), chap.12, shows GW's evolution on long enlistments and bounties; hereafter, Knollenberg, *Revolution*.

he could and however he could. Often enough, ingenuity was all he had.

On occasion, more was needed. Throughout the war, it remained difficult to recruit sufficient men, no matter what the military situation. Washington adapted to the necessities in a number of ways, one indicative of a surprising change in his social and moral outlook, which became obvious only later in the 1790s. Almost from the beginning of the war, black men were taken into the army, first in separate units, later in integrated units. Most were freedmen, but a few were slaves who served with a promise of freedom at the end of their enlistment. Although none served in any southern companies, approximately 5,000 served in northern units, both army and militia. They were treated with fairness and equality by the commander in chief, who accepted, apparently with equanimity, this striking departure from the social and legal environment in which he had grown up.[11]

With spring, more than 14,000 men were available for duty around Boston, and again Washington's thoughts turned to an attack on the city, one that would wipe out the enemy. Again the council of war restrained him. A detachment under Colonel Henry Knox, later to be chief of artillery in the American forces, had brought artillery to Cambridge from the captured royal fort at Ticonderoga. It was decided to emplace the guns on Dorchester Heights, which commanded Boston from the south, thus forcing the enemy either to come out against the Americans or to evacuate the city. Owing to the cold weather, fortifications could not be dug, but Colonel Rufus Putnam suggested using chandeliers, wooden frames filled with hay and brush, as the basis for a prefabricated fort. After appropriate preparations and a three-night artillery bombardment, the instant citadel was put in place on the night of March 4, with no hostile reaction. A violent storm broke off preparations for an attack until the Dorchester lines were so strong that an assault would be suicidal. The British commander, Sir William Howe, had already decided for strategic rea-

---

[11] Fritz Hirschfeld, *George Washington and Slavery: A Documentary Portrayal* (Columbia, Mo., 1997), chaps. 13–15; hereafter, Hirschfeld, *Slavery*. See also Benjamin Quarles, *The Negro in the American Revolution* (Chapel Hill, N.C., 1961).

sons to evacuate the city at the first opportunity. On March 8, Washington was told informally of the impending departure of the enemy, thus confirming his prediction that now the British either had to fight or leave. By March 17, the answer was clear; all the troops, what equipment they could not destroy, and approximately a thousand loyalists sailed from the harbor. The siege of Boston was over.

Although Congress congratulated their victorious general with a gold medal and Harvard College awarded him the degree doctor of laws, *honoris causa,* retrospection tempers the enthusiasm shown at the time. Washington's best efforts had been able only to make the British uncomfortable in Boston; their decision to evacuate had been made before the emplacements on Dorchester had appeared and was the result not of American strategic brilliance but rather of Howe's calm assessment of the assets and liabilities of Boston, chiefly the latter, as a base. Washington had done well to hold the varied—in numbers, training, and equipment—units of his army together and to maintain the siege, especially after having had, in essence, to replace one army with another. His use of ships as well as his realization of the superior mobility of the enemy because of their command of the sea showed the beginnings of what would be an excellent grasp of the importance and use of sea power. He had also grown in his understanding of the men he had to deal with both in the army and in the legislatures, but he was going to have to learn to be more discreet. Some of his letters to cousin Lund Washington, who was managing affairs at Mount Vernon for him, and to other relatives and friends had become public knowledge; they were exceedingly critical, unfairly so, of New England morals and courage. All the general could lamely but truthfully say was that he had changed his mind. Also, he himself, rather than his counselors, would have to learn to rein in his impetuosity. Further, his desire to mount an attack on Boston was not founded on an accurate understanding and calm assessment of the enemy's strength and disposition or of his own army's abilities, but on his eagerness to end the war with a splendid coup de main. An experienced gambler at least calculates the odds, even if he cannot wait until they are favorable. Washington would learn the importance of intelligence the hard way. He also showed his old tendency to do too much of his own paperwork; paradoxically, by tying him up with busy work, this tendency decreased his authority over his subordinates when they were sent to distant areas. Soon Charles Lee in New York, and later in South Carolina, as well as Schuyler were communicating directly with Congress; thus, unity of command was lost, and material for future misunderstandings and quarrels was supplied. But this problem was grist for future mills to grind. For now, the general was amply pleased that "my reputation stands fair, that my conduct hitherto has given universal satisfaction." That "satisfaction" was the only compensation he was asking for his services, and he would not always be paid as generously as he was after Boston. On April 4, he left for New York City, Howe's expected destination.[12]

New York City, then clustered at the southern tip of Manhattan Island, was one of the most important commercial cities in the colonies and was second only to Philadelphia in population. Its island location, ringed by the Hudson (sometimes called the North) and East Rivers, along with the certain ability of the enemy to command the waters around it, made it almost impossible to defend. Only the unlikely prospect of blocking the Hudson River could deny the city to the enemy for very long. Congress ordered Washington to defend the city, and, despite the difficulty of the task, it is hard to disagree with them. If the city *could* have been held, it would have prevented any British effort to split the colonies along the Hudson River as they attempted in 1777; it also would have denied them an excellent base for operations in the middle colonies, with the loyalist sympathies of many of the area's inhabitants a bonus. At that point, the implications for morale of abandoning the city without a fight could have been disastrous to the fragile patriot cause, although, as events proved, if the cause could survive the actual loss of the city, it could probably survive anything. Thus, the question was not should the city be denied to the enemy, but rather could it be denied to them?

Charles Lee had already studied the site and made suggestions for improving the city's defenses, but these suggestions were only partially implemented when Washington arrived. After several

---

[12] GW to John Augustine Washington, Mar. 31, 1776, *Papers/Rev*, 3: 569.

weeks on the scene, Washington hoped it could be put in a "very respectable posture of Defence," although he was concerned about shortages of men and powder. Ironically, at the critical moment, both were plentiful—but defeat still came.[13]

In mid-May, there were only 6,700 men fit for duty in the American camp against an estimated rock-bottom 8,000 needed for its defense. Faced with the continued deterioration of the army in Canada, Congress told Washington to make do with a draft of 20,000 militia from the northern colonies, with half again as many men held in reserve in New Jersey. Despite these official decisions, Washington had only 7,400 fit for duty six weeks later, with a good bit yet to be done on the city's defenses. In late June, all this became more than academic when a British fleet entered the harbor and anchored off Staten Island; by the afternoon of June 29, more than one hundred vessels had entered the road. Washington reported the event somberly to Congress and promised "to make the best disposition I can for our troops, in order to give [the enemy] a proper reception, and to prevent the ruin and destruction they are meditating against us." With this promise, he began to clear the field as well as he could.[14]

After tiptoeing around the measure for months, on July 2 Congress approved Richard Henry Lee's resolution that "these United Colonies are, and of right ought to be, free and independent States." Two days later, Thomas Jefferson's justification, after editing by his colleagues, of what had driven George III's hitherto loyal subjects to this ultimate step went out to the world (and to many still unconvinced Americans). Washington was not one of those who needed convincing. Since he had assumed command, he had often acted as if the colonies were already independent, and by so doing he helped to bring about Congress's decision. In January, he had approved "the sound doctrine and unanswerable reasoning" of Tom Paine's argument for the neces-

---

[13] Bruce Bliven's *Battle for Manhattan* (1956, repr., Baltimore, 1964) is a good popular account of the campaign. Charles Lee, "Report on the Defense of New York, March 1776," in *The Lee Papers*, 2: 354–56, vol. 5 of *Collections of the New-York Historical Society* (New York, 1872); hereafter, *Lee Papers*. GW to Charles Lee, May [9], 1776, *Papers/Rev*, 4: 245.

[14] GW to John Hancock, June 29, 1776, *Papers/Rev*, 5: 148.

sity of America's independence, which the English-born pamphleteer had put forward in *Common Sense*. In April, Washington had dropped the distinction he had previously maintained of always calling the enemy the "ministerial army," not the Royal Army; now he thought the distinction "idle," thus anticipating Congress's decision by three months. As he had in the past and would again in the future, he had let himself slide into a basic decision by allowing events to mount up until there was only one way to go; when he sent a copy of the Declaration to the Massachusetts assembly, he noted that it was "Impelled by Necessity and a Repetition of Injuries insufferable, without the most distant prospect of relief"; in short, there was nothing else to do. Congress had taken a few months longer to get to that point than had its general.[15]

But then the necessity of the case was much more obvious to the general, facing as he did more than 20,000 enemy troops, including a number of German mercenaries, hired from their princes under terms suggesting the rental of horses, not men. They were dubbed Hessians, after one of the larger contingents from Hesse-Cassel. General Sir William Howe, coming down from Halifax, where he had reorganized the troops he had taken from Boston, was in command. He was very much the model of an eighteenth-century general, proceeding slowly and very carefully, always maneuvering his force so as to gain the maximum advantage before the guns spoke, then securing a victory with the smallest possible loss of his expensive soldiers. That these tactics would not yield the destruction of the American army was probably agreeable to Howe, who hoped to end the rebellion by convincing the former colonists that resistance was hopeless; after that, reconciliation would only be hindered by memories of bloody battles. Howe opened his campaign by attempting to communicate with Washington in a letter addressed to "George Washington, Esq." Because the letter did not address Washington as general, Adjutant General Joseph Reed refused to accept it. After two more attempts, an officer finally inquired orally, would "His Excellency, General Washington" (the customary ad-

---

[15] GW to Joseph Reed, Jan. 31, 1776, to Massachusetts General Court, July 9, 1776, *Papers/Rev*, 3: 227–29, 5: 250.

dress within the Continental forces) receive Howe's adjutant? An appointment for the next day was made immediately. The insistence on proper titles looks laughable until one realizes that by insisting on a recognition of his position, Washington was also insisting on a recognition of the Continental Congress's right to confer his commission. At the interview, the British emissary, James Patterson, could offer only the king's pardon. An indignant Washington spurned it, protesting that the Americans had done nothing for which they had to be pardoned.[16]

Seeing that there was no alternative to battle, Howe began to move his army to Long Island. The Americans had anticipated this move and placed themselves on a naturally strong height, just across the East River from the city, present-day Brooklyn Heights. The position was pierced by four roads, three of which were adequately guarded. Unfortunately the fourth, the Jamaica Road, patrolled by only a small militia force, was the one Howe's main force took, probably guided by loyalists. On the morning of August 27, while redcoats annoyed the American lines from the front, Howe neatly outflanked the Americans by moving over the Jamaica Road, at the extreme left of the rebel lines. The Battle of Long Island was over almost before it began, and the Americans lost two brigadier generals, James Sullivan and William Alexander (the latter of whom claimed a Scottish peerage and insisted on the title Lord Stirling), as well as approximately 1,400 other officers and men; the British loss was less than 400. Several changes of command, inadequate knowledge of the area and reconnaissance, an uncertain command situation, and too few men defending too long a line were certainly mitigating factors in the American defeat, but the fact remains that Washington had made a very poor disposition of his resources, and his men had suffered for it.

The Americans retreated to earthen fortifications on Brooklyn Heights and faced twice their number of enemy troops, with the East River blocking any further retreat. Howe shunned the cost of a frontal attack and began a slow but man-saving siege; fur-

---

[16] The incident is described in Freeman, 4: 139–40. Phelps, *GW and Constitutionalism*, 36–37, interprets the incident and notes that Congress specifically approved of GW's actions.

ther, if the navy could come up the East River, the Americans would have no place to go but to enemy prison camps. An American council of war on August 29 reached the only possible decision: evacuate the men immediately. An unusual late-summer northeaster came to the rescue and held the enemy ships back with its contrary winds. A motley collection of small boats manned by Colonel John Glover's regiment of fishermen from Marblehead, Massachusetts, took all the men and their equipment off during the night of August 29–30. The force had been saved, but to what purpose? It was very like the famous move from the frying pan into the fire. Now Washington's force was concentrated on Manhattan Island, which had only one bridge to the mainland—Kingsbridge, at the island's northern tip—and an uncharacteristically quick move by Howe could gather it in before Glover's men could work another miracle. Congress turned down Washington's request for permission to burn the city in order to deny its buildings to the enemy. Even if it were captured, they counted on its quick recovery. Thus, Washington was apparently committed to the defense of an indefensible city with an army in which he no longer had any confidence; "I had no doubt in my mind of defending this place . . . if the men would do their duty, but this I despair of." Desertion from the militia became commonplace and also began to infect the men recently enlisted for the year.[17]

Even before September 14, when permission arrived from Congress, Washington had begun to evacuate the island; the process was interrupted by a British landing from the East River on the next day. The untrained, ill-equipped militia at the landing site broke and ran, an example that the other troops in the area unfortunately followed. Washington, riding to the scene from his headquarters, rallied some soldiers into making a stand, but as soon as the redcoats appeared, the American soldiers resumed their panicky, disorderly flight, causing Washington to despair: "Good God! Have I got such troops as these?" as he sat his horse, almost waiting for the oncoming enemy to capture

---

[17] GW to John Hancock, Sep. 2, 1776, *Papers/Rev*, 6: 199–200. Resolution of Sep. 3, 1776, in Worthington C. Ford, ed., *Journals of the Continental Congress* (Washington, D.C., 1906), 5: 753.

him. Collecting himself, he ordered a defensive line secured along Harlem Heights, hilly ground to the north of a valley running northeastward across the island approximately ten miles above the city, with what troops remained under some discipline. General Israel Putnam, acting on his own, had already gotten the men in the city, south of the enemy's landing place, moving north along the west side of the island. Practically all of them escaped before the British had thrown their line across to the Hudson, but large quantities of materiel were lost. Thus, Washington still had most of his army, but the day had seemed to confirm his earlier fears that they would not fight.

A small encounter the next day between American and British scouting parties south of the Heights led to a larger action when British cavalry, chasing a small group of Americans, sounded the "tally-ho," the signal for a fox chase. The insult angered the Americans sufficiently that they gave the redcoats as good as they were getting and showed that they could fight and fight well. The Battle of Harlem Heights "inspirited our troops prodigiously," according to their commander, but he needed more convincing evidence before he could be inspirited. For the moment, he was doubting even himself, and he poured out his hurt and confusion to cousin Lund: he did not know what to do, could see no good coming of his continued service, yet he was assured that he would irreparably harm the cause by resigning. He could gain neither fame nor success under the present system of recruiting and had neither comfort nor peace—"I never was in such an unhappy, divided state since I was born." Then the torrent of feeling eased, and characteristically but anticlimactically he concluded by cautioning Lund not to show the letter to anyone else. The task was his, and he would stay with it to the end, whenever and whatever that might be.[18]

The army lingered at the Heights for almost a month until Howe jolted Washington out of his despairing lethargy with an attempt to land on the mainland above Kingsbridge. All troops except the men manning Fort Washington, one of a pair of forts meant to deny the Hudson to the British, were immediately re-

---

[18] GW to Philip Schuyler, Sep. 20, 1776, to Lund Washington, Sep. 30, 1776, *Papers/Rev*, 6: 356–58, 440–43.

moved from the island. Once off Manhattan, Washington had to move to the high ground north of the Croton River, or he might be pinned against the Hudson. Before he could get there, however, he and Howe met on October 28 in the inconclusive Battle of White Plains. The encounter was a success for the Americans in that the men fought well, leaving the field to the enemy only when their artillery ran out of shot and powder, and it gave them enough time to beat a safe retreat to the heights above the Croton. It also suited Washington's wish to avoid a major battle "or put anything to the risk, unless compelled by a necessity into which we ought never to be drawn."[19] Now, although the army was in a naturally strong position, desertion and supply problems continued, and Congress had again delayed enlistment plans for the next year's army. Soon Washington would be in the same position he had been in at Cambridge, but this year the situation was much more fluid; everything could very easily be lost. Battered by two months of almost unrelieved defeat and retreat, the commander followed the advice of a council and did what he had always strenuously resisted: divide his army. He left 3,000 men with Major General William Heath to guard the supply route from New England, and 7,000 remained temporarily with Charles Lee (back from a successful defense of Charleston, South Carolina), while he took 2,000 with him into New Jersey, where he expected to find a reserve of 5,000 militia. In the previous summer, Congress had planned a "Flying Camp" of militia forces to be used as the commander in chief felt necessary. Congressional resolutions were one thing, their execution quite another, and the camp had never been formed, but no one had told Washington. On November 13, all he found at Fort Lee, the New Jersey twin to Fort Washington, were 2,700 men under the command of Major General Nathanael Greene, giving him a little less than 5,000 with him, including the men across the river at Fort Washington, whom Greene assured him could easily be evacuated should that "impregnable" position be threatened.[20]

An armchair general could have easily seen that Fort Washington was a poorly designed fort in an impossible location, but

---

[19] GW to John Hancock, Sep. 9, 1776, *Papers/Rev,* 6: 249.
[20] Freeman, 4: 221–41.

armchair generals have quiet and time, both missing completely from the life of the harried and bewildered commander of the American forces. Greene was left in charge of both forts while Washington puzzled out his next move. Suddenly a massive enemy attack, using a crack unit of Hessians commanded by Colonel Johann Rall, was hurled against Fort Washington on November 16, and the post's defects became obvious. Within hours, its commander, Colonel Robert Magaw, had no recourse but to surrender the almost 2,800 men and a large store of materiel that Greene had left there. A few days later Washington blamed Congress for wanting the river blocked and Greene for reinforcing the fort only days before its fall, but the fairest assessment of the incident he ever made came in 1779, when he admitted "that warfare in my mind, and hesitation" had helped bring about the loss. Despite Greene's command, Washington had had three days on the scene during which he should have done something about the risky situation across the Hudson: the responsibility was his.[21]

Washington began to plan shifting his slightly more than 2,000 men down toward another American force on the Raritan River when Howe, moving uncharacteristically fast, sent a force across the Hudson above Fort Lee early on November 20, while he himself went south, hoping to catch the Americans there. Local tradition has it that a plowman, working early, saw the redcoats and rode ahead to warn the garrison. Taking only their powder and shot, the Continentals got away just in time, clearing a critical crossroads, the Liberty Pole in the English Neighborhood (now Englewood, New Jersey), just as the British advance party came in sight. Except for the few shots exchanged there, the Americans escaped unscathed. Crossing the Hackensack River on the "New Bridge" and burning it after them, the Americans reached a haven for the night, but, pinned between the Hackensack and Passaic Rivers, in flat country with no natural defenses, Washington had to keep his small force moving south. For the next two weeks, with only a few days' rest, the men slogged through the mud of a rainy, cold November until they had passed through New Jersey, crossed into Pennsylvania, and put the Delaware River between themselves and the British.

---

[21] Knollenberg, *Revolution*, 132–38.

Washington now tried to concentrate his forces and ordered Charles Lee to bring his units totaling 7,700 men to the Delaware, but that worthy—impressed with his success in the South and aware of Washington's manifest mistakes in the New York campaign—procrastinated and presumed to deal with his commander as an equal. He decided to stay where he was and took it upon himself to order General William Heath, who had explicit orders from Washington to guard the Hudson Highlands, to move his 2,000 militia down to the Delaware. Heath properly refused. Further, Washington inadvertently discovered that Joseph Reed, his adjutant general, was secretly corresponding with Lee about their commander's indecision and lack of strategic sense. Washington, who felt he needed both men, swallowed his pride and let the incident pass. The success or failure of the war was more important than his own feelings. Lee was soon removed from the action by his own folly; sleeping, for comfort's sake, too far from his men, he was captured by an enemy patrol on December 13.

Although Washington genuinely regretted the loss of Lee, it did have two fortunate effects. If Lee had been present, he would almost certainly have argued strongly against what the commander was planning. Even if he failed to prevent the later actions at Trenton and Princeton, and they turned out successful, as they did, he would nevertheless have been given much of the credit, thus taking from Washington the prestige and acclaim that suddenly and properly fell on him. Lee's capture also freed John Sullivan, his second in command, recently exchanged, to bring on his force of 2,000 men to the main army, encamped on the Pennsylvania side of the Delaware above Trenton. The Americans had taken all available boats, so Howe settled his men down along the river below Trenton and back up the road to New Brunswick, and began to collect loyalty oaths on a wholesale basis from repentant New Jersey patriots, including even one of the state's signers of the Declaration of Independence.[22]

---

[22] John R. Alden, *General Charles Lee: Traitor or Patriot?* (Baton Rouge, 1951), 145–55; hereafter, Alden, *Charles Lee*. See also John F. Roche, *Joseph Reed* (1957, repr., New York, 1968), 98–103. The retreat across New Jersey and the Battles of Trenton and Princeton are covered in Leonard Lundin, *Cockpit of the Revolution: The War for Independence in New Jersey* (Princeton, 1940), and W. S.

Despite Howe's settled appearance, Washington was convinced that he would move on Philadelphia as soon as the river froze, giving him an easy passage across it. And the enlistments of most of Washington's men would expire with the year. Of the 8,000 (including some of Heath's men, units from Philip Schuyler in northern New York, and Pennsylvania militia) he could concentrate along the Delaware, only 1,400 to 1,500 would be left on January 1, 1777. He had to blunt or stop the British advance and gain time to gather a new army. Faced with such desperate circumstances, the only hope paradoxically was to resume the offensive and throw the enemy off stride, perhaps long enough to discourage any more fighting that winter. As early as December 14, Washington had thought of attacking the Hessian units across the Delaware in Trenton and Bordentown, and began gathering information on their numbers and disposition. Complicated plans for a three-pronged advance were made; Pennsylvania militia would strike at Bordentown, while a second force would strike at Trenton from the south; this combination was to coincide with an attack by Washington's force from the north. Christmas night, masked by a snow-and-sleet storm, Washington moved his 2,400 men, supported by eighteen cannon (much more than usual, but he knew his men needed all the help they could get), across the icy river. Before the men split into two columns, proceeding by separate roads, Washington moved among them, solemnly urging them to stay near their officers. For once, a divided American force kept well synchronized, and both columns went into action at the same time. Neither of the other units crossed the river, so 400 of the Hessian garrison escaped to the south before the town was surrounded. Two hours of close-quarter fighting brought the surrender of the rest of the garrison at the cost of only four American wounded. More than 100 Hessians were killed or wounded, and 1,000 were captured. Surveying his situation, Washington decided to stay with his original plan and recross the river immediately. Alone, his own men tired and chilled to the bone, with prisoners to handle, he could not do much more, for the moment, in New Jersey.

Stryker, *The Battles of Trenton and Princeton* (Boston, 1898). Freeman, 4: chaps. 9–14.

Washington's brief but circumstantial account of the victory noted the men's spirited behavior; when it "came to the charge, each seemed to vie with the other in pressing forward," and no unit could be singled out without doing injustice to the others.[23] If Trenton did anything, it helped to cure the lack of confidence Washington had had in his own men since Manhattan. Of course, it did much more than that. Although really little more than a raid against a poorly posted, inattentive, and ill-supported unit, Trenton immediately revived confidence in the cause and in its commander. Militarily well timed, it came at exactly the right time psychologically to inspirit the Americans, who had believed that all was about to be lost, and to discourage the British, who had believed that all was about to be won. Both sides quickly recast their plans for the immediate future. Comforted by their easy progress through New Jersey, the British had assumed they could hold large areas with token forces and wait for the rebellion to collapse for lack of popular support. Now Howe called back one of his more active subordinates, Lord Cornwallis, as he was ready to embark for Britain and sent him with reinforcements down to Princeton, eleven miles from Trenton, while the remaining Hessian units were pulled back from the Delaware. Washington, without the luxury of reserves to call in, had more difficult decisions to make.

Before he could do anything, he had to ensure that he would have an army after the first of the year. Without knowing that Congress had granted him dictatorial powers for six months, he offered his Continental regiments a ten-dollar bounty for an additional month's service. He moved around to the different encampments and spoke to the men in small groups. Responding to his description of the next few weeks as "the crisis which is to decide our destiny" and to his assurance that "we know not how to spare you," enough men signed to furnish a hard core of Continentals to bolster the Pennsylvania and New Jersey militia coming out for two month's service.[24]

A move across the Delaware could appear to be an advance but still leave several escape routes should the numerically superior

[23] GW to John Hancock, Dec. 27, 1776, *Papers/Rev*, 7: 454–55.
[24] Freeman, 4: 330–32, 331, n. 45.

enemy be encountered in an unfavorable situation. On the first day of 1777, Washington's men joined Pennsylvania militia at Trenton. Early the next day, a strong American scouting party led by Colonel Edward Hand encountered Cornwallis, advancing from Princeton; for the rest of the day, they fought a stiff delaying action, permitting Washington to arrange his army behind the Assumpink Creek. By late afternoon, the two forces faced each other across the rivulet, spanned by a narrow stone bridge. Cornwallis decided he had the "old fox" bagged between the creek and the Delaware, and could wait for the next day to claim his trophy. Meanwhile, the Americans, leaving behind some men to keep the fires lit and to make noise so that Cornwallis would sleep on undisturbed, marched south and then looped around to the north to strike at enemy units left behind in Princeton and perhaps continue on to New Brunswick, where a seventy-thousand-pound war chest and large quantities of materiel had been left.

The ruse worked. American forward units encountered a surprised British officer bringing his men forward to Cornwallis, on the outskirts of Princeton early on the morning of January 3. Despite an early reverse and the death of Brigadier General Hugh Mercer, the Americans rallied under Washington's personal direction and forced the enemy to break and run. Other enemy units were pinned down and forced to surrender, including 194 in the College of New Jersey's Nassau Hall, where one well-placed cannon shot, according to tradition, decapitated a portrait of George II inside the front door of the hall and ended its use as a redoubt. The shot was fired by Colonel Alexander Hamilton's New York artillery company; his competence soon placed him on Washington's staff, where he would stay until 1781.

Assessing the situation in a hurried conference held without even dismounting, Washington and his generals decided the men were too fatigued to continue on to New Brunswick, especially when Cornwallis's relatively fresh troops would soon be close on their heels. Destroying a bridge to slow down the British, the Americans put some distance between themselves and the enemy before resting and then moving to winter quarters in Morristown, safely beyond the Watchung Mountains in northern New Jersey. With Washington on his flank and the lesson of the

Trenton-Princeton campaign fresh in his memory, Howe moved his men back, leaving only garrisons at New Brunswick and Perth Amboy. To all intents and purposes, New Jersey was again a patriot state. More important, the American cause had been revivified beyond all reasonable expectations, with most of the credit going to Washington.[25]

To say that the 1776 campaign had educated Washington is to restate the obvious; any serious general is constantly learning— and relearning—the lessons of war. But Washington needed a good bit more of this learning than most of the generals he faced, and he obtained it in the same school they attended, that of experience. His mistakes during the fighting in and around New York City were many and obvious, but they were mitigated by the military unsuitability of a city for which it was psychologically necessary that a fight be made; he certainly could have done better, but the decision to fight for the city was correct. Throughout the campaign, the lack of competent officers threw too much of the burden on the commander in chief, who also had to contend with disloyalty and carping criticism—all of which were factors in the fatigue and indecision he showed at various times. Washington's loss of confidence in his men probably hindered him from trying to make a stand instead of retreating, but he had begun to learn the assets as well as the liabilities of the American soldier, especially the usefulness of the militia when bolstered by seasoned Continentals, as they had been at Princeton.[26] The fine performance of the troops was one of the major ingredients in the American victories of December 26 and January 3; in the words of one of Washington's favorite plays, Joseph Addison's *Cato*, the soldiers not only attained success, they deserved it. And so did their commander. Against Howe's ponderous, slow-moving caution, Washington had been able to snatch if not victory, at least survival—and a bit more—from probable defeat. The weariness and indecision that had marked him fell away as he

---

[25] GW to John Hancock, Jan. 5, 1777, *Papers/Rev,* 7: 519–23; Henry Knox shared GW's belief that a successful raid on New Brunswick could have ended the war, *Papers/Rev,* 529–30, n. 10.

[26] See Mark V. Kwasny's *Washington's Partisan War, 1775–1783* (Kent, Ohio, 1996) for an excellent description of GW's use of militia, concentrating on the middle states.

made and remade plans as the necessity of the moment required and as he took intelligent risks, not careless risks such as at Fort Washington. However, as successful as Trenton and Princeton were, they do not make Washington one of the great captains of history. The contribution he made to the American victory was in the quality of his leadership. As has already been seen, he was often discouraged, and his letters to his family read like a catalog of prospective horrors—"the game is nearly up" was one of his favorite expressions—but he never gave up, and associates remarked how his command improved during times of acute stress. During the last four months of 1776, Washington experienced enough frustration and defeat to justify a resignation, but he instead extended himself and his men, and brought about a spectacular turn of fortune. Trenton and Princeton are perhaps most important as examples of the commander in chief's refusal to accept defeat.

The army spent an uncomfortable winter at Morristown, plagued by both food shortages and disease. Washington invoked his dictatorial powers on more than one occasion to coerce farmers to sell provisions. When smallpox threatened, the general, already immune, called in physicians from Philadelphia and had everyone in camp inoculated, a preventive procedure that many still feared, but that in this instance was generally successful. Martha again joined her husband for the winter, along with other officers' wives. When the endless administrative chores threatened to swamp him, Washington would seek relief by horseback rides followed by festive dinners, even though there was little to celebrate. On these occasions, according to Martha Bland, the wife of one the staff officers, the commander "throws off the hero and takes on the chatty, agreeable companion. He can be downright impudent sometimes, such impudence, Fanny, as you and I like." But such moments were rare as the "impudent" gallant wrestled with the eternal problems of numbers and supply. The core of less than 1,000 Continentals were supplemented by New Jersey militia who spent their tours of duty harassing the British garrisons in New Brunswick and Perth Amboy. Washington kept the size of his small force such a closely guarded secret that even some congressmen complained of keeping "hordes" of men in idleness. Congress had optimistically (foolishly?) provided for an army of 75,000 regulars, but the provision was effective only on paper, as just about all such provisions were. Eventually 8,000 men enlisted under its resolution arrived at Morristown. The cause seemed finally to be shaking off the "strange-unaccountable languor" Washington complained of to Patrick Henry in April.[27]

Moving out of winter quarters in May, Washington placed his army just above New Brunswick and, through June, refused Howe's invitation to move down onto the coastal plain that began below New Brunswick. Unwilling to advance toward Philadelphia with the Continentals on his flank, Howe called the dance off early in July and left New Jersey. Washington had realized that the cause could be "advanced otherwise than by fighting," especially if one considered "the consequences which may follow"— that is, the loss of the army—and was keeping "the one great end in view," victory. He would pursue the means to attain it whatever they were, hoping for the approval of "the candid part of Mankind" when it was achieved. Although he was not nearly as unfeeling about his reputation as these words suggest, he had bought precious time with his defensive maneuvering and demonstrated much more patience and self-control than the colonel of the Virginia Regiment had, precisely the qualities needed if the cause were to be victorious.[28]

Now it was Washington's turn to be confused by Howe. Knowing of the enemy's thrust down Lake Champlain under Brigadier General John Burgoyne, Washington was uncertain whether Howe would take ship and move up the Hudson toward Burgoyne or sail around New Jersey to hit Philadelphia. Marching and countermarching through central Jersey while Howe sent out puzzling signals broke down the already shaky American supply system. The uncertainty regarding Howe's destination was a fine demonstration of the mobility the Royal Navy gave him, but Washington did not need it. On August 22, he learned that

---

[27] George F. Scheer and Hugh F. Rankin, *Rebels and Redcoats* (1957, repr., New York, 1959), 256; Freeman, 4: chap. 15; GW to Patrick Henry, Apr. 13, 1777, *Papers/Rev*, 9: 146–48. Members of Congress saw the same "languor"; see William Duer to Abraham Ten Broeck, Apr. 17, 1777, in Burnett, *Letters*, 2: 331–32.

[28] GW to Joseph Reed, June 23, 1777, *Papers/Rev*, 10: 113–15.

Howe's fleet was moving up the Chesapeake Bay. Howe had been scared away from the Delaware River by reports of its navigational hazards and of the American defenses, and now he was going to strike at Philadelphia from the south. Making a virtue of necessity, Washington had the army cleaned up, a fresh sprig of green placed in every man's hat, and marched them through the city as they moved to fend off Howe. Although admiring, Massachusetts Congressman John Adams had to note: "Our soldiers have not yet quite the air of soldiers," but their general had learned that spirit could make up for cosmetic deficiencies.[29]

In some respects, Philadelphia presented the same dilemma New York had; militarily of no great significance, it still could not be abandoned without a fight. As the seat of Congress, it was the closest thing to a capital the young republic had, and it was also an important commercial and manufacturing center. There the resemblance ended; although it was situated on a peninsula between two rivers, there was no great advantage for British sea power because the rivers were shallow and difficult to navigate; otherwise, approaches to the city were over flat or rolling terrain. Along the route of Howe's advance from the south, the closest thing to a natural barrier was the Brandywine Creek; deep enough to be crossed only at several fords, it entered the Delaware at Wilmington. Facing an army of 18,000, Washington arranged his force of 11,000 along the creek's banks on September 10 and awaited the enemy. He knew he was expected to make a fight for Philadelphia, even if in popular opinion it held only loyalist Quakers, and the Brandywine was as good a place as any to fight. Early the next day, in a hazy dawn that promised more of the stifling heat of the last few days, the American center was attacked; the line was held, but contradictory intelligence reports from the American right, commanded by John Sullivan, confused Washington, and he halted an attack on the enemy center and went himself to investigate. He found Sullivan under a heavy attack, caught while changing position to meet the enemy; all he

---

[29] John Adams to Abigail Adams, Aug. 24, 1777, in L. H. Butterfield, ed., *The Adams Papers, Series II: Adams Family Correspondence* (Cambridge, Mass., 1963), 2: 325.

could do was help the badly mauled Americans to disengage. The intelligence reports were accurate; it was Washington's poor knowledge of the terrain that made them seem contradictory. When the crisis came, his response was slow; for much of the day he acted "as if he had been in a daze." Yet, for all the commander's shortcomings, the day was not a complete disaster. Although the Americans suffered twice as many casualties as the enemy, they remained on the field until ordered to leave and then left in good order, although they later got badly mixed up. Further, the defeat seemed to discourage few; the feeling among the men seemed to be that the next encounter might be a victory. A British review of the year's operations concurred: "the rebels were not disheartened; and Mr. Washington exerted himself with ability and diligence to repair his defeat."[30]

The militia reformed, and some additional units were brought in from the Hudson Valley. Washington maneuvered his ill-fed, ill-clad men (more than 1,000 were barefoot), trying to parry the enemy's thrusts toward Philadelphia. In the confused maneuvering that followed, Howe feinted toward Reading, where a large American supply store was located, pulling Washington and his forces well away from the city, then he neatly countermarched and entered the capital on September 23. Now the unimportance of the city became obvious to everyone. Congress had long since fled, and all important supplies had been removed; only the shell of the city with its loyalists was left for the enemy. Further, it remained to be seen if Howe could hold the city. American forts, erected to guard obstructions in the narrow channel of the Delaware, were putting up a stiff resistance. If the navy could not supply Howe, he might have to give up the city. The river forts, almost unsupported, held out until mid-November, by which time Washington had shown the British he was far from beaten.

Howe had placed the main portion of his army at Germantown, about ten miles northwest of the city, where their detached location almost invited an American attack. With the available men, Washington contrived a complex four-pronged pincers movement whose strength was concentrated in the center. Al-

---

[30] Freeman, 4: chap. 18, describes the day; the quotations are on 488 and 491.

though hindered by poorly drawn orders, the attack began well early on October 4, and the Americans drove the enemy back almost into their main camp. Then things began to fall apart. A quick-rising fog confused the advancing Continentals, some of whom fired on each other; ammunition ran short just as they encountered fresh enemy units; and a precipitate retreat left Nathanael Greene's column alone so that it had to retreat hurriedly. Militia units, the outside pincers, were either beaten back or else never reached the scene. Although the American retreat was disorderly, a rear guard was organized and kept the redcoats at a distance.

Analyses of Germantown often focus on the complexity of the battle plan as the reason for defeat, but the fog, the men's confused firing on each other, and the shortage of ammunition were at least equally responsible. It is not often enough remembered that the Americans almost won the battle, complicated plans and green officers notwithstanding. (This was a tactical weakness of Washington, whose fondness for multiple column movements was shown for the first time when he encircled the Jumonville party in 1754 and then again in a similar plan only partially executed for Trenton.) As with Brandywine, solace could be found in defeat; the Americans fought well, and as Washington reported to Congress, "the day was rather unfortunate than injurious." Further, news of the battle, reported none too accurately in France, and news of the surrender of a large British-Hessian force to Major General Horatio Gates at Saratoga in mid-October created such a favorable impression at the French court that an alliance was signed in February 1778.[31]

A month of apparently aimless maneuvering north and west of Philadelphia followed until Washington settled the men down at Valley Forge, eighteen miles up the Schuylkill River from Philadelphia. He had wanted to take them into the interior near Congress, which was now safely ensconced at York, one hundred miles to the west, or else down to Wilmington, but strong protests from Pennsylvania kept him in the Philadelphia area. He obeyed

---

[31] See John S. Pancake, *1777: The Year of the Hangman* (University, Ala., 1977), 199–204, for the river forts. Ward, *War*, 1: chap. 33, is an excellent description of Germantown; GW to John Hancock, Oct. 5, 1777, *Writings*, 9: 310.

the civilian authorities, although, as he noted almost sarcastically, it was easy enough to draw up remonstrances when warm and well fed, much easier than seeing to it that Pennsylvania contributed her share to the army's supplies. The area selected for the camp had been drained dry of supplies, and "wintering in this desert," as the foreign volunteer Johann deKalb described it, would be difficult enough for an army with an effective supply organization. Now, in addition to the perennial problem of recruiting a new army and the constant problems of indiscipline and poor officers, Washington would have to be his own supply officer.

Valley Forge has become a symbol of the trials that the Continental army underwent because of the too-often ineffectual support Congress gave it, and it is difficult to exaggerate the privations that the men endured. Entering the camp in poor condition because of their inadequate clothing and constant marching, they were able to provide themselves only with shelter; by building rough log huts, they secured at least a measure of comfort. But there were rarely enough foodstuffs on hand for Washington to relax; the slightest interruption to the flow of supplies, and the men were reduced to meager allotments of flour or corn meal, with sometimes nothing at all. Local foraging was fruitless, and before the winter was over, the net had been cast as far as North Carolina to bring food to the men. The Continental commissariat had recently been "reformed," and the men administering it were inexperienced or incompetent; hence, much of Washington's time was taken up with composing begging letters to state authorities to obtain food wherever he could. The overwork caused by this constant problem may have helped bring on the irritability he displayed during the episode known as the Conway Cabal.[32]

The Cabal took its name from Brigadier General Thomas Conway, an Irish-born French officer, one of the many French officers who came over both recommended and unrecommended, expecting to show the ignorant Americans the finer

---

[32] E. Wayne Carp, *To Starve the Army at Pleasure: Continental Army Administration and American Political Culture, 1775–1783* (Chapel Hill, N.C., 1984), chap. 2, esp. 44–45.

points of the art of war. Conway had demonstrated his competence at the Brandywine and Germantown, and was angling for promotion to major general over the heads of several senior American officers. Congress did promote him and also made him inspector general, attached to the Board of War, a group of full-time administrators who took the place of congressional committees and would try to satisfy the needs of the army. Washington objected to Conway's promotion because of the injury it did to the American brigadiers, so Congress delayed it. But the commander in chief became suspicious when he learned that Conway was corresponding with Horatio Gates, whose unqualified success at Saratoga contrasted strikingly with the ambivalent results of the Philadelphia campaign. The former quartermaster general, Thomas Mifflin, was also connected with Conway when he and Gates were appointed to the board. It is doubtful that these three did anything more than exchange letters critical of Washington's conduct of the war. Nor was there widespread discontent with their general among the Congress, although some recognized that there was danger in the idolization of any military figure, even one as principled as Washington. John Adams rejoiced at the Saratoga victory, not only for its military benefits but also because it permitted "a certain citizen to be wise, virtuous, and good, without thinking him a deity or a saviour." More to the point, Elbridge Gerry complained that the extreme reaction from Washington's officers, especially his staff, to the Conway promotion was hindering Congress in its constitutional prerogative of selecting officers. One should also remember that both Congress and the officer corps had ambitious men who could be mean-spirited and irresponsible. For his part, Washington seemed convinced that there was indeed a plot to see Gates "exalted on the ruin of my reputation and influence." His anxiety on this score was compounded of several ingredients: the overwork mentioned previously, his sensitivity to criticism, and his regard for his public standing. Even as colonel of the Virginia Regiment, Washington had not received criticism well; now, although he often claimed he was willing to accept informed criticism, he usually rejected civilian comment as uninformed, and he considered military comment the symptom of a plot. His concern about his reputation was more understandable. In accord with his Stoic values, he was serving for the coin he regarded above all others—the good opinion of his fellow citizens—and anything that menaced this payment would always provoke a strong reaction from him. As he saw it, in spite of his best efforts on behalf of the cause, he was not being paid fairly. The furor began to die down when Conway, seeing the untenability of his position, resigned in January 1778; with this marplot removed from the scene, Washington recovered his composure as he continued to wrestle with the never-ending problems of keeping the army together and planning for the new campaign.[33]

The difficulties of securing men, provisions, and weapons and of dealing with the sloth, inefficiency, or recalcitrance of the states (and sometimes all these factors combined) ensured that Washington's tasks would continue to be arduous and aggravating. These difficulties also complicated the preparation of the men for the new campaign, training them to be soldiers. But help sometimes presents itself in strange forms, and Washington should not be faulted for failing to recognize it when late in February Friedrich von Steuben presented himself at Washington's headquarters as an unpaid volunteer. Although Steuben's background and experience in the army of Frederick the Great had been embellished, his ability was real, and he quickly devised a common and simplified system of drill and maneuver to replace the various systems that different regiments had adopted. Showing a surprising adaptability, Steuben soon realized that Americans were not Europeans: "The genius of this nation is not in the least to be compared with that of the Prussians. . . . I am obliged to say 'This is the reason you ought to do that' " before his new pupils accepted new methods. His work was soon rewarded with appointment as inspector general and promotion to major general. Although it is possible to overestimate the work he did at Valley Forge—after all, he did not find an untrained mob there—the army that marched in pursuit of the enemy in the

---

[33] Knollenberg, *Revolution,* chaps. 5–8, for this episode; see also Freeman, 4: chaps. 20–25; Flexner, 2: chaps. 27–30; Higginbotham, *War,* chap. 9; and John G. Rossie, *The Politics of Command in the American Revolution* (Syracuse, N.Y., 1975), chap. 13.

spring of 1778 was a more dependable force, and Steuben contributed materially to that improvement.[34]

Nor was that the only improvement that came to the cause during the otherwise grim winter of 1777–78. The Americans no longer stood alone; in February, convinced the rebels were capable of sustaining their effort against Britain, France had signed treaties of commerce and alliance with Congress's representatives in Paris. Washington's reaction was typically both hopeful and cautious: "Calmness and serenity, seems likely to succeed in some measure, those dark and tempestuous clouds which at times appeared ready to overwhelm us. The game, whether well or ill played hitherto, seems now to be verging fast to a favorable issue." Now care would have to be taken that the Americans did not relax and let their new allies take over. There was very little to relax over. As usual, with the spring already half gone, the supply system was in disarray and only a little more than one-half of the 20,000 troops authorized for the year were in camp. These men would have to deal with the 10,000 British troops in Philadelphia and with an additional 6,000 divided between New York and Newport, Rhode Island. As before, militia would have to supplement the regulars.[35]

Work provided a refuge from doubts for Washington, and there was enough of that to go around. Charles Lee was back in action, having been exchanged for a British general, so the brigades had to be rearranged, and questions of seniority and so on worked out. Nothing satisfied Lee, who was angling for promotion to lieutenant general on the basis of his self-professed merit. Temporarily settling this vexing question, Washington called a council of war, which advised him to sit tight and improve the army as much as possible. However, spies' reports that Sir Henry Clinton, the new British commander, was getting ready to evacuate Philadelphia were becoming frequent: the city was too far from the sea and too difficult to supply, and he was moving back to New York. In leaving the city, Clinton allowed himself to be burdened with numerous loyalists and wagon loads of their prop-

---

[34] John M. Palmer, *General von Steuben* (New Haven, Conn., 1937), 114–16, 129, and chap. 22; hereafter, Palmer, *Steuben.* Higginbotham, *War,* 222, 247.

[35] GW to Robert Morris, May 25, 1778, *Writings,* 11: 453.

erty, which meant that he had to guard an extended line of fifteen hundred wagons while the army moved across the plain of central New Jersey. Prepared to move, the Americans followed close behind as the British wagon train crossed the Delaware on June 17. Washington scented the possibility of striking a substantial blow at the long, straggling columns, a possibility about which his generals were seriously divided. Local militia did all they could to delay the march, burning bridges, removing forage, and striking at detached enemy units when possible. Clinton's army was the largest British force in North America; its destruction might mean an end to the war. Lee was most insistent that the Continental army was not ready to fight on even terms with the British, yet because of seniority he commanded the advance guard. The other commanders remained divided, and a council of war on June 24 ordered the advance unit "to act as occasion may serve." The main body was to stay back "so as to act as circumstances may require." They were playing it by ear, but Washington's ear had begun to hear whispers of a stunning defeat on the scale of Saratoga. However, he did not change the vague orders.

On June 28, the encounter came in sultry heat that reached near one hundred degrees at Monmouth Courthouse, southeast of New Brunswick. Fighting with his back against a field scarred by three morasses, the only way through a narrow causeway, Lee soon became convinced he had struck the main body, not the rear guard, of the enemy, and so ordered a retreat. As Washington came to the battle, a confused withdrawal had already begun. He brusquely asked Lee why he was retreating, to which Lee stammered something about poor intelligence. Turning from Lee, Washington organized a temporary line and then brought the main body of his troops into a strong defensive position in back of the morasses, and there the two armies fought it out to a stalemate. The Americans, expecting to renew the battle the next day, slept on their arms, but the morning light revealed that Clinton had quietly pulled out during the night. The field was empty.

Disappointed at the indecisive results—even the casualties were roughly equal, approximately 360 on each side—Washington did not claim a victory in his report to Congress. But there was an item for the credit side; the men had fought well, especially in their maneuvering under fire. Steuben's drilling was already paying dividends. Now a strange sequel to the battle occurred. The brusque exchange between the two generals had not been mentioned in Washington's report. Lee, believing he had saved his men from destruction, demanded an apology from Washington for his conduct on the day of the battle, insinuating that Washington's judgment was clouded by the "dirty earwigs" who had attached themselves to the general. In the exchange that followed, Lee wrote of his chief's "tinsel dignity," along with other slighting references, and wound up demanding an examination of his own conduct by a court-martial. Washington, surprised and hurt by Lee's letters, obliged him, and charges were drawn up accusing Lee of disobeying orders by not attacking, of making an *"unnecessary, disorderly, and shameful retreat"* (emphasis in original), and of being disrespectful to his commander. Held in various places as the army maneuvered and then moved into quarters near Paramus, New Jersey, the resulting court-martial settled nothing because the testimony on the conduct of the accused was confused and contradictory. Lee was found guilty and suspended from command for a year, a mild punishment that did not fit the seriousness of the first two charges. And this was as it should have been. The real point of the situation was in the third charge. Lee, ever confident of his own superior ability and contemptuous of Washington's conduct in command, had directly challenged the commander in chief. The court-martial was really asked to choose between Washington or Lee, between the symbol of American resistance to Britain and an arrogant Englishman whose attachment to the cause many suspected. Congress confirmed the verdict, and Lee never resumed his command. Ironically, Washington's fault was the greater at Monmouth; when he had very much wanted a vigorous attack to be made, he had permitted a man who openly doubted the ability of the American troops to stand up to the British and to command with vague orders. However, the army and Congress were not considering the merits of generals, but rather of leaders, and there Washington was clearly the superior.[36]

---

[36] W. S. Stryker's *The Battle of Monmouth* (Princeton, 1927) is an exhaustive treatment of the event and of the court-martial; Alden, *Charles Lee*, is a fair presentation of Lee's side of the story; see also Charles Lee to GW, June [30],

The unpleasant memories of the near thing at Monmouth and the Lee court-martial probably passed quickly away when Washington learned of the arrival of a French fleet off Sandy Hook. Gratifying as this first token of French assistance was, the event nevertheless touched off one of the most frustrating periods of the war for Washington. To have the help a powerful ally could offer and yet do nothing with it because of the inadequacy of the American forces and an inability to agree on a common plan of operations prevented any of the benefits of the alliance from being realized for almost two years. His first thought was to enlist the French force in an attempt against the garrison in New York City; he firmly believed that if the enemy could be dislodged from there, the war would be over. But this plan had to be set aside when the French admiral, Comte d'Estaing, would not pass a bar in the outer harbor. The admiral did help in an attack on Newport Island that began well but then ended abruptly, unsuccessfully, and acrimoniously when the French withdrew and left John Sullivan and an American force almost stranded on the island. The Americans were gotten off safely, but Sullivan let all who would listen know that he felt himself to be abandoned, so the alliance was off on an uneasy course.

Thus, the campaigning season of 1778 ended with little more accomplished than the recovery of Philadelphia—certainly not brought about by American arms—and the first, inglorious attempt to cooperate with the French. With the men placed in winter quarters, Washington rode to Philadelphia to confer with Congress about the next campaign. The stay produced little more than frustration for the general. He viewed with dismay the high living of congressmen and others, as well as their apparent unconcern about the deficiencies of the army and about the fast-falling value of Continental currency. All this he lamented, but quietly and privately to friends in Virginia, whom he urged to cooperate in sending the best Virginians to Congress so that at least one state would do its part. As he doubtless realized later, he was living through what was probably the war's lowest point, when the Americans seemed incapable of helping themselves

1778, GW to Charles Lee, June 30, 1778, Charles Lee to GW, June [30], 1778, *Lee Papers*, 2: 435–37, 3: 1–208, for the record of the court-martial.

and the French incapable of offering nothing save vague promises. Spring saw the same old story: too few men, too few supplies—always scarcity where plenty was needed, apparently because few civilians could or would match the dedication of the soldiers and their dispirited commander. The constant toil of fighting a war on the cheap was telling on Washington. In April 1779, he complained that it was "a melancholy thing to see such a decay of public virtue, and the fairest prospects over cast and clouded by a host of infamous harpies who, to acquire a little pelf, would involve this great Continent in inextricable ruin." Although he was overstating things, as he usually did when he vented the deep pessimism lying just below his usually calm exterior, it is also important to note that he never showed the least disposition to take matters into his own hands and, with the army, to give law to Congress, which had allowed, if it had not caused, such a situation. If the new republic was generally fortunate in its servants, it was thrice blessed with a commander who could, despite such discouragement, continue to serve loyally and without public complaint.[37]

The year 1779 saw almost as little for Washington's army as 1778 had. Except for some minor actions in the lower Hudson Valley and a successful campaign by Sullivan against the Iroquois, the focus of action had shifted to the South, where first Horatio Gates failed to stop the British, who had already taken Charleston, and then where Nathanael Greene parried with the enemy in an exhausting campaign that covered most of the Carolinas before it was finished. Perhaps realizing that Congress's war chest could not support an extensive effort, Washington did not push strongly for more than a holding action in the North. And that is all he got.

The frustration of the summer of 1779 was followed by one of the most difficult winters the Continental army ever faced. Encamped in the woods near Morristown, New Jersey, the men were ill-served by a supply system that was often ineffectual in good weather, but that broke down completely under the pressure of heavy snows and low temperatures. Steuben described the New York Brigade as "the most shocking picture of misery I

---

[37] GW to William Fitzhugh, Apr. 14, 1779, *Writings*, 14: 363–65.

have ever seen, scarce a man having wherewithal to cover his nakedness." And these were the men who had to be talked into reenlisting before May 1780 when the service period of 8,000 men would expire. The deep snow and frigid temperatures combined with the collapsing supply system to bring about a dangerous state of indiscipline in the men. With so many officers being on furlough, the men could not be kept in the camp, and they roamed the neighborhood, taking what they pleased. Washington was forced to condone a requisition on the countryside, always considered the last resort because he realized that one of the special strengths of the American cause had to be the favor of the country people or all indeed was lost. By this and other expedients, the army was again pulled through and prepared, as well as it could be, for the summer's campaigning. If Washington had been willing to let 1779 slip by without a strong American effort, he was not going to let 1780 by. If the French were not convinced that the Americans were serious, he feared they might let the alliance slip into ineffectuality. A special urgency was given to this issue when the Marquis de Lafayette—a young French volunteer who had originally joined the Americans in 1777 just before Brandywine and had since endeared himself to Washington by his blend of youthful enthusiasm and competence—returned from France with the news that a large French army would presently arrive. Congress "reformed" the supply system yet again, replacing requisition or purchase by Continental agents with one of direct requisition in kind from the states. With adequate transport, such a system might have worked, but transport was as inadequate as the clothing and food the men were not receiving. In protesting the system, which made Congress little more than a collecting agency for the army, Washington penetrated to the basic flaw in the Confederation, one that would not be corrected until 1789:

> Unless the states will content themselves with a full and well-chosen representation in Congress, and vest that body with absolute powers in all matters relative to the great purposes of war and of general concern by which the states unitedly are affected, reserving to themselves all matters of local and internal polity for the regulation of order and good government, we are attempting an impossibility and very soon shall become (if that is not already the

case) a many headed monster, a heterogeneous mass, that never will or can steer to the same point.

As expected, the system was a failure, and the army limped along for another year with inadequate supplies.[38]

Most of the summer of 1780 was spent waiting for the French army, which, when it arrived, proved smaller than expected. Washington's first conference with its commander, Comte de Rochambeau, in September at Hartford, Connecticut, was polite but vague: "We could only combine possible plans on the supposition of possible events and engage mutually to do everything in our powers against the next campaign," the American general recalled later. When Washington asked for some French troops to go south with American units to assist there, Rochambeau refused, saying that he could place his units only under Washington's personal command. Thus, one clear gain did come from the meeting; the American general realized that his command of the combined forces was "upon a very limited scale." If the French general was going to cooperate, it would be only on something he felt bound to succeed.[39]

One step ahead, two steps backward. As Washington rode back to his headquarters in Tappan, New York, from his talks with the French general, he decided to inspect the progress of the fortifications at West Point over which he had recently placed Benedict Arnold, who was slowly recuperating from a wound suffered at Saratoga. There he found the works in disarray and the post's commander absent. Within a few hours, he had learned the reason for both of these strange occurrences. Arnold had been in a treasonous correspondence with the enemy designed to bring about the handing over of the vital post. The plot had been uncovered by the accidental capture of a British officer sent behind the American lines to confer with Arnold. Informed of the capture by an unsuspecting American officer, Arnold had fled to the safety of the vessel that had brought the captive officer to the

---

[38] Palmer, *Steuben*, 218; GW to William Irvine, to Royal Flint, Jan. 4, 1780, *Writings*, 17: 347–49, 351–52; Flexner, 2: 362; GW to Fielding Lewis, May 5 [July 6], 1780, *Writings*, 19: 132.

[39] "Answers to Queries," "Summary of a Conversation," Sep. 20, 1780, *Writings*, 20: 76–78, 79–81.

area. Although the event was one of the more spectacular of the war, it actually had few significant consequences except for those immediately involved. Washington could have been affected if anyone had cared to comment on his placing Arnold in such a vital post, but no one did. He put the best face he could on the incident by commenting to Rochambeau that the remarkable thing was not that there was a traitor—that was only to be expected—but that there had been so few.[40]

Washington should have kept the good spirits he expressed to Rochambeau; he would need them to get through the coming winter. His confused outlook was expressed in a kind of summing up in early October:

> I see nothing before us but accumulating distress. We have been half our time without provision and are like to continue so. We have no Magazines [of munitions], nor money to form them, and in a little time we shall have no Men, if we had money to pay them. We have lived upon expedients till we can live no longer. In a word, the history of the war is a history of false hopes and temporary devices, instead of system and economy. It is in vain, however, to look back, nor is it our business to do so. Our case is not desperate, if virtue exists in the people and there is wisdom among our rulers.

Virtue and wisdom, just the qualities Washington had seen so conspicuously lacking in Philadelphia.[41]

Patience and discretion were also needed, for January 1781 brought one of the most terrifying developments any general could face: mutiny. Anthony Wayne's Pennsylvania Line Regiment, quartered near Morristown, had enlisted for three years or the duration. Disgusted with their conditions of service, the men decided their enlistments were for three years only and, under the direction of a committee of sergeants, marched toward Philadelphia. Before Washington could react to the emergency, the

---

[40] Carl VanDoren, *Secret History of the American Revolution* (New York, 1941), chaps. 6–15. James Kirby Martin's *Benedict Arnold, Revolutionary Hero: An American Warrior Reconsidered* (New York, 1997) studies Arnold's career up to the discovery of his treason, by way of explaining it. James T. Flexner's *The Traitor and the Spy: Benedict Arnold and John André* (New York, 1953) is also useful. GW to Rochambeau, Sep. 20, 1780, *Writings*, 20: 97.

[41] GW to John Cadwalader, Oct. 5, 1780, *Writings*, 20: 121–22.

Pennsylvania authorities entered the situation and negotiated a settlement favorable to the men. Although Washington feared the settlement might "not only subvert the Pennsylvania Line but have a very pernicious influence on the whole Army," there was nothing he could do but wait for the next incident. Before the end of the month, it came. A New Jersey unit encamped at Pompton decided to extort its back pay from the state authorities. The officers had talked the men back into their quarters before a picked unit of 500 men under Major General Robert Howe arrived. On Washington's orders, "a few of the most active and incendiary leaders" were executed, and the men returned to their duties. The example he had wanted to give to the army had been given, but Washington did not delude himself. Further mutinies could be prevented only "by rendering the situation of the soldiery more tolerable than it has heretofore been." Patriotism only went so far; good food and warm clothing were also needed.[42]

Washington was also feeling mutinous, but he vented his feelings by a few uncharacteristic displays of ill temper. In February, Alexander Hamilton resigned from Washington's staff in a huff because the general had brusquely rebuked him for a tardy response to a summons; there was fault on both sides, but the initial harshness was the older man's. The following month, after an ineffective and belated attempt by a small French fleet to land some men in the Chesapeake area to relieve the heavy pressure on Nathanael Greene in North Carolina, Washington vented his anger in an imprudent letter to cousin Lund. As in 1775, the letter fell into British hands and was published. Rochambeau diplomatically hinted that the letter was a forgery, but the American commander refused to take the hint and bluntly stated that because the letter was private, it should not be noticed. Fortunately for the future of the alliance, Rochambeau decided not to take offense, and the affair ended there.[43]

With the failure of the French attempt to land troops in the Chesapeake, Washington was free to argue that an old dream of

---

[42] Carl VanDoren's *Mutiny in January* (New York, 1948) is a full recounting; Freeman, 5: 245–50.

[43] Flexner, 2: 411–15; GW to Rochambeau, Apr. 30, 1781, *Writings*, 22: 16–17.

his, an attack on New York City, would be the most effectual means of relieving the pressure on Greene in the Carolinas by possibly inducing the British to pull men north. A Franco-American conference in May resulted in plans for just such an attack.[44] The next month Rochambeau moved his units south from Connecticut, and on July 2 the attempt was made. For a variety of reasons, most of them stemming from the natural superiority of the area for an enemy who commanded the waterways around Manhattan, it failed. With this failure, Rochambeau was now free to push his favorite plan, moving the whole army to the Chesapeake area. In the late summer of 1781, a specific objective presented itself when the British commander in the South, Lord Cornwallis, concentrated his forces on a peninsula between the York and James Rivers, a safe situation as long as the Royal Navy retained its command of the sea. Cornwallis at Yorktown presented an opportunity to Washington and Rochambeau almost as attractive as Clinton's forces had in New York City; all they had to do was puzzle out how to take advantage of it. The major pieces needed to solve the puzzle were the allied armies concentrated around New York City, additional men and provisions, a small French squadron at Newport with the heavy artillery needed for a siege, and, most important, a fleet strong enough to stop any attempt by the Royal Navy to take off Cornwallis. On August 15, Washington learned that the last element was, incredibly, about to be supplied. Comte de Grasse was bringing a large battle fleet up from the West Indies and would be off the Chesapeake Capes in early September. Also, he had 3,000 soldiers with him who would be landed if necessary. Moving more quickly than one would have thought possible, the first American units left for the Chesapeake on August 19, followed presently by the French. As Washington moved across New Jersey, he constantly fretted about the possibility of de Grasse's not arriving in time: "I am distressed beyond expression. . . . If you get anything new from any quarter, send it . . . for I am almost all impatience and anxiety." On September 5, Rochambeau and his staff, sailing

---

[44] Approximately at this time, GW resumed his diary, which he had dropped at the beginning of the war; "Yorktown: A Victor's View," May–Nov. 1781, *Diaries*, 3: 356–438.

down the Delaware from Philadelphia in order to inspect the river forts that had given Howe such difficulty in 1777, were amazed to see Washington on the dock at Chester, jumping up and down and waving. They understood the loss of his usual composure when he relayed what a special messenger had just told him: de Grasse had arrived in the Chesapeake and was already unloading the troops at Jamestown, opposite Yorktown on the narrow peninsula of the James and York Rivers. With some superb staff work and logistics (and some luck), both armies moved men and materiel along until the men from the north joined the Pennsylvania Line, under Lafayette's command, at Williamsburg, ten miles from Yorktown. By the time the northern armies arrived, de Grasse had fought and won the Battle of the Chesapeake Capes on September 9; this victory not only gave the allies temporary but essential naval supremacy, but also covered the arrival of the Newport fleet with the vital siege guns. Incredibly, all the various pieces had been fitted together; the finished picture showed a British force of more than 9,000, with some supporting transport vessels bottled up at Yorktown by approximately 11,000 American regulars and militia, and almost 9,000 French regulars.[45]

What followed was almost anticlimactic. The siege, conducted mainly by the French, who had the necessary equipment and expertise, was opened on September 28; Cornwallis resisted it sluggishly, almost fatalistically, and made no attempt to break through the allied lines. With the lines drawn close about his camp and the fire of more than one hundred cannon concentrated on it, the British general proposed the opening of negotiations on the morning of October 17. Two days later, the terms had been put into regular form, but in the meantime, one concession, formally unnoticed, had taken place. Washington permitted Cornwallis to send one sloop, uninspected, away to New York City, allowing the safe evacuation of loyalists and American deserters, whom Washington would not promise to treat as prisoners of war. Early in the afternoon of October 19, the British

---

[45] GW to Lafayette, Sep. 2, 1781, *Writings*, 23: 75–77; Freeman, 6: chaps. 21–23, details GW's role; Higginbotham, *War*, 375–83. Thomas Fleming's *Beat the Last Drum* (New York, 1963) is a good popular account.

garrison marched out of the town, passing between facing lines of American and French soldiers. When Washington realized that Cornwallis did not head the British officers (he pleaded illness), but that Brigadier Charles O'Hara was offering his sword, he motioned O'Hara to present the weapon to Benjamin Lincoln, who had surrendered to Cornwallis at Charleston in 1780. In the surrender terms, the British were denied the same honors they had denied Lincoln's men at Charleston; they could not fly their flags or play songs of the victor as a mark of respect. Thus, they marched out with colors cased, playing a strikingly appropriate melody, "The World Turned Upside Down." On the morning of October 20, in a letter written in his aide Colonel David Humphreys' hand, Washington informed Congress of the victory, emphasizing, quite properly, the French contribution. Although it was the first real victory dispatch he had been able to write— Boston, Trenton, Monmouth, none were on the scale of this victory—he allowed his aide to write the letter and signed it with a simple "G. Washington." Washington could be flat on occasion.

Although Yorktown did not take away from the enemy's ability to mount another offensive, it proved to be the last major action of the war. Magnified by defeats in Florida, India, and elsewhere, plus the fact that this particular defeat had been made possible by sea power, precisely where the enemy believed themselves invincible, Yorktown brought about a loss of nerve in the British, and they began seriously to negotiate a peace treaty. Washington reacted to the victory with his habitual caution, calling it "an interesting event that may be productive of much good . . . but if it should be the means of relaxation . . . it had better not have happened."[46]

Suiting action to words, the commander busied himself until early November cleaning up the odds and ends of the victory, seeing prisoners off to nearby camps, diverting captured materiel to convenient storehouses, and the like. After a short stay at Mount Vernon, he reached Philadelphia before the end of the month. He and Martha spent the winter there, the general conferring with Congress and planning for the 1782 campaign, and

---

[46] Piers Mackesy, *The War for America, 1775–1783* (Cambridge, Mass., 1964), 435–36; GW to Robert Hansen, Nov. 18, 1781, *Writings*, 23: 352.

both of them being lionized by the smart set of the republic's capital. Recent administrative reforms in the Congress had lightened the work customarily thrust on Washington, especially the decision to appoint a full-time superintendent of finance, Robert Morris. A Philadelphia merchant, Morris let out contracts for army provisions to civilian contractors who, in the long run, fed the army better than it had ever been fed before (considering how it had been fed, that is not saying much). A secretary at war, Benjamin Lincoln, was made responsible for many of the decisions regarding the officer corps that the general previously had to make. Ironically, just as the war was winding down, the Congress was finally learning how to do its job properly.

In March, Martha went home, and Washington established headquarters in Newburgh, near the encampment at New Windsor, New York. There the spring and summer passed quietly. Yorktown had proved one thing, significant victories could be won only with the assistance of French sea power, and de Grasse's fleet was no more, having been defeated in an action off Guadeloupe in April. In August, a new British commander in New York City, Sir Guy Carleton, offered to open negotiations on the status of loyalists because a definitive peace treaty was then being negotiated in Paris. After Congress denied this overture, Washington published the denial in a general order, adding what had become an almost monotonous caution—except for its obvious truth: "The readiest way to procure a lasting and honorable peace is to be fully prepared vigorously to prosecute War." But war seemed to be the last thing on Carleton's mind as he notified Washington in September that fighting was suspended as far as he was concerned. Although Washington refused to accept the unilateral suspension, he lacked the means to undertake any large-scale action, especially after Rochambeau took his troops home in the fall. After his inactive summer, the general prophesied to Lafayette, "The winter will be tranquil."[47]

Prophecy was never his strong suit. Since the early years of the war, the officers had complained about their conditions of service, and Washington had spent many anxious hours soothing

---

[47] General Order, Aug. 19, 1782, GW to Lafayette, Dec. 13, 1782, *Writings*, 25: 42, 434.

them and petitioning Congress to redress their real grievances. The most important of these grievances was their pay, which, even if it had been remitted promptly, was made ludicrously inadequate by the depreciation of the Continental currency. Congress had promised half-pay pensions but lacked the means to redeem its word, especially after Rhode Island rejected a proposal to give taxing power to it. In March 1783, the officers' resentment boiled over, and some overt action, probably a call to the army not to disband until justice had been done, seemed imminent. Plans for this action were made with the connivance, possibly even at the instigation, of some nationalists in Philadelphia primarily interested in strengthening Congress, not in compensating the army. An anonymous call for an officers' meeting at New Windsor on March 12 precipitated Washington into action. He forbade the meeting and called one of his own for March 15. The writer of the original call sent out a second one, making it seem that Washington had approved the purpose of the original meeting. After this, whether he had intended to address the meeting or not (and he probably had), Washington could not avoid doing so. Entering "The Temple," a rough wooden hall only recently completed, he took the lectern with no great ceremony. Reading from a prepared statement, he exhorted the officers to have faith in Congress and in themselves and not to take any steps that would detract from the honor of their service. Appealing to what he considered the most perceptible gauge of honor, he urged them to stay true to their duty and to act so that posterity could say, "Had this day been wanting, the world had never seen the last stage of perfection to which human nature is capable of attaining." Then he began to read a congressman's letter, telling of recent action on their behalf. When he found the writing difficult to read, he took out reading glasses, apologizing: "Gentlemen, you must pardon me. I have grown gray in your service and now find myself growing blind." (This was a fine piece of theater; few, if any, of the officers knew he needed glasses, a realization that left some of them in tears.) He finished the letter and left, and the officers adopted a resolution expressing their faith in Congress. Washington had handled the affair magnificently; probably suspecting the nationalists' hand in the business, he nevertheless treated it as strictly an army affair and brought out of it vindication of civilian control of the military. The significance of the incident is difficult to evaluate because it lies in the fact that certain things did not happen. Thomas Jefferson put it very well: "The moderation and virtue of a single character has probably prevented this revolution from being closed as most others have been by a subversion of the liberty it was intended to establish."[48]

Less than a month later, Washington was able to announce the signing of a preliminary treaty, but he also urged the men to stay to their duty and to preserve a perfect unvarying consistency of character through the very last act because he feared they might begin to desert, believing the war over. But they stayed the course as they were gradually furloughed during the spring, taking with them certificates of service, pay warrants, and their muskets, the last a gift from a Congress that could not give them their back pay. By June, only the three-year men were left, waiting as impatiently as Washington for the British to evacuate New York City.

Thus, the army passed out of existence much as it had been formed, in fits and starts and bits and pieces. Throughout the conflict, some had suffered more from their supposed friends than from the action of their enemies. The constant shortages of provisions, clothing, even muskets, powder, and shot had been the most serious, or at least the most persistent, of Washington's problems. But there had been other difficulties no less perplexing and no more solvable than those of supply. From the beginning, there was a shortage of men willing to serve lengthy enlistments. After an early inattention to the problems posed by short enlistments, Washington asked for enlistments of three years or the duration. Although Congress supported him, Americans were not willing to enlist for more than a year, if they were willing to enlist at all. Also, patriotism was not enough. Bounties would have to be paid, and Washington reluctantly supported

---

[48] Freeman, 5: chap. 26, treats the episode from GW's perspective. Richard H. Kohn analyzes its implications in chap. 2 of *Eagle and Sword: The Beginnings of the Military Establishment in America, 1783–1802* (New York, 1975); hereafter, Kohn, *Eagle and Sword*. See also Kohn's contributions to an exchange with Paul David Nelson on the topic in the *William and Mary Quarterly* 27 (1970) and 29 (1972), and with C. Edward Skeen, 31 (1974). Phelps, *GW and Constitutionalism*, 40–47; Thomas Jefferson to GW, Apr. 16, 1784, *Jefferson Papers*, 7: 106–7.

them. Consequently, the line regiments of the Continental army, arranged by states, were seldom more than shadows of their authorized strength and furnished only a cadre around which militia or short-term soldiers could form. Disciplining such a mixed force posed problems that European armies commonly did not experience. Washington met the problems with a combination of traditional and novel methods. The traditional was well represented in his advice to Congress: "Three things prompt Men to a regular discharge of their Duty in time of Action: natural bravery, hope of reward, and fear of punishment. The two first are common to the untutor'd, and the Disciplin'd Soldiers; but the latter, most obviously distinguished the one from the other."

Thus, lashes were a common punishment in the Continental forces, but they were generally administered in doses smaller than European soldiers suffered. Desertion was punishable by death. However, American soldiers with families, farms, and other responsibilities often had serious reasons for leaving and little understanding of why *their* presence was so essential. Washington often remitted the death penalty, as he had while colonel of the Virginia Regiment. He also issued four general pardons during the war. Throughout the army, a reluctance to impose the death penalty seems to have obtained; of 225 soldiers sentenced to death, only 40 are known certainly to have been executed. Although Washington recognized that the traditional severe punishments would not solve the disciplinary problems, especially when the soldiers had genuine grievances, he showed he could work positively in meeting problems peculiar to an army freely enlisted from the general body of citizens—a people's army fighting a war of liberation. His general orders, despite their monitory tone, were frequently dotted with reminders to the men of the nobility and value of the cause for which they were fighting. These appeals to patriotism and public virtue were often the only coin Washington had for the men, and he was generous with it. He designed chevrons to be worn on the sleeve to indicate multiple enlistments and ordered that a purple heart be worn on the breast of any soldier who distinguished himself by "not only instances of unusual gallantry but also of extraordinary fidelity and essential services in any way." This decoration, revived in modern times as the Purple Heart, showed an appreciation of the necessity of maintaining morale and of recognizing the contribution that the enlisted men were making. European armies, with their soldiers enlisted from the lowest orders of society, seldom if ever recognized the merit or valor of the common soldier. Washington tried to convince his soldiers that they were serving not only themselves but also posterity by fighting for their country.[49]

The gradual incorporation of African Americans into the ranks has already been mentioned. The effect that the good performance of these soldiers had on Washington is difficult to estimate, but it may be seen in his approval of a scheme in the last years of the war. Colonel John Laurens, a South Carolina planter and aide to the general, proposed the enlistment of an African American regiment composed of slaves Congress would purchase from their owners. At the end of their enlistment, the men would be freed. Washington approved the plan, and Congress authorized the regiment, but Laurens could not find any planters willing to sell their slaves. Washington counseled Laurens that, although he sincerely wished him well, he had not expected the scheme to work because it went against "every selfish passion" of humankind. An odd phrase for a slave owner to use.[50]

With the leisure to contemplate a United States at peace, Washington decided to issue a last circular letter to the governors of the states. In this address, later known as "Washington's Legacy," he urged the strengthening of Congress as the only hope for the future stability of the republic. "For, according to the system of Policy the States shall adopt at this moment, they will stand or fall . . . for with our fate will the destiny of unborn Millions be involved." Thus, although the general rejected the nationalists' means, he agreed with their goal, a stronger Congress to hold the states together. Despite his prestige, the message was

---

[49] GW to John Hancock, Feb. 9, 1776, *Papers/Rev,* 3: 247; Allen Bowman, *The Morale of the American Revolutionary Army* (Washington, D.C., 1943), 24, 89–92; Stuart L. Bernath, "George Washington and the Genesis of American Military Discipline," *Mid–America* 49 (1967): 83–100; Maurer Maurer, "Military Justice under General Washington," *Military Affairs* 28 (1964): 8–16.

[50] Hirschfeld, *Slavery,* chap. 12, treats the history of Laurens's proposal. See also Dorothy Twohig, " 'That Species of Property': Washington's Role in the Controversy over Slavery," in *GW Reconsidered,* 119–20; hereafter, Twohig, " 'That Species of Property.' "

rejected as an intrusion into affairs that did not concern him. For now, the "legacy" would be unredeemed.[51]

The summer of 1783 passed by in unaccustomed leisure for Washington. A trip to Lake Champlain with New York's governor, George Clinton, and a stay with Congress, which was then sitting in Princeton, occupied his time until he learned that Carleton intended to evacuate New York City on November 23. By early November, only the troops assigned to march into the city were left in service. Just two days behind schedule, Washington took his small force into New York City to be welcomed by the state authorities, who had moved in a few hours earlier. Contrary winds held the British ships in the harbor for several days so that the general was not free to leave until Friday, December 4. At noon, he met with his officers for a brief and eloquent farewell. Entering the upper room at Fraunces Tavern, he passed by the buffet of food and poured himself a glass of wine. When the others had followed suit, he lifted the glass and spoke: "With a heart full of love and gratitude, now I take leave of you. I most devoutly wish that your later days may be as prosperous and happy as your former have been glorious and honorable." Then, "I cannot come to each of you, but shall feel obliged if each of you will take me by the hand." As it happened, Henry Knox stood next to Washington, who impetuously embraced him; after that, all had to be and were embraced. Nothing was said as the general went to the door and lifted his hand in silent farewell, nor was there any acclaim as he walked to the ferry slip. The silence spoke volumes.[52]

After a ceremony-plagued trip across New Jersey, Washington reached Philadelphia on December 8 and settled his accounts with Congress's finance office, thence on to Annapolis, where the legislators were sitting. The formal surrender of his commission was scheduled for December 23 at noon. For what he expected to be the last formal act of his public life, the general had written an address in which he gave Providence and his fellow citizens most of the credit for the victory; then, pausing as if he could not continue, he bade "an Affectionate farewell to this August body

---

[51] "Circular to the States," June 8, 1783, *Writings*, 26: 483–96; Phelps, *GW and Constitutionalism*, 65–74, analyzes this message.

[52] Freeman, 5: chap. 28, esp. 466–68; chap. 29 for the trip to Annapolis and for Washington's leave-taking of the Congress.

under whose orders I have so long acted, I here offer my commission, and take my leave of all the employments of public life." Thomas Mifflin, as president of Congress, accepted the commission and thanked the general, and the ceremony was all over. As at Fraunces Tavern, Washington turned and left, too moved at that moment to say anything more, although he did linger in an anteroom to speak with members and guests. James McHenry may have captured the feelings of many there when he wrote: "The events of the revolution accomplished—the new situation into which it had thrown the affairs of the world—the great man who had borne so conspicuous a figure in it, in the act of relinquishing all public employment to return to private life—the past—the present—the future—the manner—the occasion—all conspired to render it a spectacle inexpressibly solemn and affecting."[53]

Late the next afternoon George Washington reined in his horse at Mount Vernon to receive the excited greetings of family and servants. He was home.

He once suggested to Nathanael Greene that if historians dared to present the story of what had been accomplished by the Continental army, "it is more than probable that posterity will bestow on their labors the epithet and marks of fiction." The general's contribution to that "fiction" was only a part of the story, but a vital and irreplaceable part. One should not forget the labors of Congress, soldiers, states, and people, the assistance of the French, and the mistakes of the British. They are also parts of the story.[54]

George Washington was not one of history's great generals, but he was one of its great military leaders. His skills were not those of the battlefield tactician; rather, they were those of the military administrator and diplomat. His generalship consisted mainly of getting the army together and keeping it together, neither of them easily accomplished tasks. He always lacked one or

---

[53] James McHenry to Margaret Caldwell, Dec. 23, 1783, in Edward Rhodehamel, ed., *Writings of the American Revolution* (New York, 2001), 796–97, and see 795–96 for GW's and President Thomas Mifflin's speeches. Garry Wills explores the meaning of this renunciation in *Cincinnatus: George Washington and the Enlightenment* (Garden City, N.Y., 1984), chap. 1.

[54] GW to Nathanael Greene, Feb. 6, 1783, *Writings*, 26: 103–4.

more of the tools needed for victory—most especially, as things turned out, the command of the sea, which gave his enemy such mobility. The British lost control of the sea off the Chesapeake Capes for a few weeks in 1781 and lost the war. Provided with all the tools he needed, the Virginia planter might have proved himself to be one of the military geniuses of all time, but for the kind of war he did have to fight, with the poor support Congress and states were able to provide, he had the qualities needed to secure victory: patience, self-discipline, organizing ability, willingness to work hard, and faith in the eventual success of the struggle for independence. These qualities sustained him during the long nights spent writing, often in vain, to Congress and to the governors for the provisions needed for his men, for all the materiel of war so sorely needed but so seldom provided, and for more troops.

Washington also contributed to American success, in a sense, by just being there. When he was appointed commander in chief in 1775, he instantly became a symbol of the united will of the colonies to resist British tyranny. As the war dragged on, the symbolic value of Washington increased, and neither Congress nor any other American general ever seriously challenged him in this popularity. This public acclaim was especially appropriate, for it was the only compensation Washington desired. It was the tangible sign that in his leadership he had come as close as anyone can to the Stoic ideal of unselfish service to the people, that he had kept faith, both with himself and with the republic.

4

Interlude on the Potomac, 1784–1789

"Our affairs seem to be drawing to an awful crisis."
GW to Edmund Randolph, November 19, 1786

WASHINGTON tried to move back into the pleasantly busy routines of Mount Vernon as quickly as possible, but both the climate and the habits of the past eight years conspired against this goal. For six weeks, winter lay especially heavy on the Northern Neck, and travel was impossible. He had no recourse but to idle about the mansion house, postponing the pleasant task of getting reacquainted with the farms on the estate. As late as February, he was still in the habit, upon waking up, of turning over in his mind all the things he had to do that day; then, realizing "I was no longer a public man, nor had anything to do with public transactions," he would permit himself a more leisurely arising. As the weather lightened, one of the frequent sights he had on his rounds was of visitors coming down the drive, some well-remembered faces from the army, some with letters of introduction, some with no letters but a strong desire to be able to say to their children that they had sat at table with him. For more than a year, George and Martha Washington did not once sit down alone to dinner, and the host accurately described himself as running "a well resorted tavern." If the general had led Congress's army only for the esteem of his fellow citizens, he was now paying the price of that affection.[1]

Although Washington never adverted to it, the cost of his hospitality may well have weighed on him as he surveyed the state

---

[1] GW to Henry Knox, Feb. 20, 1784, *Papers/Conf*, 1: 137; *Diaries*, July 30, 1785, 4: 157; GW to Mary Washington, Feb. 15, 1787, *Papers/Conf*, 5: 35.

of his private finances. Despite his best work, Lund Washington had not been able to prevent some deterioration of the estate during the war, which was in part owing to his unwillingness to travel or to keep good accounts. Further, some of Washington's creditors had taken advantage of his willingness to accept depreciated wartime currency to pay off notes far below their true value. He had ordered Lund to accept all such offers because he would not have the revolutionary cause embarrassed if it became known that Congress's general would not accept Congress's money. But because his personal scrupulosity did not permit him to do the same thing as his own creditors, the end of the war found him considerably the loser. Lund's unwillingness to travel meant that the rents on the western properties had not been collected, and he had also confused the capital and current accounts. However, Washington had insisted on continuing the enlargement of the mansion house, with the new dining room on the northern end being a special concern. The confused state of the books prevented an accurate accounting, but he knew he was painfully short of ready cash. A year after the war's end, he was unable to lend his brother £500 and had to ask George Mason if he would make the loan as a personal favor.[2]

The most immediate source of income would be the produce of Mount Vernon, and Washington continued the diligent cultivation and intelligent experimentation that had been so characteristic of his farming before the war. In good years, he might have got as much as $10,000 to $15,000 without considering the use of the house and livestock, increase in slaves, and so on, but not all years were good, and in 1798, even with the profits from a distillery and other enterprises on the farms, Mount Vernon yielded less than $4,500, or approximately 2.25 percent on an estimated value of $200,000. The Custis estates and the rents on his western properties, uncollected since before the war, constituted the rest of his income. Washington's farming knowledge was expanded by a correspondence with Arthur Young, the British agricultural reformer, begun in 1785. Young might have been

---

[2] Freeman, 6: 7–8, 59–62; GW to George Mason, Dec. 13, 1784, *Papers/Conf,* 2: 180; Dalzells, *Mount Vernon,* chaps. 3, 4, and 5, describe the various renovations of the mansion house.

the source of plans for a seed drill, built by slave artisans, which apparently worked only under ideal conditions. Elaborate tables of crop rotation were worked out, considering not only the market value of the crops, but also the labor involved and the benefit to the soil. Although Washington described Mount Vernon's soil as a "good loam," it was actually of rather poor quality and needed constant attention to be productive. One of Washington's more unusual projects was an attempt to popularize mules in America. The animal, a hybrid of the horse and the ass, worked harder than a horse while requiring less fodder and suffering from fewer diseases than its equine relative. Washington managed to breed into one jackass, Compound, the size and strength of Royal Gift from the king of Spain and the liveliness and good humor of Knight of Malta, a gift from Lafayette. Although mules never became as popular in the United States as Washington had hoped, their subsequent history justified his enthusiasm, and at his death Mount Vernon had two mules for every draft horse. He also experimented with sheep, carefully recording an increasing yield of wool that went to the weavers at the main farm. This yield was later lost owing to the neglect of a manager during the presidential years. Despite Washington's steady interest and constant experimentation, he never considered himself an especially skillful farmer, and in his last message to Congress as president he urged the establishment of a group to spread the kind of knowledge he had found so difficult to acquire.[3]

The principal labor force at Mount Vernon was, of course, slaves. During the war, Washington had come to appreciate the competence of freed slaves serving in northern regiments and perhaps to doubt not only the efficiency but also the morality of slavery as a labor system. He does not seem to have been an especially kindly master, permitting his slaves to live in ramshackle quarters and speaking brusquely to them. He constantly suspected them of malingering; on one occasion, he spent time

---

[3] Paul L. Haworth, *George Washington: Country Gentleman* (Indianapolis, 1925), contains much information about Washington's finances and farming practices; hereafter, Haworth, *Country Gentleman*. See also Wilstach, *Mount Vernon,* and *Diaries* has many entries referring to the farms. GW to Landon Carter, Oct. 17, 1796, "Eighth Annual Message to Congress," Dec. 7, 1796, *Writings,* 35: 245–47, 315–16.

observing several sawing fence timbers, then went away for a while and, on his return, contrasted the quantity cut while he observed with that done while he was away. Not surprisingly, the latter was substantially less. However, he did know his "people" as individuals and tried to use each as his or her special abilities and temperament indicated. One, Davy, served as manager of one of the Mount Vernon farms for years. Despite Washington's respect for the slaves' competence, he took no special pains to improve either their minds or their morals. On several occasions during the 1780s, he confided his misgivings about the system to friends and visitors, once commenting that he did not even want to think about the problem. However, he could not help but think about it—and with interesting results, to be noted later.[4]

In February 1784, Washington formally resigned from the vestry of his Anglican parish. Because he apparently regarded this service as a civic rather than a religious duty, his resignation was not a sign of unwillingness to participate in a church as much as a sign of his retirement from public life. He was not hostile to religion, but he was apparently devoid of any deep personal religious faith. Much in the fashion of the eighteenth century, he considered religion as one of the important elements in the stability of American society; it was religion's "laudable endeavors to render men sober, honest, and good citizens, and the obedient subjects of a lawful government" that impressed him the most. Thus, he approved of a postwar Virginia law requiring all to pay a tax for the support of Christian churches; their work benefited all, even non-Christians, so all should pay. This opinion not only shows what moderns would consider an illiberal attitude toward religious liberty but also a utilitarian attitude toward religion itself. It was, however, in keeping with the enlightened Deism of Washington's generation. In his public pronouncements, both as general and as president, he avoided explicit references to God or to Jesus Christ, preferring impersonal terms.[5]

---

[4] Haworth, *Country Gentleman*, 193–209; GW to William Pearce, Dec. 18, 1793, *Writings*, 33: 188–95. Dorothy Twohig's " 'That Species of Property' " is the most recent and best treatment.

[5] GW to Daniel McCarty, Feb. 3, 1784, *Papers/Conf*, 1: 146. Stuart Leibiger, *Founding Friendship: George Washington, James Madison, and the Creation of the American Republic* (Charlottesville, Va., 1999), 48–49; hereafter, Leibiger, *Friendship.* Boller, *GW and Religion*, 46, 64, 108.

Once Washington had started Mount Vernon on the road back to profitability, he began to look to the other parts of his estate. In the fall of 1784, "having found it indispensably necessary to visit my Landed property West of the Apalachean [sic] Mountains," he traveled there. Almost immediately the trip took on another aspect as Washington began to survey the possibilities of opening up an easy water route between the Ohio and the Potomac. It was just as well he had a second task at hand because he managed to collect very little in back rents and even had to begin court suits to evict some squatters on land he owned in southwestern Pennsylvania, near Pittsburgh. That was as far west as he got, for reports of hostile activity by natives near the bounty lands made a visit to them unwise. He reached home on October 4, just a little more than a month after he had left.

Back at Mount Vernon, Washington wrote to Richard Henry Lee, president of Congress, regarding his impressions of the western situation; here he returned to one of his favorite topics of the war years, the necessity of a stronger union. As he saw it, commerce and politics went together; the West hung "as it were on a pivot—the touch of a feather" could incline it either eastward and allegiance with the United States or westward and independence with a connection to the Spanish in Louisiana or to the English in Canada. He asserted that trade connections via an improved Potomac River would be one of the surest bonds of union, with the welcome dividend of increased trade throughout the Chesapeake area for Virginia and Maryland. But the "great object," as he confided to Edmund Randolph, "is to connect the Western Territory with the Atlantic States; all others with me are secondary." The "great object" took definite form in May 1785, when Washington became president of the Potomac Company, jointly chartered by Virginia and Maryland to improve the river for commercial navigation; he would hold the office until he resigned it in 1789, when he accepted another presidency.[6]

---

[6] GW's trip west is in *Diaries*, 4: 1–53, and pages 54–68 have information regarding the improvement of the Potomac; GW to Benjamin Harrison, [Oct. 10, 1784], to Edmund Randolph, Aug. 13, 1785, *Papers/Conf*, 2: 92, 3: 179–81; Leibiger, *Friendship*, 49 ff. for the beginning of the postwar effort to improve the Potomac, part of a decade-long partnership between GW and James Madison; Bowling, *Creation*, 24, 111 ff.

As he viewed the country in the mid-1780s, it needed all the bonds of union that could be forged; Congress, states, and people were all responsible for sinking "our national character much below par" and for bringing the country to the point where "a step or two further must plunge us into a Sea of Troubles, perhaps anarchy and confusion." The prospect was not all black; immediate action might forestall an impending disaster. And he did not doubt what the remedy was: "I do not conceive we can exist long as a nation without having lodged somewhere a power which will pervade the whole Union." Perhaps his greatest hope was in the people, for there was "virtue at the bottom." But something had to be done, for "affairs seem to be drawing to an awful crisis."[7]

That this "awful crisis" might occur Washington was firmly convinced, and a good many other Americans agreed with him. Many pressing problems—the natives' unrest and the British occupation of posts in New York and the Northwest, to name only two—were hanging fire because Congress lacked the power to deal with them. But it also ought to be noted that Congress was not the nation, that there was much prosperity to be found in the states, and in the areas where there was distress the future was still bright. Further, in the agrarian economy of the late-eighteenth-century United States, farmers who complained about low prices for their produce still had food, shelter, and a rough but adequate existence. Many of the problems that Washington and others bemoaned were only potentially troublesome, things that a great nation ought not to tolerate but that, more realistically, the United States of the mid-1780s might well have to live with for a while.

In an attempt to iron out trade problems in the Chesapeake Bay area, Maryland and Virginia held a meeting in March 1785. At Washington's invitation, the commissioners met at Mount Vernon (he was not a delegate) and achieved sufficient success to lead Virginia to issue a call to all the states to meet at Annapolis, Maryland, in September 1786 to discuss trade problems. This meeting drew delegations from only the middle states in addi-

---

[7] GW to Thomas Johnson, Nov. 12, 1786, to Edmund Randolph, Nov. 19, 1786, *Papers/Conf*, 4: 359–60, 387.

tion to Virginia; the delegates decided not to attempt a settlement of the trade problems they had been convened to discuss
but instead issued a report stating that they believed the Union's
problems were sufficiently grave to justify a general meeting of
the states. Copies were sent to Congress and to all the states.
In February 1787, Congress would accept the report and call a
meeting of all the states in Philadelphia the following May to
propose revisions to the Articles of Confederation that would
make them "adequate to the exigencies of Government & the
preservation of the Union." This bare recital of facts hides a
good bit of activity by those who wanted to strengthen the
Union—the federalists, as they were soon to call themselves.
They as well as those who wanted to preserve the weak union of
the Articles as given or at least to keep change to a minimum
(antifederalists) knew that Washington's opinion would count for
much with the people should a strong movement to strengthen
Congress develop. His opposition would stop it in its tracks. Anyone who had corresponded or spoken with Washington knew
what he thought. Indeed, his last circular letter to the governors
at the end of the war had made clear his opinions on this topic.
His convictions on what had to be done to keep the country
strong would hardly keep him from attending the proposed
meeting.[8]

Rather, the obstacles came from Washington's sense of his own
honor and from particular circumstances. He took his promise
to retire from public life, which he had made at the war's end, to
be a bar to any kind of public office. But as an index of his strong
convictions on the necessity of some kind of drastic reform, he
left the door open should the country voice "its affection and
confidence"; in other words, he would accept a draft. Then an
additional complication was introduced; the Society of the Cincinnati, a hereditary fraternity of former Continental army officers, was also meeting in Philadelphia in May 1787. At the war's

---

[8] "Proceedings of Commissioners to Remedy Defects of the Federal Government [Annapolis 1786]," "Report of Proceedings in Congress, Feb. 21, 1787,"
in C. C. Tansill, ed., *Documents Illustrative of the Formation of the Union* (1926,
repr., Washington, D.C., 1965), 39–43, 44–46. Leibiger's *Friendship*, 58–70, is
a succinct treatment of GW's coming to agree to participate in the Philadelphia
meeting.

end, when the society had been founded, many Americans had objected to it, especially to its hereditary character, and Washington, its first president-general, had proposed changes that some state chapters had rejected. He decided to distance himself as much as he could from the society. Using poor health and his own business as excuses, he had already sent his regrets to the meeting's organizers. Now, how could he attend the meeting of the states without being disrespectful to the Cincinnati? Although he did not want to be associated with what was seen as aristocracy and privilege, neither did he want to gratuitously insult well-meaning former comrades.[9]

As 1786 drew to a close, Washington's concern about the Philadelphia meeting become more pointed; in December, he was nominated by the Virginia Assembly to head the state's delegation. Governor Edmund Randolph explained that this nomination was made because Virginia wanted to lend her greatest strength to the effort. Washington's answer was not quite a declination: he told Randolph he doubted he could go because of his health—he was much bothered by rheumatism at the time—and because of the coincidence of the Cincinnati meeting. Both Randolph and James Madison, then a member of Congress, refused to press him into a definite decision, preferring to let the matter ripen a bit. Events elsewhere conspired to speed up the ripening process. In Massachusetts, an imprudent fiscal policy, aimed at quickly paying off the commonwealth's debt, had increased taxes beyond the ability of some farmers, especially those in the Connecticut River Valley, to pay. The farmers resisted legal processes to collect the levies and closed the courts in several counties. In late 1786, several hundred, led by a Captain Daniel Shays, moved against the armory at Springfield, and the movement seemed about to blossom into a full-scale rebellion complete with angrily shouted leveling mottoes. State forces under Benjamin Lincoln put down the resistance, and the movement quickly collapsed, but not before Washington had been thoroughly alarmed by exaggerated reports from Henry Knox and others. The "re-

---

[9] GW to Theodoric Bland, Nov. 18, 1786, GW to James Madison, Nov. 18, 1786, and David Humphreys to GW, Jan. 20, 1787, *Papers/Conf,* 4: 377–79, 382–83, 529.

bellion" seemed to him further evidence of the angry temper of the people and of the inability of the states, even apparently well-governed ones such as Massachusetts, to deal with their problems. It may have been the events in Massachusetts that turned him into a supporter of a stronger government. He reproved Henry Lee, who had naively suggested that "influence"—perhaps Washington's?—should be employed to calm the farmers: "I know not where that remedy is to be found and, if attainable, that it would be a proper remedy for our disorders. *Influence is no government*" (emphasis added). But, despite the wisdom of that last sentiment, Washington realized he did have influence, and as 1787 wore on, he put the question to himself: Should he use his prestige to support a meeting that might prove to be ill attended and ineffective? Would he be risking his own reputation in a cause that would be doomed from the start? There was a selfish ingredient in this anxiety because he seemed unwilling to risk what he prized most highly to help preserve the independence and integrity of the Union. In February 1787, Congress approved the meeting, calling it for "the sole and express purpose of revising . . . the federal constitution adequate to the exigencies of Government and the preservation of the Union." The chances of success at the meeting had became much greater—indeed, in Washington's judgment, it was perhaps "the last peaceable mode of essaying the practicability" of the present government. But the time had come for him to make a decision, and in April he accepted his state's call to go to Philadelphia. Now the battle line had been drawn. Although he still had his doubts, he wanted the meeting to "adopt no temporizing expedient, but probe the defects of the constitution to the bottom and provide *radical cures*" (emphasis added). Whether its suggestions were adopted or not, it would "be looked to as a luminary, which sooner or later will shed its influence." Everything should be risked, for everything was at stake.[10]

Washington arrived in Philadelphia on Sunday, May 13, in-

[10] GW to Edmund Randolph, Dec. 2, 1786, *Papers/Conf,* 4: 471; Flexner, 3: 63–68; David Satzmary, *Shays' Rebellion: The Making of an Agrarian Insurrection* (Amherst, Mass., 1980); GW to Henry Lee Jr., Oct. 31, 1786, to John Jay, Mar. 10, 1787, to James Madison, Mar. 31, 1787, to Edmund Randolph, Apr. 9, 1787, *Papers/Conf,* 4: 318–20, 5: 79–80, 116, 135–36.

tending to lodge at "Mrs. House's," but Robert Morris, once the superintendent of finance for the Congress, convinced him to stay at his city mansion. The next day, the one appointed for the meeting to open, found only two states' delegations—Virginia and Pennsylvania—in attendance at the State House. Washington filled the time meeting with his Virginia colleagues until May 25, when a quorum was present and the meeting could organize itself. As one of the first items of business, Washington was made president; this appointment did not restrict his participation because much of the business was done in committee of the whole. In that format, the president stepped down, and a president pro tem was appointed to preside. The convention also voted to follow Congress's practice of allowing one vote per state. On May 29, the first full day of deliberations, Edmund Randolph offered a set of proposals that, in effect, would have supplanted the Articles. On the next day, on motion of Gouverneur Morris, the delegates approved the formation of a national government with an executive, legislature, and judiciary—an explicit replacement, not a revision, of the Articles. As Washington had wished, he would see "radical cures" tried. True to his previous behavior in the burgesses and in the Continental Congress, he did not participate in the debate and spoke only once on a matter of detail. At the very end, he asked the delegates to approve a motion by Nathaniel Gorham to make the minimum size of electoral districts of the House of Representatives thirty thousand people, down from the draft provision of forty thousand. He supported his request by stating that government should be as close to the people as possible. The convention unanimously agreed. Washington kept the secrecy of the meeting (mandated on its second day) so closely that his journal contained only the places he ate and the various entertainments he attended, along with an excursion up the Schuylkill during a recess. He was the only delegate to attend every day that the convention was in session.[11]

---

[11] *Diaries*, May 13, 1787, 5: 155, 155–87, for GW's activities during the convention. Max Farrand, ed., *The Records of the Federal Convention of 1787*, rev. ed., 4 vols. (New Haven, 1966); hereafter Farrand, *Records*. Of the many treatments of the convention, I prefer Clinton Rossiter's *1787, The Grand Convention* (1966, repr., New York, 1968); the supporters and opponents of the movement for the Constitution are labeled *federalists* and *antifederalists*, respectively.

Although Washington has never been known as a political theorist, he did have several well-considered principles that he applied to political affairs. Some of these principles are seen in the votes he cast within the Virginia delegation to decide how its vote would be given. Government had to be strong, so he voted to suppress the states' interests; the executive also had to be strong, so he voted in favor of a single executive who was not elected by and thus dependent on the legislature; he also approved making a three-fourths rather than two-thirds vote of the Congress necessary to override an executive veto, but he lost on this point. He also lost within the Virginia delegation when he approved export taxes, generally thought to be against the interest of the southern states. He was ready to be more nationalist than his Virginia colleagues. And as his request on the size of House districts indicated, he wanted government to be close to the people, although he may also have been looking ahead to the effort to get the convention's work approved by voters wedded to small electoral districts and immediate representation. Other than these few rules, however, he seemed to be ready to accept any "tolerable compromise" that would strengthen the Union and restrain the states from excesses.[12]

Washington's contribution to the success of the Constitutional Convention lay principally in his being there; that he attended, presided, and signed the result of the convention convinced countless Americans of the value of the new Constitution. Further, he may have helped to shape the presidency in the new government, for as it became obvious that the executive position was to be entrusted to one person, some of the delegates, expecting Washington to be the first president, "shaped their Ideas of the Powers to be given to a President by their opinions of his Virtues." He also spent a good number of his evenings dining and conversing with other delegates; here he may well have

---

[12] Arthur N. Holcombe, "The Role of Washington in the Framing of the Constitution," *Huntington Library Quarterly* 19, no. 4 (Aug. 1956): 317–34; Harold W. Bradley, "The Political Thinking of George Washington," *Journal of Southern History* 11 (Nov. 1945): 469–86; see also Phelps, *GW and Constitutionalism*, 102–16, arguing that GW achieved a broad constitutional agenda at the convention; GW to Thomas Jefferson, Aug. 31, 1788, *Papers/Conf*, 6: 493.

urged, subtly or otherwise, particular provisions that implemented his basic ideas on government, mentioned above.[13]

The convention finished its work on September 17, and the members left for their homes, most to help secure their state's ratification of the Constitution, some few to oppose it. In this contest, Washington played a discreet role typified by the covering letter he enclosed with copies of the draft constitution he sent to other Virginians on his return to Mount Vernon: "I wish the constitution which is offered had been made more perfect, but I sincerely believe it is the best that could be obtained at this time; and, as a constitutional door is opened for amendment hereafter, the adoption of it under the present circumstances of the union is, in my opinion desirable."

He used this basic argument, expanded and sometimes modified to suit the recipient, again and again as he kept up his large correspondence. He made no objection when some of his letters were printed in the newspapers except when he did not expect this publication and fretted about the clumsy style and possible misspellings of what he had thought of as a strictly private letter. He gave James Madison explicit permission to tell any interested parties that he supported the Constitution and wished to see it ratified. All in all, he successfully walked the line between backing the document he had helped write and not appearing to be running for the presidency.[14]

During the contest, many referred to their confident expectation that Washington would accept the position. Over and above this expectation was his obvious approval of the new frame of government. The only way to counter that approval was to discredit either his judgment or his integrity, and few attempted to do that. James Monroe certainly claimed too much when he said that Washington's "influence carried this government," but, equally certain, Washington's approval, his probable presidency, and his cautious campaigning were substantial advantages for the federalists as they carried the Constitution successfully

---

[13] Pierce Butler to Weedon Butler, May 5, 1788, in Farrand, *Records*, 3: 302.

[14] GW to Benjamin Harrison, Patrick Henry, Thomas Nelson, Sep. 24, 1787, *Papers/Conf*, 5: 339–40; Freeman, 6: 129–30; GW to James Madison, Jan. 10, 1788, *Papers/Conf*, 6: 32–33.

through the ratification contest. That contest ended late in July 1788, when New York, as the eleventh state, ratified. Rhode Island, after polling its town meetings with a negative result, had ignored the meeting in Philadelphia, and North Carolina had adjourned its ratifying convention without coming to a final decision. Be that as it may, more than the requisite nine states had ratified, and whether the two hold-outs joined sooner rather than later, the Constitution was going into effect and with a good chance of success, for, as Washington predicted:

> When the people shall find themselves secure under an energetic government, when foreign Nations shall be disposed to give us equal advantages in commerce from dread of retaliation, when the burdens of war shall be in a manner done away by the sale of western lands; when the seeds of happiness which are sown here shall begen [sic] to expand themselves, and when every one (under his own vine and fig tree) shall begin to taste the fruits of freedom— then all these blessings (for all these blessings will come) will be referred to the fostering influence of the new government.

But then, more realistically, he added: "Whereas many causes will have conspired to produce them." For many reasons, the grand experiment in self-government that, for Washington, had started at the encampment at Cambridge in 1775 was going to receive a fair trial.[15]

Now that the trial was about to begin, Washington would have to make up his mind on a question that had been hovering in the background, sometimes popping to the foreground, since the convention: the presidency. He had good personal reasons for wanting to stay at Mount Vernon, not the least of which was the place itself; in addition, he wondered if the antifederalists who had opposed the Constitution would accept him and how people generally would view his breaking of his 1783 promise to retire from public life. In his consideration of the problem, he balanced duty and reputation: nothing would take him away from Mount Vernon "unless it be a *conviction* that the partiality of my countrymen had made my services absolutely necessary, joined to a *fear* that my refusal might induce a belief that I preferred the conservation of my own reputation and private ease to

---

[15] GW to Lafayette, June 18, 1788, *Papers/Conf,* 6: 338.

the good of my country" (emphasis in original). So his realization of the position he had in the esteem of the people and a fear that his refusal might lessen that esteem brought him to acceptance. He may also possibly have considered his opinion of the dire situation he saw the country in at that time. Finally, perhaps (and it is a big perhaps) he missed the challenge and excitement of public life. In the end, the choice was almost made for him; when he heard that the strongly antifederalist New York governor, George Clinton, was being considered for vice president, he let it be known that he considered John Adams much the better man for the job. If he was concerned about the vice presidency sufficiently to influence the choice of its occupant, how could he refuse the presidency? Thus, there was no grand announcement of his willingness to accept the call of his fellow citizens, just a slow, steady march of events until he silently or at least implicitly accepted what had become inevitable. Because there would be no formal notice until March at the earliest, he did not have to make any statement when he learned in mid-February that enough states had voted for him to make certain his election. His acceptance could be seen in the preparations he started to make for the move to New York, where the new government would be seated: visiting his mother, for what turned out to be the last time; giving instructions to George Augustine Washington, his nephew and manager; and sending Tobias Lear, his personal secretary, to the capital in early April. After he had taken these steps, no one near him could have been surprised at his answer when Charles Thomson, the secretary of the Congress, handed him a formal notice of his election on April 14. In a gracefully phrased reply, he bowed to "this fresh proof of my country's esteem and confidence" and informed Thomson he would be ready to leave for New York in two days. The furlough was over; the next campaign had begun.[16]

---

[16] Freeman, 6: chap. 6, describes GW's activities July 1788 to Apr. 1789. See Zagarri, *Humphreys' "Life,"* 40–51, for Humphreys' version of GW's weighing of the pros and cons of accepting his likely election. See also Alexander Hamilton to GW, Aug. 13, 1788, Sep. [n.d.], 1788, in Harold C. Syrett, ed., *The Papers of Alexander Hamilton* (New York, 1966), 5: 202, 221, for the arguments thought effective by someone who knew GW well; hereafter, Syrett, *Hamilton Papers*.

5

A Commission from the People, 1789–1793

> So much is expected, so many untoward circumstances may intervene, in such a new and critical situation, that I feel an insuperable diffidence in my own abilities.
>
> GW to Edward Rutledge, May 5, 1789

As THE PRESIDENT-ELECT began his journey to the new government's capital on April 16, he confided to his diary that his mind was "oppressed with more anxious and painful sensations than I have words to express . . . with the best disposition to render service to my country in obedience to its call, but with less hope of answering its expectations."[1] This was certainly true, but it was also probably true that he half-welcomed his new position. What better proof of the public's esteem and of the standing of his reputation than his election to the presidency without a dissenting vote? The journey to New York City was punctuated with dozens of demonstrations of the public's affection, reaffirming the official decision of the Electoral College. No crossroads village could let Washington through without at least a formal welcome by the local dignitaries and, if possible, a parade of the militia and an artillery salute. One of the most elaborate welcomes was staged, fittingly enough, by the nation's largest city, Philadelphia, but the ceremony that seemed to affect Washington the most was in one of the smaller cities, Trenton, New Jersey. There, the bridge over the Assumpink Creek had been decorated with thirteen bunting-bedecked arches (despite the fact that North Carolina and Rhode Island had not yet ratified, this number was the usual practice), the same bridge where the general had sat

---

[1] *Diaries*, [Apr. 16, 1789], 5: 445.

his horse in January 1777 while he watched Colonel Edward Hand's unit delay Cornwallis's vanguard. Now, in the warm spring sunshine, thirteen girls dressed in white sang:

> Virgins fair and matrons grave,
> Those thy conquering arm did save.
> Build for thee celestial bowers,
> Strew your hero's way with flowers.

And strew they did, while they continued with more verses. As sentimental as the words seem to modern ears, they had a powerful effect on Washington, for he wrote a thank you note to the "gratulatory choir" that evening in which he explicitly referred to the contrast between the scene that day and that of 1777. This reaction was unusual, perhaps unique, for he had a habit of visiting sites connected with the war—Valley Forge during the Philadelphia convention, for instance—but not of recording the memories, if any, that the visit stirred up. Unbeknownst to them, the Trenton choir had stirred him deeply and strongly.[2]

With the usual ceremonies, the party moved across New Jersey until they reached Elizabeth on the morning of April 23, where they were met by a delegation representing both the new Congress and the state of New York. The president-elect boarded a specially built barge manned by thirteen master pilots of the port and was rowed through Newark Bay and across the Hudson River to Manhattan. Other vessels fell in behind as the barge moved along; one sloop was filled with singers who serenaded the presidential party with songs of the type—and quality—heard in Trenton. As Washington stepped out of the barge at the Battery in New York City, he was greeted cordially by Governor George Clinton. The welcome of the strongly antifederal Clinton seemed a good omen for the future of the new government. Washington was escorted through a tightly pressing crowd to a house set aside for his use, to rest and prepare for a banquet that evening. A line heard frequently throughout the day seemed to typify the prevailing sentiment: "Well, he deserves it all."[3]

---

[2] GW to the Ladies of Trenton, Apr. 21, 1789, *Papers/P*, 2: 108; Freeman, 6: chap. 7 for the journey to New York, chap. 8 for Inauguration Day.

[3] Thomas E. V. Smith, *The City of New York in the Year of Washington's Inauguration, 1789* (New York, 1889), chap. 8.

But that statement referred to the past; the future was what interested Washington. He readily agreed to Congress's arrangements for the inauguration: April 30 would be the date, and Congress's seat, the refurbished City Hall, now christened Federal Hall, the site. The day proved to be intermittently sunny and mild—another good omen for the future? At 12:30 a coach and four pulled away from the presidential mansion; its occupant wore a suit cut from cloth woven in the United States, the buttons decorated with an eagle to complete the patriotic motif. At Federal Hall, he was formally introduced to Congress, gathered in the second-floor Senate chamber, by Vice President John Adams, who had already been sworn in. He then stepped out onto the balcony, where Robert R. Livingston, chancellor of the state of New York, administered the oath of office, the new president adding "So help me, God" to the official formula. At its conclusion, Livingston gestured as if he were presenting Washington to the people and exclaimed: "Long live George Washington, President of the United States!" The crowd, quiet for the oath-taking, broke into loud cheers, punctuated by church bells and a thirteen-gun salute.

The presidential party then moved inside for the inaugural address, a brief and general speech of about twelve hundred words. Washington referred to the seriousness of his task and requested pardon in advance for any unintentional errors. Evidence was given that the United States was being guided by the "Almighty Being" who directs human affairs—for example, "the important revolution" just accomplished "through the tranquil deliberations and voluntary consent" of the people. The Congress needed no guidance from him as to necessary legislation, and he was certain "no local prejudices or attachments, no separate views nor party animosities" would divert them from their work (he would not always be certain of this). He made only two specific suggestions. Congress should consider amendments to the Constitution to correct deficiencies pointed to during the ratification controversy. (This consideration would result in the passage of the first ten amendments, the Bill of Rights.) He also requested that his compensation, following his wartime practice, would be confined to his expenses only. Then came a brief statement imploring the blessings of the "benign Parent of the

Human Race" on the republic, and the speech was over. One observer, Senator William Maclay of Pennsylvania, noted the president's awkwardness in delivering the speech and regretted that he was not first in speech-making, as in everything else, but it was something Washington disliked and he never improved substantially in it. A thanksgiving service at St. Paul's Church followed. After a private dinner, Washington toured the city with his secretaries, Tobias Lear and David Humphreys, to view the fireworks and illuminations at the end of the day's celebrations.[4]

With the inaugural ceremonies finished, Washington could settle down to the work of beginning a new government. What the president and Congress had ahead of them was something that no one before them had tried and few after them would accomplish so successfully: the self-conscious formation of a new government based on popular consent. It speaks volumes for their ability that they did not permit their doubts that it could be done at all to paralyze them into inaction. Washington reflected these fears when he later wrote: "Few who are not philosophical Spectators, can realise the difficult and delicate part which a man in my situation had to act. . . . I walk on untrodden ground. There is scarcely any part of my conduct w[hi]ch may not hereafter be drawn into precedent." Governments are not formed simply of taxes and armies and bureaus; people who were concerned not only with the substance but also with the accidents of the new government anxiously observed even the most trivial aspects of Washington's behavior.[5]

The president of the United States at that time occupied a unique position in the Atlantic world, where there was no other elected head of state. The House and Senate disagreed over how to address the president formally, with the upper house wanting to send its reply to the inaugural address to "His Highness, the

---

[4] "First Inaugural Address, Final Version," [Apr. 30, 1789], *Papers/P*, 2: 173–77, and 158–73 for fragments of GW's first draft. Kenneth R. Bowling and Helen E. Veit, eds., *The Diary of William Maclay and Other Notes on Senate Debates*, vol. 9 of *The Documentary History of the First Federal Congress* (Baltimore, 1988), 13; hereafter, Bowling and Veit, *Diary of William Maclay*. James Madison helped prepare the speech; see Leibiger, *Friendship*, 103–5.

[5] GW to Catharine Macaulay Graham, Jan. 9, 1790, *Papers/P*, 4: 552. Jack D. Warren Jr.'s *The Presidency of George Washington* (Mount Vernon, Va., 2000) is an excellent brief study of its subject.

President of the United States of America, Protector of their Liberties," but the lower house stood firm on "the President of the United States." In ordinary discourse, Washington was addressed as "Excellency," as he had been during the war. ("Mr. President" came to be used during the Jefferson administration.) Blending advice solicited from various quarters in and out of government as to how he should entertain, Washington decided to hold a weekly reception—a levee at which all social visits would be made; this practice would give him the time he needed for his official business and appointments while at the same time permitting any decently dressed person a chance to speak with the president. Mrs. Washington held a similar reception on Friday evenings for the ladies, which Washington usually attended also. Observing the president at these gatherings, Abigail Adams, the vice president's wife, was impressed with his happy "Faculty of appearing to accommodate and yet carrying his point. . . . He is polite with dignity, affable without familiarity, distant without Haughtiness, Grave without Austerity, modest, wise, and good." Her comments reflect Washington's greater ease with women and the degree of respect he usually accorded them; he was more relaxed with the ladies than at his own receptions, which were also usually crowded with strangers. Every Thursday, government officials—congressmen, generally—attended a formal dinner at the president's house; these dinners were culinary triumphs but could be social trials, at least if Senator Maclay is to be believed, but the senator had come to New York sniffing suspiciously for stray scents of aristocracy and monarchy, and would not allow himself to be disappointed.[6]

The grave, formal tone of the administration, which Washington thought necessary so that the new government not seem cheap or familiar, was also a reflection of the public mask he customarily wore as a disguise for his own shyness and feelings during occasions that were uncomfortable for him. He relaxed only with a few old friends at Mount Vernon. Maclay was not the only one to feel that the tone was excessively formal, and by 1790

[6] Abigail Adams to Mary Cranch, Jan. 5, 1790, in Stewart Mitchell, ed., *New Letters of Abigail Adams, 1788–1801* (Boston, 1947), 35; hereafter, Mitchell, *New Letters*. Bowling and Veit, *Diary of William Maclay*, 70, 136–37, see also 8–9 for an example of Maclay's suspicions regarding anyone not from Pennslyvania.

even Virginians were making barbed comments about the aristocratic airs of the "Republican Court." Although the president did not worry about the formality of his administration, he was concerned about his limited social circle, and before his first term ended, he asked Tobias Lear to give him impressions of public opinion because his secretary mixed with all kinds of different people, many more "than could fall to the lot of a Stationary character who is always revolving in a particular circle." Unfortunately, Washington would not always see this limitation as a problem.[7]

Congress ignored Washington's request about his compensation, reasoning that the office should not be tailored to the wishes of one person, and gave the president a salary of $25,000 a year. However, he treated this salary as if it were compensation for expenses and had Lear enter the salary paid against expenses accruing. Because he always spent more than his salary, some years as much as $5,000 more, he always drew the total amount. Mount Vernon's expenses were lower in his absence, so this additional amount was no great burden, and the flow of cash from his salary may actually have helped his personal finances. The heavy expenses of Washington's household were increased by his decision to live as "respectably" as circumstances permitted, as illustrated by his move in February 1790 to a mansion on Broadway, even though it had become likely that the capital would be moving to another city. His first house was too small and not furnished well enough for his taste. When the new executive mansion, recently completed by the land speculator, Alexander Macomb, was refurbished, its new tenant took personal charge of the decorating. Much the same happened when the capital was moved to Philadelphia in November 1790, with Washington closely supervising the leasing and decorating of Robert Morris's mansion on Market Street. Fifteen to twenty servants, supplemented when Congress was in session, were employed in the house and stables; as many as seven slaves from Mount Vernon might also be used, but they did not work where the public would see them. During 1790, the expenses of the table alone ran to

---

[7] GW to David Stuart, July 26, 1789, *Papers/P,* 5: 359–63; GW to Tobias Lear, May 6, 1794, *Writings,* 33: 354.

approximately $165 a week, and these expenses remained about the same during Washington's presidency. All in all, the president adhered closely to his intention of giving the office in its social aspects as dignified an air as was possible, despite the protests of some anxious democrats that this practice "squinted" toward aristocracy and monarchy.[8]

Still, there was something to the tone of the administration, at least as it was reported in the press, to give a thoughtful citizen pause as one viewed the new government. The Federalist press used only superlatives in reporting the president's actions and did not stint in awarding honorific titles. Martha was usually styled "Lady Washington," as were the wives of others prominent in the administration, no matter how humble their origins. The silliness as well as the falseness of much of this reporting is illustrated in the *Federal Gazette* description of Washington's reaction to a popular melodrama, *The Maid of the Mill:* "the great and good Washington manifested his approbation of this interesting part of the opera by the tribute of a tear." Although retrospection shows that there was little to fear from this, contemporaries might be pardoned their anxiety. As Jefferson later noted, hangers-on "had wound up the ceremonials of the government to a pitch of stateliness which nothing but [Washington's] personal character could have supported, and which no character after him could maintain." And it says much for Washington's conduct of the presidency that most of the criticism directed at him in the first term concerned just such relatively trivial aspects of the office as its social tone.[9]

For, if government were more than taxes and armies and bureaus, it was those things also, and they were anything but trivial. Although the secretaries of the old Congress continued in office, its rudimentary executive organization could not long serve the expanded tasks of the new government. In congressmen's eyes, revenue came first, and a bill levying tariffs on imports and a

---

[8] Stephen Decatur Jr., *The Private Affairs of George Washington: From the Records and Accounts of Tobias Lear, Esq., His Secretary* (Boston, 1933), xi, 12–13, 49, 101, 108–9, 118, 156–57, 329–30.

[9] Haworth, *Country Gentleman*, 246–47; Thomas Jefferson to James Madison, June 9, 1793, *Jefferson Papers*, 26: 241; Rufus W. Griswold, *The Republican Court; or American Society in the Days of Washington* (New York, 1863), passim.

tonnage tax on all ships entering American ports was presented to the president early in July. As originally drafted, the rates would have discriminated against British goods and ships in retaliation for their discrimination against America's, but this provision was taken out. Although Washington would have liked to see Britain receive a taste of the power of the new government and disagreed with the policy of the bill, he signed it on July 4, 1789. He understood Congress was considering another bill that would do what he wanted, and a veto so early in his administration would be a poor start to what he hoped would be a cooperative enterprise between the executive and the legislature. He viewed the new government as one that mixed the various levels and interests of the United States into a harmonious and cooperative body that sought, in Edmund Burke's phrase, "a permanent, aggregate interest of the community," not whatever a diverse executive and legislature would mutually accept. He would change his mind by the end of his administration.[10]

The Congress gave the president three executive departments to assist him. The State Department was to handle both domestic and foreign affairs because the latter were expected to be simple and uncomplicated; the War Department would take up the work of its predecessor, and the Treasury Department was to take in hand the complex task of bringing order to the nation's finances. An attorney general, to act as the government's chief legal officer, was also provided, as was a rudimentary system of federal courts, capped by a six-man Supreme Court. Congress's work done, Washington's began as he tried to find suitable men to fill these posts and others. War was the easiest because Henry Knox, Washington's chief of artillery during the war, was willing to continue in this post that he had filled for the old Congress. Washington readily appointed him. John Jay, secretary for foreign affairs for the old Congress, was appointed to head the Supreme Court; he had recently proposed closing the Mississippi to Amer-

---

[10] Freeman, 6: 216; Phelps, *GW and Constitutionalism*, 150–51, 155–57. Ralph Ketcham, *Presidents above Party: The First American Presidency, 1789–1829* (Chapel Hill, N.C., 1984), chap. 11, esp. 226; hereafter, Ketcham, *Presidents*. See David P. Currie. *The Constitution in Congress: The Federalist Period, 1789–1801* (Chicago, 1997), 24–33, 36–41, 209–17, 252 ff., 260 ff. for GW's relations with Congress.

ican commerce in a draft treaty with the Spanish, so Washington feared western animosity toward Jay would keep him from being an effective secretary of state. In filling the other seats on the Court and in these high offices, Washington paid attention to qualifications and sectional distribution. Although he did not intend to be partisan, he was not going to ignore the sectional feeling in the country. After Jay, the two obvious choices for the State Department were John Adams and Thomas Jefferson, but serving as vice president ruled out Adams. Although Jefferson was then serving as American minister in Paris, he was coming home for a leave late in the year, so Washington waited to ask him to take the post. Even then, it took a combination of several letters and a visit to Mount Vernon before Jefferson said yes. Jay filled in until Jefferson took up his duties in March 1790. Although Washington and Jefferson had not associated much, both had served in the Virginia Assembly and came from the colony's gentry, so, in a way, they knew each other well. The head of the Treasury Department should have been one of the more difficult posts to fill, calling as it did for a combination of fiscal competence and statesmanship, but Washington had spoken of his wartime aide Alexander Hamilton for the post and appointed him as soon as the department was formed in September. (Robert Morris, qualified through his service as superintendent of finance during the war, was serving as a senator from Pennsylvania, where he preferred to remain.) Edmund Randolph as attorney general completed Washington's official family. The president knew all of the men reasonably well and expected a harmonious relationship to develop among them.

When making appointments, Washington considered not only merit and residence. Wherever possible, he practiced a kind of crude "veteran's preference" and gave positions to those who had fought for independence, but this history alone would not qualify anyone for a position. In only one case did Washington consider political factors. Rhode Island finally entered the Union in May 1790 (North Carolina had come in the previous November), and in that state Washington consciously appointed those who had worked for the ratification of the Constitution. He always kept in mind that political division came in part from sectional feeling. In 1795, he took an overview of all his appointments, arranging them carefully by state to be certain none had reason to feel aggrieved.[11]

Washington had a clear view of the role his secretaries were to play in administration. "The impossibility that one man should be able to perform all the great business of the State, I take to have been the reason for instituting the great Departments, and appointing officers therein, to assist the supreme Magistrate in discharging the duties of his trust." Thus, the secretaries were his agents to perform whatever tasks he saw fit to assign to them. So in addition to presiding over his department, a secretary might find himself doing anything from giving advice on all sorts of matters to writing a state paper. If the variety of their work blurred the lines of responsibility, Washington did not become concerned because he viewed administration as a kind of communal enterprise; a gain for one was a gain for all. He kept track of what the secretaries were doing within their respective departments by reading all letters going out over their signatures along with the letters they were answering. Jefferson summarized the advantages of this practice when he instituted it in his own administration in 1801: "thus he was always in accurate possession of all facts and proceedings in every part of the Union, and to whatsoever department they related; he formed a central point for the different branches; preserved a unity of object and action among them; exercised that participation in the suggestion of affairs which his office made incumbent on him, and met himself the due responsibility for whatever was done."

Although Washington readily assumed responsibility for what his assistants did, he did not interfere in their work. When the French minister, Comte de Moustier, tried to approach Washington directly, the diplomat was coolly informed that the president believed it to be the practice "in most polished nations . . . that business should be digested and prepared by the Heads" of departments. He early conceived of the cabinet as a unit and authorized Jefferson, Hamilton, and Knox to meet during his southern tour in 1791 to take action should an emergency arise in his absence. If the vice president were in town, he should also be invited. But meetings of all the secretaries with the president

---

[11] List of Government Officers, [Mar. 1795], *Writings*, 34: 165–67.

were usually restricted to serious matters, and only five meetings were held during the first term, most of them near its end. Washington had hoped to use the cabinet as a consultative body, similar to the councils of war of the revolutionary struggle. However, when the wars of the French Revolution began to complicate American foreign policy, meetings became occasions for disagreement between Hamilton and Jefferson, and their consultative quality was lost. By this time, April 1793, Attorney General Randolph attended the meetings, but Adams had stopped coming. These meetings were confined to policy questions; administrative matters were handled between the president and the relevant secretary.[12]

In keeping with his wartime practice, Washington did not confine himself to his official advisors; rather, he canvassed widely and then considered the various answers, sometimes at length, before coming to a decision. Thus, he consulted not only the cabinet but also Adams and Jay on how to treat an informal emissary from the English who presented himself in July 1790. He asked Madison for guidance on any number of points, and in 1792, when Washington was considering retiring, the Virginia congressman drafted a farewell message. During much of the first term, Madison acted as a kind of informal counselor to the president to an extent not generally realized. The president often asked individuals about someone in their locale who was being considered for an appointment and used general news from unofficial correspondents to give him a notion of how the people saw the government.[13]

Although at first glance Washington's decision-making procedures seem to be unsystematic, he followed a general rule of involving only as many people as needed to arrive at a sound, well-buttressed conclusion. And when he made up his mind, that was the end of the debate, if there had been one. If he called for a

---

[12] Circular to Heads of Departments, Nov. 6, 1801, in Paul Leicester Ford, ed., *Writings of Thomas Jefferson* (New York, 1897), 8: 99–101; GW to Comte de Moustier, May 25, 1789, to Alexander Hamilton, Thomas Jefferson, Henry Knox, Apr. 4, 1791, *Papers/P*, 2: 390, 8: 59–60. Leonard White, *The Federalists: A Study in Administrative History* (1948, repr., New York, 1965), chaps. 1, 3, and 9.

[13] *Diaries*, Apr. 27, 28, July 8, 1790, 6: 68–69, 87–89; Leibiger, *Friendship*, chaps. 4, 5, and 6.

cabinet vote, which was not often, he almost always followed the result; with a cabinet containing two men of such surpassing ability as Jefferson and Hamilton, along with their competent associates, a majority decision was likely to be a sound one. As it happened, Hamilton's responsibilities were in an area with which Washington was unfamiliar and also involved primarily congressional action; the secretary usually worked alone or with congressmen directly. Further, in forming the department, Congress had given itself the right to call on the secretary to "digest and prepare" reports on fiscal matters, so they had a kind of private line with each other that bypassed the president. Jefferson's responsibilities, on the other hand, involved issues that had to be settled mainly within the executive branch and that involved foreign affairs, a topic on which the president had clear and strong ideas. Thus, Jefferson's work was more likely to involve close work with the president and could be undone by a cabinet vote. As disagreements developed between the two principal secretaries, they were exacerbated by these circumstances. The president's hope of a happy official family was not to be fulfilled.

Washington took a relatively active role in the legislative process. For example, during the First Congress, he sent frequent messages to the legislators, raising substantial issues for their attention; more than 80 percent of these issues dealt with the American Indians and the West. The major tool the president had in shaping legislation, other than his right to advise Congress, was his executive veto. As noted already, Washington believed he could veto on grounds of policy as well as unconstitutionality. In the interest of working cooperatively with the legislators, he would not exercise this power lightly. It happened that the first occasion on which Washington exercised the veto was on the ground of unconstitutionality. Following the first census in 1790, Congress reapportioned itself during the first session of the Second Congress (October 1791–May 1792), dividing each state's population by the constitutional minimum of thirty thousand (Art. I, sec. 2); so far, it was a simple exercise in division. But the remainders were then divided among the states, starting with those with the largest remainders. These states were also the largest states, primarily northern. In the process, not only was the South shortchanged, but some states received more than one representative per thirty thousand population, and there was no common divisor. In canvassing his advisors, Washington found that Hamilton and Knox advised him to accept the bill because Congress's interpretation of the constitutional provision was a reasonable one. However, Randolph, Jefferson, and Madison convinced him that although the veto could be made to appear a sectionally motivated action in favor of the South, a desire not to appear biased toward his own section should not prevent him from following the constitutional standard. Washington asked the three Virginians to draft the veto message that was sent down on April 5, 1792. Within nine days, a bill applying the uniform ratio of one representative per thirty-three thousand inhabitants was given to the president for his signature. This quick action showed the legislators' ready agreement with the first use of the executive veto. At the end of his administration, in March 1797, Washington vetoed a bill discharging a troop of dragoons then on the frontier; he did so on grounds of policy, and Congress again quickly modified the bill to meet his objections.[14]

He took full advantage of his right to advise the legislature and gave them a long shopping list in his first Annual Address, January 1790, when he recommended improvement of the army and militia, support of manufactures, improved roads, and, especially, the necessity of promoting education, among other topics. The message was delivered personally, with ceremony Washington must have approved, for he noted the details carefully in his diary—including even the place where the cloth of his suit was woven. However, he could also indicate his sentiments by failing to mention something. In a 1791 report, Hamilton recommended, among other things, a system of bounties to encourage manufacturing; the president never mentioned the report in his speeches and only later commented that he thought the bounties both ineffectual and unconstitutional. The report was never acted upon. As events will show, his expectation of leading a co-

---

[14] Charlene Bangs Bickford and Kenneth R. Bowling, *Birth of the Nation: The First Federal Congress, 1789–1791* (Madison, Wis., 1989), 80; hereafter, Bickford and Bowling, *First Congress*. Freeman, 6: 343–48; Leibiger, *Friendship*, 156; Phelps, *GW and Constitutionalism*, 149–54, treats both vetoes.

operative effort of executive and legislature in implementing a consensus of the national interest would not be fulfilled.[15]

This expectation was seen in his attempts to follow the constitutional provision that the president should seek the "Advice and Consent of the Senate" (Art. II, sec. 2) in making treaties. In August 1789, Washington and Secretary Knox went to the Senate to seek their advice on instructions for commissioners being sent to negotiate a treaty with the southern American Indian tribes (Indian affairs were the province of the War Department). The senators proved unable to deliberate with the president, and Senator Maclay recommended that the matter be referred to a select committee. At this recommendation, Washington exclaimed, *"This defeats every purpose of my coming here!"* (emphasis in original), and explained that he had brought Knox along so that the instructions could be considered expeditiously in an oral exchange. By mutual consent, the business was put over to the following Monday. But the overly suspicious Maclay "knew" that the president had come down only to overawe the Senate with his presence: "form only will be left to Us—This will not do with Americans," and he reported the president as leaving "with a discontented Air. had it been any other, than the Man who I wish to regard as the first Character in the World, I would have said with sullen dignity." Monday's session went no better than the first, and as Washington left, he was reported as saying that he would be "damned" if he ever went "there" again. Of course, no president ever has gone "there," and the advice clause is a dead letter, treaties being negotiated with a free hand by the president. Thus, as with the cabinet, Washington's hope of using the Senate as a consultative body was disappointed.[16]

Washington was responsible for another diminution of the Senate's power in foreign relations when, in October 1789, he asked Gouverneur Morris, then in Europe on business, to go to London and informally ascertain the British government's views on a number of points left over or inadequately dealt with by the peace treaty. (Neither the United States nor Britain had a minis-

---

[15] To the United States Senate and House of Representatives, Jan. 8, 1790, *Papers/P,* 4: 543–46; *Diaries,* Jan. 8, 1790, 6: 4.
[16] Bowling and Veit, *Diary of William Maclay,* 130–32; Phelps, *GW and Constitutionalism,* 167–72.

ter in the other's capital.) Although this request weakened the constitutional prerogative of the Senate to approve all persons nominated to represent the country abroad, Morris's negative report, received in July 1790, permitted the administration to take a strong line with a British agent who came to New York later that summer.[17]

Thus, the Constitution was being fleshed out and put into execution by a combination of attention to it, discreet departures from it, continuation of old practices, and trial and error. By the time of Washington's first Annual Address to Congress (January 1790), the government had a revenue, the executive departments had been established and, with the exception of state, manned; attention was being paid to foreign relations, and Congress was presently to take up the area where the most improvement was needed—the unpaid debt left over from the War for Independence. Washington may justifiably have taken personal satisfaction when he congratulated the legislators "on the present favorable prospects of our public affairs."

This optimistic judgment was in part based on a kind of vacation the president took during a congressional recess. He had toured the New England states "to acquire knowledge of the face of the Country, the growth and agriculture thereof—and the temper and disposition of the inhabitants toward the new government." Accompanied by servants, he left New York on October 15, 1789, and traveled through Connecticut, Massachusetts, and New Hampshire for almost a month, avoiding Rhode Island (which had yet to ratify). He carefully noted in his journal not only the condition of the roads, the style of cultivation, and the like, but also extensive information on commerce and manufacturing, showing his appreciation that even these unfamiliar ways of making a living figured in the nation's prosperity. Also into the journal went an unconsciously amusing recounting of Massachusetts governor John Hancock's abortive attempt to upstage the president by receiving the first visit, "which he knew was improper." The affair ended with Hancock being melodramatically carried into Washington's presence to maintain the governor's pretense of being too ill with gout to call on the president. This

---

[17] *Diaries,* Oct. 7, 8, 1789, 5: 454–56; Freeman, 6: 269–71, 284.

minor annoyance aside, the rest of the trip went well, and Washington did not even object too strongly to being marooned in a Connecticut town by the state's blue laws, although he had to spend Sunday listening to two "very lame" sermons by the local parson. He made a similar tour of the South in the spring of 1791, when he also attempted to learn the people's reaction to Hamilton's funding plan, which had been enacted the previous summer. If the new government were to gain the loyalty of its citizens, if a sense of American nationalism were to develop, just such expedients as this were necessary. As Jefferson once noted, one of Washington's chief services for the new nation was as the focus for loyalty until a less personal, more general feeling could develop. The tours helped to fulfill that function in the most effective way possible—by his presence.[18]

Although the government seemed to be going well, all was not good in Washington's personal life. His mother died of breast cancer during the summer of 1789; in consoling his sister, he wrote that he hoped their mother was "translated to a happier place." Nor was he as healthy as he wished; he suffered a painful abscess on his thigh during the summer of 1789 and during the following winter was stricken with a cold that developed into pneumonia. After he apparently lingered between life and death for a week, the fever broke, and he quickly recovered. He commented fatalistically that such things came in threes; his next illness would probably carry him off. Although he was not plagued by ill health during his presidency, he was in poorer health than during the war, when the physical and mental demands had probably been greater. The difference might be explained as much by his inability to exercise as by his advancing age; he had constantly to work off the tensions of his duties by horseback riding and other forms of exercise that had been an integral part of his wartime duties. The only physical feature visitors commented on was his teeth, which had been poor for years and were now almost completely gone, being replaced by a variety of dentures, none of which were adequate, some of which were downright painful. Eighteenth-century dentistry was about

---

[18] *Diaries*, Oct. 5, Oct. 15–Nov. 17, 1789, 5: 452–53, 460–97, for the New England tour; Mar. 21–June 12, 1791, 6: 99–163, for the southern tour.

as ineffectual as eighteenth-century medicine. "His Excellency" had kept his figure, weighing about 170 to 180 pounds, well proportioned to his height of more than six feet and probably owing as much to his moderate eating and drinking habits as to his exercise. But he felt himself growing old and feared he would not much longer be physically and mentally equal to the demands of his office.[19]

And those demands were about to increase substantially. Congress had commissioned Secretary Hamilton to draft a plan for funding the debts of the old Congress. The "First Report on the Public Credit," submitted in January 1790, was in the main unexceptionable. Hamilton proposed to pay off the old debt, estimated to total almost eighty million dollars—foreign, congressional, and state debts included—at face value, with bonds for the domestic debt bearing interest of a little more than 4 percent; whatever interest the foreign debt contracts called for would be paid. The present holders of the debt certificates were to be the recipients of the bonds. Thus, Hamilton rejected the idea of scaling the debt down or discriminating in favor of the original holders, who, in most cases, had sold their certificates for a fraction of their face value. There was sentiment in favor of both expedients, but neither was able to muster many votes in Congress. The Constitution had been put into effect in part to pay off the debt, and, considering the wide range of policies from which Hamilton could have chosen, he had served the fiscal needs of the nation well. But his proposal, on grounds of both equity and policy, that the national government assume the debts incurred by the states in fighting the war, snapped the patience of the agrarian sectionalists, who, although none too happy with the new, stronger central government, had borne with it up to that point. Madison was prominent in the opposition to assumption. His political activity, even when advancing the new Constitution, had always been in what he considered Virginia's best interests; thus, his opposition to assumption was not a switch from nationalism to sectionalism, but a shift from one way of protecting Virginia to another. The southern states generally, with the exception of South Carolina, felt they had little to gain and much to lose by assumption.[20]

Washington played no direct role in the controversy. Because he was careful to say nothing while Congress was deliberating, one can make only surmises. In 1783, he may have favored discrimination on the ground of equity to the soldiers who were forced to sell their pay warrants; he had certainly felt strongly about it then. By 1790, he might have concluded that the nation's credit took precedence. In 1789, he had drafted a plan calling for the federal government to collect all taxes; he felt this approach would be more just and would increase the loyalty of citizens to the central government. Washington would favor anything constitutional and reasonable that would increase the power of that government, so he might have approved of assumption. The only comment he made was to regret the controversy that arose over it. To him, the quarrel was sectional, not fiscal, and involved no constitutional questions. At one point, he complained that his fellow Virginians were extraordinarily "irritable, sour, and discontented" about assumption, so he had little patience with them.[21]

But Washington was not so nationalistic that he had no regional attachments, and the quarrel over assumption took a turn that in his opinion served well the needs of both the nation and the Chesapeake area. In order to get assumption through Congress, Hamilton found it necessary to buy votes by locating the proposed capital somewhere on the Potomac River and changing the manner by which the accounts between the old Congress and the states were being settled. The latter point was an item of concern to Virginia, which had paid off most of its debts but believed itself to be Congress's creditor by a large sum. These matters arranged, separate bills were passed providing for assumption and for a capital city to be located on the Potomac. The government would move there after a ten-year stay in Philadelphia, beginning in November 1790, to allow government buildings to be built.

Thus, the Potomac would get a city that some southerners ex-

[20] Leibiger, *Friendship*, 129–33.
[21] GW to David Stuart, June 15, 1790, *Papers/P*, 5: 286–87.

pected to grow into an important commercial center that would be able to serve the growing needs of western commerce through an improved Potomac River. This was just the kind of development, both commercial and industrial, that the president felt was most needed in the South and for which he had been working since before the war. None of the Jeffersonian fears of the social and political evils large cities reputedly brought with them was expressed by the master of Mount Vernon. Although he could not see himself living anywhere other than there, he realized that to grow and prosper the nation needed more than an agrarian economy. During the New England tour, he had shown much interest in the factories he had visited, and he approved of discrimination in favor of American manufactures and commerce so that they might be built up. Just as the nation needed a balanced economy, so too did the Chesapeake region. Maclay's comment that the president, rather than lobbying legislators, was the primary, though hidden force behind the Potomac residence bill reflected Washington's strong, thinly veiled desire to see the capital located on the Potomac, for political as well as economic reasons. There was a strong protest from interested groups, especially New Yorkers, and the president was attacked in newspaper statements and cartoons for signing the residence bill.[22]

Although assumption had not presented any constitutional difficulties to Congress, that was not the case with Hamilton's next proposal. In December 1790, he urged the legislature to establish a national bank to serve as the government's fiscal agent and to bring the benefits of a large, well-funded bank to the private economy. The Bank of the United States was to have a capital of ten million dollars, 20 percent of which would be paid in by the government, which would also share in the bank's governance to that extent. A portion of the capital would consist of government bonds, and the bank's charter would last as long as the bonds were outstanding. No one except diehard agrarians were against banks in general or even this bank in particular. The difficulty lay with the federal government's power to establish it. A proposal to permit the government to issue charters of incor-

---

[22] Bowling and Veit, *Diary of William Maclay*, 308, 321; Bowling, *Creation*, chap. 7.

poration had been voted down at the Philadelphia convention, and while Congress debated the bank bill, the Tenth Amendment—specifying what all had understood to be the case, that any power not expressly delegated by the Constitution, was reserved to the states or to the people—was being ratified. The constitutional question was not strongly debated in Congress, where the only change the bank bill incurred was a twenty-year term to its charter.

Washington received the bill on February 16, 1791, and now had ten days to sign it, or it would become law without his signature. He had already questioned the cabinet separately on the point, and both Randolph and Jefferson had criticized the bank on grounds that the power to incorporate was not expressly delegated. Knox simply agreed with Hamilton, who was now given his adversaries' statements and instructed to answer the constitutional objections. The secretary came back on February 23 with a fifteen-thousand-word defense of the bank's constitutionality that relied on a liberal interpretation of the clause granting Congress authority "to make all Laws necessary and proper for the carrying into execution all the foregoing Powers" (Art. I, sec. 8). Hamilton argued that "necessary" included all means convenient and not ruled out by either the Constitution or morality. The defense demonstrated the kind of development that the Constitution would have to undergo if it were to be an adequate instrument of government for an expanding and changing country. Jefferson and Madison opposed the bill not only because of the constitutional question but also because they had come to distrust Hamilton's objectives, believing that he wished to distort the Constitution into a virtually unlimited grant of power to a government modeled on Britain's as much as circumstances permitted. For the moment, their objections were focused on the claimed unconstitutionality of the proposal.

What the effect of this debate was on Washington is difficult to say. He may not have had any constitutional doubts about the bank because he generally favored a broad conception of the government's powers and roles. But southerners had another reason to object to the bank: Would the location of its headquarters in Philadelphia affect moving the capital to the Potomac in 1800? Washington's selection of the exact site for the capital had

been partially outside the bounds indicated in the original residence bill. At this time, there was a bill in the Senate retroactively
approving the president's choice. The senators resolved to consider the bill on the same day Washington had either to sign or
veto the bank bill. After reading Hamilton's defense, he signed
the bill without comment. He may have been following Jefferson's advice (contained in his opinion on the bank) to sign out
of respect for Congress's judgment if his own mind were still
undecided. Or the deciding factor may have been his desire to
see a government worthy of the name come out of the Constitution. Jefferson was proposing a base only, a scope so circum-
scribed that the president may have been unpleasantly reminded
of the Articles of Confederation. Or Washington may have
wanted to ensure the Potomac site with a measure that had much
public benefit to recommend it.[23]

The day after the bank bill became law, Washington signed a
tax bill placing excise taxes on a variety of items, chief among
them "spirituous liquors of domestic manufacture," that is, rum
and whiskey. There were no constitutional questions asserted
here; rather, those that developed were political. Sectional interests had been upset, then accommodated in the assumption controversy, but with the bank and the excise bills there had been
no accommodation. The opponents of these measures were clustered in the southern states, and as early as March 1790 Virginian David Stuart had warned Washington that his home state felt
alone and friendless against a "Northern phalanx . . . so firmly
united as to bear down all opposition." Washington's reply reproved the South, Virginia especially, for not seeing and steadily
pursuing their real interests; if the North had more votes, the
South would have to accept it until they could do better. Dis-
unionist talk such as Stuart had related undermined the basis of
the Union: mutual accommodation. Washington would have to
repeat this reproof again and again as he tried to deal with the
effects of fast-increasing party feeling on his administration. As
he saw it, the future belonged to the United States; all the states

---

[23] Stanley Elkins and Eric McKitrick, *The Age of Federalism: The Early American
Republic, 1788–1800* (1993, repr., New York, 1995), 223–34; hereafter, Elkins
and McKitrick, *Age of Federalism*. Bickford and Bowling, *First Congress*, 72–75;
Bowling, *Creation*, 215–19.

had to do was stay together and let the development of half a continent carry them to greatness. There was much that was flexible in the future, and opposition to a specific measure of the administration did not indicate disloyalty to the government, nor could one or even several bills undermine the Constitution. The reproof also reflected his conviction that sectional feelings were one of the major causes of political division.[24]

But Madison and Jefferson could not bear with the direction of public affairs because they were afraid the country would not remain a republic long enough to realize its glorious future. Years later Jefferson recorded his dismay at the preference for monarchy he found among people within and without the government when he arrived in New York in 1790; he also believed that Hamilton's fiscal system was designed first to confuse people and then to enrich legislators. Seeing the country galloping into monarchy, Madison in the legislature and Jefferson in the executive branch began to cooperate in opposing as well as they could the policies they saw as warping the Constitution into a grant of nearly absolute power that could end only with the duplication in America of the corrupt and unrepresentative government of Britain. Neither believed Washington was helping this trend along. "Unversed in financial projects and calculations and budgets, his approbation of [Hamilton's policies] was bottomed on his confidence" in the man, Jefferson observed. The president not only retained confidence in both secretaries, but he also refused, at first, to be disheartened at opposition in Congress. When the First Congress finished its work in March 1791, he blithely observed to Humphreys, now minister to Portugal, that "our public credit is restored, our resources are increasing, and the general appearance of things at least equals the most sanguine expectation that was formed of the effects of the present government." Although "great harmony and cordiality" prevailed throughout Congress, Washington admitted to Humphreys that, on the bank and the excise bills, "the line between the southern and eastern interests appeared more strongly marked than could have been wished. . . . But the debates were

---

[24] David Stuart to GW, Mar. 15, 1790, GW to Stuart, Mar. 28, 1790, *Papers/P*, 5: 236, 286–88.

conducted with temper and candor." Few congressmen would have subscribed to so rosy a view of affairs.[25]

Nor would Washington if he had been thinking of his private affairs. His nephew George Augustine had been a satisfactory steward; the young man had recently married and seemed settled for the foreseeable future at Mount Vernon. But when Washington visited there in the fall of 1791, he found the estate suffering from the combined effects of drought and his nephew's serious illness. Just as the president had whipped things back into shape, he had to return unexpectedly to Philadelphia. The return was unexpected only because he had absentmindedly set Congress's convening one week later than it was actually scheduled. With self-reproach for his poor memory, he sent off a flurry of instructions to the secretaries about his Annual Address, and leaving the estate in the hands of his head farmer, Anthony Whiting, a recent emigrant from Britain, he left for the capital.[26]

Despite Washington's concern about his speech, it proved, when he delivered it on October 25, to be mainly a list of items previously recommended to Congress but not yet acted upon. He did express hope that the "misconception" over the excise tax held in certain parts of the country would soon be corrected and advised the legislators to deal promptly with any legitimate grievances that were discovered. He also informed them of the selection of a site on the Potomac for the new capital and gave them an optimistic report on its progress.[27]

This almost casual reference to the new capital concealed a good bit of satisfaction on Washington's part. From the passage of the residence bill on, the president took a great interest in the progress of the federal city. He had selected a site at the junction of the Eastern Branch and the Potomac, reaching beyond the southern edge of the area marked out by Congress. In the 1780s, when the old Congress had thought about a permanent home

---

[25] *The Anas, 1791–1806*, selections, Feb. 4, 1818, in Merrill Peterson, ed., *Thomas Jefferson: Writings* (New York, 1984), 665–66, 670; hereafter, Peterson, *Jefferson: Writings.* GW to David Humphreys, Mar. 16, 1791, *Papers/P,* 7: 583.

[26] Freeman, 6: 330–35; GW to Alexander Hamilton, to Henry Knox, Oct. 14, 1791, *Papers/P,* 9: 78–79, 84.

[27] "To the United States Senate and House of Representatives, Oct. 25, 1791," *Papers/P,* 9: 110–16.

for itself, a site near Washington's choice had been tentatively selected, so the area had already been seen as a suitable location. The small commercial towns of Georgetown and Alexandria, included within the ten-mile square ceded by Maryland and Virginia, were looked to as nuclei for the commercial center the capital was expected to become. In 1791, the name *Washington* was selected for the city and *District of Columbia* for the entire square, and commissioners were appointed to purchase land, lay out streets, supervise the construction of the federal buildings, and so on. Although the commissioners frequently conferred with the president and seem never to have done anything with which he disagreed, their appointment removed from his shoulders the immediate responsibility for the work. He followed its progress eagerly, always visiting the city when he was staying at Mount Vernon. As late as February 1792, he was sufficiently nervous about the continued opposition to removing the government from Philadelphia to worry that any slowdown resulting from the discharge of the project's superintendent, Pierre L'Enfant, would be a "deathblow." Senator Maclay had not been correct in 1790 when he believed Washington to be the chief mover of a southern capital, but if he had written those lines two years later, he would have been considerably closer to the truth. The president consistently supported—often in opposition to his fellow Virginians, Madison and Jefferson—a grand (some would call it grandiose) plan for the capital city and its public buildings, a plan suitable for the great national republic that he believed the country would become.[28]

Congress took up the president's shopping list and began to act on it in desultory fashion while he fretted over news from Mount Vernon. His nephew continued to decline, but Whiting was showing surprising competence. The situation was similarly mixed in Philadelphia: George Hammond presented himself to the president in November as the first British minister to the United States, but the next month news of the defeat of an American force under Major General Arthur St. Clair by natives in the

---

[28] Bowling, *Creation*, esp. chap. 8, "Washington Takes Command." C. M. Harris, "Washington's Gamble, L'Enfant's Dream: Politics, Design, and the Foundation of the National Capital," *William and Mary Quarterly* 56 (July 1999): 527–64.

Ohio country reached Washington. Britain, still in possession of posts on American soil, might have sent a minister, but would they negotiate in the face of American weakness? St. Clair's defeat also led to a congressional investigation, the first of its kind. The executive office complied with a request from the House for executive papers pertaining to the expedition, although it was realized that this compliance might present difficulties in the future. The investigation exonerated both St. Clair and the administration, and actually helped to build up support for a stronger force.[29]

As the last full year of his presidential term opened, Washington did some calculating. He had celebrated his sixtieth birthday in February, marking sixteen years of his adult life spent in public service, first for the king, then for the republic. He certainly deserved retirement. He was also concerned about his reputation; as he told Jefferson, accepting a second term "might give room to say, that having tasted the sweets of office, he could not do without them." What he saw as the effects of old age on his health and memory also bothered him, and, with his inability to exercise, his office was "more irksome, and tranquility and retirement become an irresistible passion." He seemed determined not to accept election to a second term.[30]

Confirming and strengthening Washington's decision to retire was the quarreling of his secretaries at the more frequent cabinet meetings now being called to save some of the time used in individual consultation. These quarrels were duplicated in Congress and in newspapers that quickly developed partisan attachments either to the opposition "Republicans," as they had begun to call themselves, or to those who supported Hamilton's policies, the "Federalists." Washington did his best to stay aloof from these contentions, in part from personal preference, in part because he did not believe his office permitted partisan activity. But the Republican attacks on Hamilton's fiscal system began to tell on the president also, and he complained to Jefferson in July that "in condemning the administration of government, they con-

[29] Freeman, 6: 334–42.
[30] "Memoranda of a Conversation with the President," Mar. 1, 1792, *Jefferson Papers*, 23: 185.

demned him, for if there were measures pursued contrary to his sentiments, they must conceive him too careless to attend to them, or too stupid to understand them." He was especially critical of the *National Gazette*, whose editor, Phillip Freneau worked as a part-time translator in the State Department. The *Gazette*, Washington felt, was trying to promote disunion by exciting opposition to the government. If Jefferson really feared monarchy, what would be more likely to bring it on than the chaos caused by the breakup of the Union? Jefferson replied by repeating his criticism of the funding system for corrupting the legislature and, among other evils, for milking the South in order to pay off the bonds held by the North.[31]

Jefferson's charges, however, sufficiently upset Washington that he rephrased them and, in August, asked Hamilton to answer them. The Treasury secretary conceded nothing other than that some might have been hurt speculating in government bonds, but he saw no way of preventing that. To the charge that he was promoting monarchy, the secretary gave the same answer Washington had already given: that the easiest way to do this was to promote instability, and the easiest way to do the latter was to "resist a confirmation of public order." Washington tried to reconcile his two aides with almost identical letters to each in which he pleaded that "instead of wounding suspicions and irritable charges, there may be liberal allowances, mutual forbearances and temporizing yieldings on *all sides*" (emphasis in original). In replying, Hamilton did concede that he had helped with the recent attacks on Jefferson in the Federalist press, but he called it mere self-defense against charges that Freneau, Jefferson's minion, was daily leveling against him. Jefferson simply repeated his charges, including Hamilton's interference in State Department affairs (true), and denied that he had any share in Freneau's writing (technically true). He concluded by stating his intention to retire in March 1793. Despite each secretary's obviously half-hearted promises to keep the peace in the cabinet,

---

[31] "Notes of a Conversation with George Washington, Jul. 10, 1792," *Jefferson Papers*, 24: 210–11. See James Roger Sharp, *American Politics in the Early Republic: The New Nation in Crisis* (New Haven, 1993), part 1, "The Breakdown of an Elite Consensus, 1789–1792," for a detailed recounting; hereafter, Sharp, *American Politics*.

Washington could see that the two men disliked and distrusted each other intensely and were not soon likely to change their minds.[32]

Paradoxically, this evidence of personal and partisan discontent, reflecting as it did sectional discontent, was probably helping to change Washington's mind about retiring. It underlined the point Jefferson made in May: "The confidence of the whole union is centered on you. . . . North and South will hang together, if they have you to hang on." Everyone Washington talked with—Hamilton, Madison, Lear—concurred in this feeling. The latter had occasion to go to New England during the summer and reported that all there wanted the president to continue. The need for union was self-evident to Washington; in May, when directing Madison in the drafting of his "valedictory," he told him to stress the common bonds uniting the country: "that we are *all* the children of the same country" (emphasis in original), and the interests of all Americans were the same; the economic interests of all sections could be made to march together to the mutual enrichment of all. These statements are truisms, and they are more valuable for what they show of Washington's concerns than for the advice they contain, for he was also worried about the harsh criticism of public officials in the press: "there ought to be limits to it; for suspicions unfounded, and jealousies too lively, are irritating to honest feelings." Thus, on the one hand he was being told that all believed him to be the hinge on which the Union turned, but on the other hand his agents and the policies of his administration were being severely criticized, and he was certainly the "indirect object" of some of this criticism. As ever, the currents seemed contradictory and confusing, not a clear guide at all.[33]

While preparing for what he had hoped would be his last speech to Congress, he also had to worry over objections to the excise that were surfacing in some sections, especially in western Pennsylvania. An executive proclamation warning all citizens to refrain from opposition to the law was sent out, but the president

---

[32] Freeman, 6: 364–71, cites all the relevant letters.
[33] Freeman, 6: 371; Leibiger, *Friendship*, 157–65; Thomas Jefferson to GW, May 23, 1792, *Jefferson Papers*, 23: 539.

feared that more stringent measures, perhaps even troops, would be necessary before matters quieted down. This was just the kind of trouble, his advisors assured him, that only his presence kept from flaring up into something more serious. His Annual Address, delivered to Congress on November 6, referred to the complaints of the Pennsylvanians but only to assure the legislators that the laws would be enforced. The message concerned mainly American Indian affairs policy, detailing the steps taken to defend the frontier but also pleading for congressional support for a more just and humane policy toward the natives. His statements here were an interesting contrast to those he had made as colonel of the Virginia Regiment when he had seen the natives only as malignant obstacles to Virginia's progress westward. Despite his resentment over the newspaper attacks on the administration, Washington also asked Congress to consider whether or not postal rates were discouraging the circulation of papers; he was ready to criticize the press, but he was not ready to do without it.[34]

The last time Washington had had to make a fateful decision was in 1789; then it had been impossible to say at what point he had decided to accept the presidency. Similarly, in 1792, he said nothing and did nothing and by that means slowly but inextricably slid into his second term. As late as November 4, a close friend of the president was not certain he had decided to stay. But the Electoral College met on schedule the first Monday in December, and from that point on Washington was going to serve another term, the prospect of his declining it after election being inconceivable.[35]

One thing helped to make Washington's election to a second term a pleasant event; as the votes were made known in early January, it was seen that no one had voted against him. In urging him to stand for election, Hamilton had derided the idea that anyone would vote against him, so apparently this prospect had worried the president. Negative votes would have been a kind of

---

[34] "Proclamation," Sep. 15, 1792, GW to Alexander Hamilton, Sep. 16, 1792, "Fourth Annual Address to Congress," Nov. 6, 1792, *Writings*, 32: 150–51, 153, 205–12.

[35] Flexner, 3: 378–80, indicates the friend was Eliza Powell; GW and Martha were very friendly with Powell and her husband.

confirmation of his fears that his presence had become a disuniting force. The electors' second votes were divided between John Adams, seventy-seven, and George Clinton, fifty. Clinton's votes were a half-hearted Republican attempt to unseat the man whom some wrongly credited with trying to push monarchy onto the American people. Except for the gratifying unanimity of Washington's reelection, little else promised that his second term would be either easy or tranquil, however.

In February 1793, Washington secured from his secretary of state a promise to stay until the end of the year, although he would not promise to try to get along with Hamilton. Jefferson protested that he had never conspired against his colleague, and if Virginia were restless, as Washington had heard from Henry Lee, it was only because of the constant losses southern interests suffered at the hands of the stock jobbers in Congress. This accusation wrung from Washington the almost anguished cry that although everyone was urging him to remain, few realized "the extreme wretchedness of his existence while in office." Just a few weeks later, as he celebrated his sixty-first birthday, he learned of the death of his nephew George Augustine. In addition to the loss of a dearly loved relative, Washington now had to secure a new estate manager. Whiting, already acting in that capacity, would have to do for the time being. Washington directed him, as he had his nephew, by means of long letters written every Sunday morning; they were incredibly detailed and showed, in addition to his intimate knowledge of his farms, that his memory, at least as far as Mount Vernon was concerned, was as good as ever.[36]

In assessing his first term, Washington may well have judged it to be rather close to what he expected it to be: a mixed blessing. The administrative and social chores of the office had been burdensome, but the realization that he was helping the new nation through a difficult adolescence had been a more than adequate compensation. But the major difficulties he had experienced were completely unexpected; the party animosities in Congress and their spread into his official family seemed to him useless demonstrations of an incomprehensible fear of the legitimate

---

[36] "Notes of a Conversation with George Washington, Feb. 7, 1792," *Jefferson Papers*, 25: 153–55.

operations of the new government. To Washington, experience was the best and only teacher; Americans must be willing to trust the Constitution and its government not to stray beyond the bounds marked out for it. What he feared most was anarchy, the sad state from which he believed the country had been rescued in 1789.

The primary task of the new president had been twofold: to get the new government functioning and to plant it firmly in the affections of the people. Washington had clearly succeeded in the first and—if the discord in cabinet and Congress as well as in the newspapers was any indication—partially failed in the second. This partial failure should not be allowed to obscure the substantial success he did achieve. The government had been organized and was working efficiently and effectively; the office of the president had been satisfactorily executed along the lines of the conception of it held by Washington and by most of his successors. If the new government could enjoy a few more years of tranquility, perhaps the difficulties foreseen by the Republicans would disappear as the strength of the United States translated itself into increasing prosperity and freedom for its citizens. An America isolated from the consuming furies of Europe, set free by the French Revolution, might have had that tranquility, but Washington's America was not isolated.

6

The Task Completed? 1793–1797

> What with the current affairs of the Government, the
> unpleasant aspect of matters on our Indian frontiers,
> and the momentous occurences in Europe, I am not
> only pressed with the quantity of business, but the na-
> ture of a great part of it is peculiarly delicate and em-
> barassing.
>
> GW to Gouverneur Morris, June 13, 1793

AS A SIGN OF THE division already affecting the country, the cabinet could not agree on the ceremonial details of Washington's
second inauguration. The president followed Randolph and
Knox's advice and took his oath before both houses of Congress
in a brief, almost commonplace ceremony in the Senate chamber. Before taking the oath, he stated that he would at a later
date "express the high sense I entertain of this distinguished
honor," but for now he was content to note "That if it shall be
found during my administration of the Government I have in
any instance violated willingly or knowingly, the injunction
thereof, I may (besides incurring Constitutional punishm[en]t)
be subject to the upbraidings of all who are now witnesses of the
present solemn Ceremony."[1]

It was a curious statement for such an occasion, and whatever
else it might indicate, it certainly showed that the sense of adven-
ture and imminent high accomplishment of 1789 had evapo-
rated amidst the division in the cabinet, the opposition in
Congress, and the partisan contention in the country at large.
Originating in disagreement over Hamilton's fiscal system, the
tension was exacerbated by a disagreement among Americans
over the aims and accomplishments of the French Revolution.

---

[1] GW to the Secretaries of Treasury and War, Feb. 27, 1793, "Second Inaugural Address," Mar. 4, 1793, *Writings*, 32: 361, 374–75.

At its start, most Americans wished well the country that had so materially aided theirs in its struggle for independence, but among those who knew France well there were early doubts that this revolution would proceed smoothly. Conditions in the two countries were so different that it seemed no comparisons could be drawn. Washington contented himself with cordial but vague replies when French correspondents informed him of conditions there. "Of one thing, however, you may rest perfectly assured, that nobody is more anxious for the happy issue of that business than I am, as nobody can wish more sincerely for the prosperity of the French Nation, than I do," he assured the Chevalier la Luzerne in April 1790. As the revolution progressed, both the hopes and fears of Americans were confirmed more or less in agreement with the original positions they had taken, for that progress was sufficiently complicated to permit anyone to take comfort or alarm. A fondness for France and a willingness to believe that somehow things there would work out seemed to accompany an antipathy for Hamilton's fiscal system and for Britain. Other issues developed, but finances and relations with Britain and France remained primary. These issues were the ones that divided the pro-British Federalists from the pro-French Republicans, the "Anglo-men" from the "Gallo-men," the "monocrats" or "paper men" from the "democrats" or "Jacobins," to use some of their favorite pejoratives for each other. Actually, Hamilton's supporters were more or less bound to a pro-British attitude, for their mentor's system relied on a high volume of trade for a steady flow of revenue from the tariff, trade in which, independent or not, Britain remained the republic's major partner. Once Britain joined the alliance of monarchs fighting to contain the revolution, it could also be supported as one of the chief fighters for a proper concept of liberty and order. But this characterization gave the Republicans yet another reason for disliking the former colonial master.[2]

---

[2] GW to Luzerne, Apr. 29, 1790, *Papers/P,* 5: 359. Louis M. Sears's *George Washington and the French Revolution* (Detroit, 1960) is a competent survey. See Sharp, *American Politics,* chaps. 5–7, and Elkins and McKitrick, *Age of Federalism,* chaps. 9–11, for the general domestic picture. Frank T. Reuter's *Trials and Triumphs: George Washington's Foreign Policy* (Fort Worth, Tex., 1983) is an excellent brief treatment for the general reader.

Washington managed to remain largely aloof from these developing party tensions during his first term, especially as they translated themselves into a preference for either Britain or France. Maintaining this seeming indifference was not easy because these powers, plus Spain, retained an interest in North America. A 1790 war scare between Britain and Spain, the Nootka Sound Controversy, touched off a cabinet discussion on a U.S. response to a possible attempt by Britain to move troops across the American West to attack the Spanish in the lower Mississippi Valley. The discussion settled only one thing: there was nothing the country could do to resist such an expedition should it be sent. Besides illustrating the powerlessness of the country, the discussion also showed Washington's anti-British disposition, for although he realized that all the United States could do was protest, he wanted the protest to be in the strongest possible language. But these feelings did not influence his conception of a proper foreign policy, as he confided to Lafayette in August:

> Gradually recovering from the distresses in which the war left us, patiently advancing in our task of civil government, unentangled in the crooked politics of Europe, wanting scarcely any thing but the free navigation of the Mississippi (which we must have and as certainly shall have as we remain a Nation)—I have supposed, that, with the undeviating exercise of a just, steady, and prudent national policy, we shall be the gainers, whether the powers of the old world may be in peace or war; but more especially in the latter case. In that case, our importance will certainly encrease, and our friendship be courted.

To paraphrase a cliché much loved by diplomatic historians: Europe's distresses just might be America's successes.[3]

The pursuance of a "just, steady, and prudent national policy" was no easy thing, however. The British retained seven military posts in the United States on the presumed ground of American nonfulfillment of the 1783 treaty; in truth, the posts aided them in their dominance of the fur trade. Washington was convinced that their presence, especially in the Northwest, encouraged the

---

[3] GW to Lafayette, Aug. 11, 1790, *Papers/P,* 6: 232–33. For general background, see Charles R. Ritcheson, *Aftermath of Revolution: British Policy toward the United States, 1783–1795* (1969, repr., New York, 1971).

native tribes in their intermittent warfare against American settlers in the region. Another difficulty, previously noted, was the
commercial discrimination Britain practiced against the United
States. Nothing having been accomplished in any of these areas,
Washington looked forward to the coming of a British minister,
but Hammond lacked instructions on any of the topics that upset
the United States.

In the Mississippi Valley, Spain's control of New Orleans
blocked the easiest route for American goods from the West; the
Spanish were also suspected of inciting the native tribes in the
Southwest. Indeed, the valley was a kind of focus for the American policies of all three Atlantic powers; each wished to keep the
United States east of the Appalachians. But for Washington, as
for most Americans, the West was the surety that the United
States would one day, and that day not far in the future, be a
great power. The European war brought on by the French Revolution postponed any vigorous action by Britain or France (Spain
was capable of no more than a weak holding action) to realize
their Mississippi dreams until the United States had a firm hold
in the area. Although the long-term effects of the wars of the
French Revolution and Napoleon may have been beneficial for
the United States, in the short run they were anything but, as
Washington discovered in April 1793.[4]

When Washington left for Mount Vernon late in March, he
knew of Louis XVI's execution and of the declaration of the First
French Republic, whose government had sent a new minister.
Edmond Charles Genet (later famous, or infamous, as your historical politics may dictate, as "Citizen Genet") was already on
the way to his post as minister to the United States. Should he
arrive in Washington's absence, Jefferson was directed to receive
him correctly but with no undue cordiality. In Virginia, Washington busied himself with Mount Vernon's tangled affairs and the
funeral of his nephew while the news from Europe remained
vague, with Jefferson disparaging rumors of a general war in Europe involving Britain as the garbled reports of the new repub-

---

[4] See Arthur P. Whitaker, *The Mississippi Question, 1795–1803* (1927, repr.,
Gloucester, Mass., 1962), for a general treatment, and John F. McDermott, ed.,
The Spanish in the Mississippi Valley, 1762–1804 (Urbana, Ill., 1974), for more
recent treatments of aspects of the topic.

lic's condemnations of monarchy and statements of philosophy, nothing more. The president hoped Jefferson was correct, but for the moment he was more interested in why the governor and judge of the Northwest Territory were still in Philadelphia and not at their posts; the government was not going to stop because of events three thousand miles away. Hamilton was the first to advise the president that reliable reports of a European war, involving Britain, had come to the capital. Washington replied that he would return as soon as possible; until then the secretaries should ponder how to keep the United States neutral. "A strict neutrality" would be needed to keep individuals from involving the country with either of the principal—to the United States—belligerents, Britain and France.[5]

Reaching Philadelphia on April 17, Washington plunged into the work of evaluating the effect of the war on American policy. As he did so, he discovered that his secretary of state had only a few general thoughts on a proper policy for a neutral country. Quite the contrary with Hamilton, who presented the president with a list of questions regarding American conduct toward France and the validity of the 1778 treaties with that country. Lacking any other advice, Washington used the list almost verbatim as an agenda for a cabinet meeting on the morning of April 19. Although Jefferson resented his colleague's role, he had only himself to blame; the secretary of the treasury had done his homework, the secretary of state had not.[6]

The meeting was able to settle only two of the thirteen questions Hamilton had posed. Despite Jefferson's objections, it was decided to issue an official statement of policy. The secretary of state believed this response to be possibly unconstitutional and

[5] Notes to the Reception of Edmond Charles Genét, Mar. 30, 1793, *Jefferson Papers*, 25: 469–70; GW to Thomas Jefferson, Apr. 12, 1793, *Writings*, 32: 406–7.

[6] Charles M. Thomas's *American Neutrality in 1793: A Study in Cabinet Government* (New York, 1931) is a complete analysis of GW and his associates' handling of the neutrality issue; Hamilton's authorship is on page 28; hereafter, Thomas, *American Neutrality*. Notes on Washington's Questions on Neutrality and the Alliance with France, Apr. 18, 1793 [May 6, 1793], *Jefferson Papers*, 25: 665–66, for Jefferson's resentment. See also John J. Reardon, *Edmund Randolph: A Biography* (New York, 1974), part 3, for Randolph's role; hereafter, Reardon, *Randolph*.

imprudent, unconstitutional because only Congress had the power to declare war—could the president unilaterally declare neutrality or no war?—and imprudent because Jefferson hoped that perhaps Britain might bid for neutrality with a liberal policy toward American shipping. The president and his other advisors saw only peril, not opportunity, in silence. With a nod to Jefferson's sensibilities by directing that the word *neutrality* not be used, Washington commissioned Randolph to draft the proclamation. The attorney general was becoming more significant in the president's circle of advisors, mostly as a result of Jefferson and Hamilton's partisan squabbling. Randolph had cast the deciding vote on a number of significant issues—which meant sometimes voting against the secretary of state because Knox supported Hamilton uncritically. Now Jefferson felt he could not be certain how the attorney general would go, and he had become resentful, styling his colleague a "chameleon." Chameleon or no, Randolph supported Jefferson more than Hamilton. Nevertheless, he had earned the president's gratitude for sometimes giving him a middle ground between the extremes of Hamilton and Jefferson. Faced with Knox's literary incapacity, Washington naturally turned to the only available person who could draft an announcement without its becoming the object of interminable wrangling. (Previously, he might have asked Madison to do this job, but the two men were being separated by Washington's resentment of the younger man's partisanship.) More such work would be Randolph's lot in the future.

The second question, whether or not a new French minister should be received, had already been answered when Washington had directed the American minister to Paris, Gouverneur Morris, to extend recognition to the republic. Next the cabinet was asked whether the minister should be received unconditionally. Here Hamilton was implicitly questioning the validity of the 1778 treaties now that France was a republic, not a monarchy. Jefferson countered, with Randolph's support, that treaties were made by nations, not by governments, and could not be affected by the death of a king, even when the death was accomplished by the guillotine. When Hamilton supported his stand with a quotation from Emmerich Vattel, the writer on international law, and Jefferson challenged its relevance, Randolph took advantage of the disagreement to suggest an adjournment so the authority could be consulted. Washington probably appreciated Randolph's tact in postponing, possibly preventing, a squabble between Hamilton and Jefferson. Another meeting was called for the following Monday, April 22.

By that time, Randolph had a draft of the policy statement ready, so the meeting was spent going over it instead of Vattel. The statement advised all nations that the United States would "pursue a conduct friendly and impartial toward the belligerent Powers"; despite the avoidance of the word *neutrality*, it immediately became known as the Neutrality Proclamation. Within a week, Jefferson had, in a report to Washington, refuted Hamilton's aspersions on the validity of the treaties, even showing where his colleague had misconstrued Vattel, and there was no further discussion on that score. There was a good bit more talk, however, on how the United States could live up to its obligations as a neutral. The problem was, given the limited number of federal officials and the political unreliability of some state and local officers, how a rule forbidding the fitting out of privateers in American ports could be enforced. Randolph suggested using customs collectors, but only as useful adjuncts to federal attorneys. Jefferson resented the use of any Treasury Department officials, but he did not realize that this suggestion was a Washington-Randolph modification of a Hamilton plan that would have used customs collectors only. Whereas partisanship was lessening Jefferson's effectiveness, Randolph's apparent independence was increasing his value.[7]

As Washington and his advisors wrestled with the problems of a neutral during a general war, they carved out a new concept of neutrality that saw the country through a difficult period of the 1790s safely. The prevailing definition of neutrality did not rule out favoring one side. Now, however, the United States aimed to be "friendly and impartial" toward all belligerents. In doing so, they made a serious attempt to ensure that private Americans did not violate their country's neutrality. To the privileges of a neutral were now added duties. Washington, Jefferson, Hamilton, and Randolph all contributed to this redefinition of neutral-

---

[7] Reardon, *Randolph*, 225–27.

ity. Both of the secretaries were partisans of one of the belligerents; although Hamilton was more pro-British than Jefferson was pro-French, neither could be neutral. At this time, Washington was the balance who kept American policy from tipping too far in either direction. As he saw it, the United States wanted "to have nothing to do with the political intrigues or the squabbles of European nations, but on the contrary to exchange commodities and live in peace and amity with all." He succeeded sufficiently to earn the compliment of a British foreign minister years later who held up the American policy of neutrality of the mid-1790s as a model for Britain to follow.[8]

Enforcement of American neutrality regulations was one of the most difficult tasks the administration confronted. Already the British minister had complained about the fitting out of several French privateers in southern ports. These complaints reminded Washington that although the French minister had landed in Charleston, South Carolina, in early April, he had not yet appeared in Philadelphia. At length, on May 16, after a triumphal progress by land, Genet made a grand entrance into the capital, welcomed enthusiastically by local Republicans and by a salute from a visiting French warship. After festivities at the City Tavern, Genet presented himself to Jefferson for an appointment to perform what should have been his first public act in the United States, the presentation of his credentials to the president. Accompanied by the secretary of state, he did this on May 18. Few details of the occasion survive, but apparently Washington, as he frequently did, contented himself with as few words as possible, thus putting off the voluble Frenchman; the president had long since discovered that silence had its uses. Genet had expected to find in America a sympathetic partner in the struggle against monarchical government that all right-thinking people would presently join. When he found instead an administration intent on keeping him at arm's length, he assumed popular support for the policy he desired and tried to communicate directly first with Congress, then with the people. These attempts were his first mistakes; he did not make too many others, for his time as minister was short.[9]

---

[8] Carroll and Ashworth, 7: 54; Thomas, *American Neutrality*, 266, 13, n. 1.

[9] Harry Ammon's *The Genêt Mission* (New York, 1973) is an excellent study of Genêt's embassy and its domestic repercussions.

Jefferson's initial reaction to Genet was admiring, almost effusive, but by early July the secretary considered the minister "Hot headed, all imagination, no judgement, passionate, disrespectful and even indecent" toward Washington. Although the president kept his counsel, he probably shared these sentiments. Genet's demands for the immediate payment of the principal of the French debt and a new alliance between the two republics could be considered and, at length, rejected; what could not be tolerated were Genet's continued violations of diplomatic protocol and, in at least one instance, bad faith. A French privateer had seized an English merchantman, the *Little Sarah;* the vessel had been condemned by a French prize court; Genet purchased it, renaming it *La Petite Democrate*, and began to fit it out as a privateer. Minister Hammond of Britain protested the original seizure, and the legality of the conversion, by American law, was questionable. Jefferson secured what he believed was a promise from Genet that the vessel would stay moored in Philadelphia for the time being until the matter could be settled. Washington was especially ill-equipped to deal with annoying matters of this sort because he was ill with a low fever for several weeks; he had erupted at Jefferson late in May about Freneau's attacks, which had previously gone unmentioned. Then he had to go to Mount Vernon in June to deal with problems created by the serious illness of Whiting; when he arrived there, he found the steward dead, and with no replacement at hand the estate had to be left in the hands of the overseers of the five farms, unsatisfactory but the best that could be done when he left in early July. Reaching Philadelphia, he discovered that Genet had put the *Democrate* down the Delaware, beyond the reach of state and federal authorities. Jefferson was quizzed sharply as to why the president had not been informed of this development earlier; then he was asked, "Is the Minister of the French Republic to set the acts of this government at defiance with impunity? And then threaten the Executive with an appeal to the people? What must the world think of such conduct, and of the Government of the U[nited] States for submitting to it?"

By the end of the month, the cabinet had agreed that Genet's recall had to be requested and that "Rules Concerning Belligerents" had to be drawn up and published. Now no one could take refuge by charging vagueness on the part of the administration. But Washington's temper continued high, and at an early August meeting considering whether or not to publish Genet's correspondence he lost it altogether, according to Jefferson:

> The President was much inflamed; got into one of those passions when he cannot command himself; ran on much on the personal abuse which had been bestowed upon him; defied any man on earth to produce one single act of his since he had been in the government, which was not done on the purest motives; that he had never repented but once having slipped the moment of resigning his office, and that was every moment since; that *by God* he had rather be in his grave than in his present situation; that he had rather be on his farm than to be made *Emperor of the world;* and yet they were charging him with wanting to be a King. That that *rascal Freneau* sent him three of his papers every day, as if he thought he would become the distributor of his papers; that he could see in this, nothing but an impudent design to insult him. (emphasis in original)

Although Washington's anger at Freneau was also directed in part at Jefferson, a few days later he talked the secretary into staying for the rest of the year; thus, even as the partisan contention deepened, the president tried to keep the cabinet at least bipartisan, if not nonpartisan. But he himself was slipping from that standard. Whereas he had been unsparing in his denunciation of Freneau, he said nothing to Hamilton about his "No Jacobin" essays, answers to "Jacobin's" defense of Genet, which had appeared in July.[10]

All this squabbling was cut short by an entirely nonpartisan phenomenon that appeared in Philadelphia in August: yellow fever. Under the pressure of an epidemic that saw deaths reaching one hundred a day by early October, government and most other organized activities almost disappeared. Washington was alarmed for the safety of his family, but Martha refused to be sent away. In order not to dispirit the people, he waited until the

---

[10] Thomas Jefferson to James Madison, May 19, June 9, July 7, 1793, Notes of a Conversation with George Washington, May 23, 1793, Notes of Cabinet Meeting on Edmond Charles Genet, Aug. 2, [1793], *Jefferson Papers,* 26: 61–63, 239–42, 443–44, 101–2, 601–3; GW to Thomas Jefferson, July 14, 1793, *Writings,* 33: 4; Carroll and Ashworth, 7: 95–111.

normal date for his fall visit to Mount Vernon, September 10, before leaving.

About this time, Washington began to connect Genet's activities, which disturbed him even at Mount Vernon, with those of the Democratic-Republican Societies, political groups that had originated coincidentally with Genet's arrival, although they had no direct, causal connection with the minister. Beginning with the Democratic Society of Pennsylvania in Philadelphia, organized in July 1793, the clubs spread throughout the country; they held public political debates, sent out propaganda, and generally espoused the cause of the French Revolution in any way they could. Although these societies were not part of the Republican Party, often the same people were active in both, and they frequently worked for Republican candidates. Washington did not view them at all dispassionately and confided to Richard Henry Lee, governor of Virginia, that their purpose was "nothing short of the subversion of the Government of these States, even at the expense of plunging this country in the horrors of a disastrous war." For now, he did not link the societies directly with France but rather lumped them with those trying to involve the country in a war, a group that included the French minister.[11]

With the arrival of cold weather, the fever abated in the capital, and by the time Congress was scheduled to convene, life was nearly normal in the city, but the losses had been heavy. Washington's fifth Annual Address was delivered on December 3. His explanation of the Neutrality Proclamation was plain and straightforward: "It seemed . . . my duty" because "our disposition for peace" might be questioned by the belligerents if they saw Americans participating in contraband trade or hostile acts. After briefly explaining the rules regarding belligerents, he handed the topic on to Congress to deal with as they saw fit. Separate messages would be sent later dealing with U.S. relations with Britain, France, Spain, and the Barbary states. Otherwise, the message noted some difficulties with the American Indians and recommended close attention to defense. The special mes-

---

[11] GW to Richard Henry Lee, Oct. 16, Oct. 24, 1793, *Writings*, 33: 133, 137–38. Eugene Perry Link's *The Democratic-Republican Societies, 1790–1800* (1942, repr., New York, 1965) is the only full-length study of the societies.

sages followed soon after and, in the case of France, detailed Genet's conduct as a justification for his recall. Britain's noncompliance with the Treaty of 1783, especially in the matter of the military posts and its bland refusal to negotiate seriously any of the outstanding difficulties, was explained. This message was a minor triumph for Jefferson, who had countered Hamilton's strong arguments that the British minister's correspondence should not be published. Washington had insisted, against a majority of the cabinet, that both records, the French and the British, should be given to the Congress (and through them to the people) as justification for the steps that had been taken. On December 16, as a kind of valedictory, Jefferson submitted a report on discrimination against American commerce by its major foreign customers and suppliers. Requested by Congress, the report showed that Britain was the major offender on this score and called for retaliatory action by the United States. At the end of the year, Jefferson resigned and was replaced by Randolph. In a graceful letter, Washington acknowledged Jefferson's work and commented that it showed the correctness of his initial appointment. The post had first been offered to Madison through Jefferson, who conveyed the former's refusal to the president. Whatever Madison's reasons for declining might have been, an opportunity to help the president keep to a middle course between the two contending groups was thereby lost. Washington depended on those around him for advice, and that circle was becoming increasingly Federalist. A Pennsylvania Federalist, William Bradford, replaced Randolph as attorney general, so now only Randolph differed from that party line.[12]

The replacement of Jefferson with Randolph as well as the hiring of a competent manager, William Pearce, for Mount Vernon probably eased the president's mind. As 1794 began, most of the major problems confronting the administration seemed to be under control, and Washington might have expected a quiet period for the immediate future. Certainly Genet would no longer plague the government; the State Department learned on

---

[12] "Fifth Annual Address to the Congress," Dec. 3, 1793, *Writings*, 33: 163–73; [Thomas Jefferson on Genét's conduct], Dec. 5, 1793, Report on Commerce, Dec. 16, 1793, *Jefferson Papers*, 27: 170–73, 532–80; GW to Thomas Jefferson, Jan. 1, 1794, *Writings*, 33: 231; Leibiger, *Friendship*, 177–79.

January 20 that a replacement was on the way. And the House began consideration of Jefferson's report on commercial discrimination, but then postponed the task until March. The signs predicting a quiet time were misleading, however.

Before the end of February, Washington learned of extensive ship seizures in the West Indies; apparently Britain was determined to cut off trade between the United States and the French islands. To compound the injury, some seamen were being impressed after their ships were detained. And the promulgation of an order forbidding neutral trade with the French was insulting; instead of a warning period, the order went into effect on the day it was announced in London so that some vessels were seized that had left port when no one outside of the British capital could have known that their voyages might be illegal. Congress's response was thundering and, for once, bipartisan; a thirty-day embargo was passed and went into effect on March 28. Adding to the legislators' agitation was the report of a speech by Lord Dorchester, governor general of Canada, to some native tribes assuring them of aid in the event of an expected war between them and the United States. News had also come to Philadelphia of British mediation of a treaty between Portugal and several North African states; this treaty had the effect of opening the Straits of Gibraltar to "Algerine corsairs," that is, the Barbary pirates. Then there were reports of the capture in the Atlantic of an American merchantman whose crew would now be held for ransom, according to the custom of "Algerines." (British and European vessels were protected by treaty.) Suspicion of Britain's intentions naturally, but in this case unfairly, arose. Now, just at the wrong time, resolutions based on Jefferson's December 1793 report came up for House debate. They found an excited and agreeable audience. Despite the prompt British withdrawal of the West Indian order (even before American protests reached London), a bill extending the embargo until the seizures had been made good and the military posts evacuated passed the House but failed in the Senate only by John Adams's tie-breaking vote. Discriminatory tariffs and the sequestration of balances owing to the British merchants were also spoken of in and out of

Congress. The construction of four frigates was begun, and coastal defenses were to be strengthened.[13]

In the spring of 1794, the nation was in the grip of war fever because of Britain's repeated and blatant insults to American sovereignty and interests. Washington kept his counsel in the midst of the excited talk in and out of Congress. Early in March, a Federalist senator, Oliver Ellsworth of Connecticut, suggested a special mission to Britain to secure a settlement and to prevent war, but the suggested emissary was Hamilton. Washington frostily told the senator that the people did not trust his secretary of the treasury. Other Federalists repeated the offer of Hamilton, but to no effect. Hearing of the suggestion, Senator James Monroe of Virginia, not knowing Washington's reaction, gratuitously told the president that the appointment would be as bad for Washington as for the country. This comment got the sharp reply that as the appointing power was the president's, he and no one else would consider carefully whom to appoint. Washington's coolness was bipartisan, but the situation was hot enough to merit the serious consideration of a special mission. Surveying the field, Washington could see no qualified person who was then free to take the mission. Rioting in Philadelphia, not the first instance of violence coming from the tense situation, underlined the necessity that something be done.[14]

John Jay was, of all those mentioned to Washington, in the best position to go to Britain, being in the relatively undemanding position of chief justice. Although Jay was not the ideal candidate, a point Randolph emphasized, no one else available had the requisite diplomatic experience. Jay accepted the offer of the special mission to London in mid-April, ignoring Washington's rather pointed suggestion that he resign his seat. In formulating Jay's instructions, Randolph lost the initiative to Hamilton, who

---

[13] Samuel Flagg Bemis's *Jay's Treaty: A Study in Commerce and Diplomacy*, rev. ed. (New Haven, 1962), and Jerald A. Combs's *The Jay Treaty: Political Battleground of the Founding Fathers* (Berkeley, 1970) treat the subject in detail; hereafter, Bemis, *Jay's Treaty*, and Combs, *Jay Treaty*. Bemis includes documents and the treaty text. See Sharp, *American Politics*, chaps. 6 and 7, for the political background.

[14] Elkins and McKitrick, *Age of Federalism*, chap. 9, convey the popular reaction.

responded first and in detail to the president's request for help. On the surface, the instructions were quite rigorous. Jay was to obtain compensation for seized vessels and a more liberal treatment for American ships, evacuation of the military posts, and payment for slaves taken away at the end of the War for Independence, but these stipulations were desirable goals only. All that Jay was required to secure was limited entry for American vessels to the British West Indies; also, he was not to violate any treaty obligations to France. Randolph also lost in deciding whether or not Jay should be empowered to sign a treaty rather than a preliminary agreement. The secretary of state feared that Jay, in the absence of express stipulations, would let the British walk away with the negotiations. Hamilton, much more than Randolph, had set the tone and scope of the mission. In mid-May, to the jeers of suspicious Republicans, Jay left for London.

Now that relations with Britain had been put beyond the reach of the angry opposition in the House, French affairs needed looking after. The French had willingly recalled Genet, but they had also requested that the United States replace Gouverneur Morris, whose obvious sympathy with the monarchists had been made more difficult for the French to bear by his too-ready wit and sarcasm. (Washington had feared just this in 1792.) Getting a new envoy was no easy job. Robert R. Livingston had to decline the post twice before Washington stopped trying to recruit him. Then, apparently working on the principle that because Britain had gotten an Anglophile minister plenipotentiary, France deserved a Francophile minister, the president turned closer to home and asked his fellow Virginian James Monroe to go to Paris. Monroe, disillusioned with what he thought was the decrepit state of the Republican bloc in the Senate, accepted. His confirmation was almost the last business considered by the upper house before the legislature adjourned a long, bitter, and exhausting session early in June.

The previous five months had been extraordinarily trying, and as his carriage took Washington southward to Mount Vernon in mid-June, he probably reflected on the one consolation he could take from his work during those months: the country was at peace. Despite the importunities of angry congressmen and the shouted slogans of riotous mobs, despite the selfish arrogance of

Britain's commercial policies, the peace had been kept. Looking abroad, even giving the most optimistic outcome of Jay's mission, the future did not look good, and he might have wondered how much longer peace could be kept.

Congress might have a respite from its labors, but the president and his cabinet soon had a new threat to the peace of the country with which to contend. Since 1791, the excise tax on "spirituous liquors of domestic manufacture" had been a grievance of the citizens of trans-Appalachia, who shared the historic British resentment of it as a "hateful tax levied upon commodities, and adjudged not by the common judges of property, but by wretches hired by those to whom it is paid."[15] They also had practical, immediate reasons for resenting certain features of the tax that, because of their unusual situation, made it especially burdensome. Among these features were that the levy had to be paid in cash on the produce of all stills and that all indictments under the law were to be tried in the nearest federal court. In the West, many farmers did not sell their whiskey, the only way to convert a bulky crop into an easily moved commodity, but bartered it to a store owner for necessities, paid debts with it, and used it to supplement the wages of extra hands hired for the harvest. Thus, the farmer/distiller frequently received little cash, if any, for his whiskey. How was he to pay the excise man with cash if he handled most of his affairs without it? And if he did not pay the excise man, he would be tried in the nearest federal court; in the case of the center of discontent, western Pennsylvania, however, that court was in Philadelphia, three hundred miles and several weeks across the mountains. Further, the levy exacerbated feelings endemic in the area that the law and its minions—courts, attorneys, constables, and the like—were there only to trap the poor farmer in their snares and rob him of his land. Anything that seemed likely to entangle him with the law was certain to be resented. Thus, Hamilton's excise law would have to be carefully explained and judiciously enforced if the West, especially western Pennsylvania, were to accept it.[16]

---

[15] Samuel Johnson, *A Dictionary of the English Language* (1755, repr., New York, 1967).

[16] Thomas P. Slaughter's *The Whiskey Rebellion: Frontier Epilogue to the American Revolution* (New York, 1986) is the most recent treatment, although Leland D.

Although Washington was no friend to tax collectors (he had recently styled Fairfax County's collectors as "among the greatest rascals in the world"), he was not sympathetic to the westerners. They were represented in the legislature that had drawn up the levy they were protesting so vehemently. Petitions to their representatives or directly to the president were the proper channels for presenting grievances. In 1792, Hamilton had wanted to suppress forcibly protests against the law, but no one had supported him then; in 1794, new trouble sprang up in part because of Hamilton's obtuseness. Despite a recent revision of the law that permitted trial in convenient state courts, the treasury secretary had warrants returnable in federal court in Philadelphia sworn out because the offenses had been committed before the law was revised. When the warrant servers were forcibly resisted and an attack was made on the home of an official of the excise near Pittsburgh, resulting in a life lost and the home burnt to the ground, it was obvious that the disturbances were much more than the usual grumbling. As early as April, Washington had labeled the westerners' protests as "the first fruits of the Democratic Society" and saw Genet as their originator. Consequently he was in no mood for conciliation and compromise when news of the trouble mentioned above came to him in July. It was soon seen that force might have to be used to suppress resistance to the law, but several details had to be considered before force could be employed: How was it to be authorized, and where was it to be found? Further, because the resistance centered in Pennsylvania, what actions would that state take?

Pennsylvania's authorities refused to see the trouble as beyond the reach of judicial authority and would not call out their own militia; this refusal made the administration fearful that perhaps no state's militia would answer a federal call. James Wilson, an associate justice of the Supreme Court, gave the necessary declaration that ordinary processes could not enforce the law, thus clearing the way for a federal summons of militia, but Randolph

Baldwin's *Whiskey Rebels: The Story of a Frontier Uprising*, rev. ed. (Pittsburgh, 1968), remains useful; hereafter, Slaughter, *Whiskey Rebellion*, and Baldwin, *Whiskey Rebels*. See Mary K. Bonsteel Tachau's "The Whiskey Rebellion in Kentucky: A Forgotten Episode of Civil Disobedience," *Journal of the Early Republic* 2 (fall 1982): 239–59, for a description of resistance elsewhere in the West.

urged delay. He argued that news of the "rebellion" rested entirely on correspondence so far and might be exaggerated; also, troops would certainly inflame party feelings and ought to be avoided, if at all possible. And this was as it should be, for the "strength of a government is in the affections of the people." Troops ought always to be the last resort. Washington had argued to much the same effect in 1792 when Hamilton had wanted to use force, so Randolph's statements probably weighed a good bit in the president's judgment. The president believed troops had to be the "dernier resort" because, in the view of some citizens, it would let "the cat out of the bag" and reveal the true purpose of having such instruments of force. Instead of calling troops out precipitately, the administration now began to exhaust other courses of action. Pennsylvania authorities were sounded out officially on August 2; they still saw no grave emergency. Next, federal commissioners were sent to the troubled area with an offer of amnesty to all who would immediately stop opposing the law. This step had the twin benefits of showing the conciliatory policy of the administration and of gathering first-hand information on the situation. Thus, if force eventually had to be used, the public might be readier to believe in its necessity. However, preparations for the calling of militia also went forward.

As the commissioners rode westward, they received conflicting reports from persons met on the road and sent their confusion back to Philadelphia. By the middle of September, the confusion had been dispelled; it was obvious that the insurgents were at least a strong minority in the area around Pittsburgh and that they were rejecting the amnesty. It was impossible to enforce the law by normal means. Washington was now convinced force was necessary, and he called out twelve thousand men from Pennsylvania, New Jersey, Maryland, and Virginia to rendezvous at Bedford, Pennsylvania. Yet another proclamation was issued explaining the necessity of the move as Washington prepared to travel west with his personal secretary (and nephew), Bartholomew Dandridge, and with Hamilton, temporarily in charge of the War Department for Knox, who was absent on pressing personal business. As Washington left the capital, he learned of Anthony Wayne's victory over the western native tribes in August at

Fallen Timbers, Ohio Territory. Now that the frontier was temporarily safe, the white settlers who refused to accept the burdens of the government that gave them that safety would have to be disciplined.

All fears about public nonacceptance of the government's actions proved needless. The militiamen turned out and, as a marching song of the New Jersey militia had it,

> To arms once more, our hero cries;
> Sedition lives and order dies,
> To peace and ease then bid adieu,
> And dash to the mountains, Jersey Blue.

The militiamen did not quite dash, but they turned out willingly enough and showed themselves to be perhaps too zealous in the performance of their duties, especially in the suppression of rebellious chickens encountered along the way. When Congress assembled, there was a general feeling that the government had done all it could to avoid force; as distasteful as the excise was, it was undeniably constitutional and had to be collected until it could be repealed. The administration's lengthy consideration of the problem before any drastic steps were taken—a consideration imposed by the politically inspired near-sightedness of the Pennsylvania authorities—fears over whether or not the militia would turn out, and Randolph's prudent and cautious arguments in the cabinet had helped substantially to bring about this general acceptance. If the administration had dashed as precipitately as the "Jersey Blue," the public reaction could easily have been quite different. After all the deliberation and delay, or perhaps because of it, the militia's march west became a grand military excursion. At Bedford on October 28, Washington left the force in the command of Governor Henry Lee of Virginia and returned to Philadelphia for the opening of Congress. As the army neared the rebellious area, resistance collapsed, and the most prominent leaders fled. Hamilton, representing civil authority, had to content himself with sending twenty obscure "rebels" back to Philadelphia for trial. They were escorted by the elite Philadelphia City Troop of Cavalry, whose wealthy members mistreated the western "savages" with contemptuous sneers and some physical brutality. The evidence against these suspects was so slight that only two were brought to trial; both were convicted, but the president pardoned them, for one was insane and the other a "simpleton." Despite the tragicomic aspect of its ending, the episode had shown the ability of the government to enforce a duly enacted law and, less obviously, had furnished an example of the judicious, prudent application of force, except for the thoughtless brutality visited on the suspects.[17]

As Washington rode west with the militia, he became more and more convinced that the troubles were owing to the Democratic Societies; "self-created Societies . . . have been laboring incessantly to sow the seeds of distrust, jealousy, and of course discontent; thereby hoping to effect some revolution in the government. . . . That they have been the fomenters of the Western disturbances, admits of no doubt. . . . I shall be more prolix in my speech to Congress."

In the speech, delivered on November 19, he amply redeemed his promise to be "prolix" on the supposed connection between the Whiskey Rebellion and the Democratic Societies, devoting about two thousand words out of a total of about twenty-five hundred in the address. The rebellion was ascribed to "certain self-created societies," and its participants were not simply resisting a tax, but "a spirit inimical to all order has actuated many of the offenders." In concluding his consideration, Washington put it to the citizens generally to "Determine, whether it [the rebellion] has not been fomented by combinations of men, who, careless of consequences, and disregarding the unerring truth, that those who rouse, can not always appease a civil convulsion, have disseminated, from an ignorance or perversion of facts, suspicions, jealousies, and accusations of the whole government."

Thus, the president clearly indicated to the public his belief that the Democratic Societies at best served no useful purpose

---

[17] GW to Edmund Randolph, Apr. 11, 1794, *Writings*, 33: 321–22; Kohn, *Eagle and Sword*, chap. 8, is an excellent description of the administration's decision making; see also Phelps, *GW and Constitutionalism*, 133–38. The events of 1794 are described in Slaughter, *Whiskey Rebellion;* Baldwin, *Whiskey Rebels;* and Carroll and Ashworth, 7: chap. 7. The description of Virginia tax collectors is in Carroll and Ashworth, 7: 38, n. 80.

and at worst were bent on bringing the Constitution and the government conducted under it into such disrepute that it would fall.[18]

Noticeably lacking from the address was any extensive reference to the topics that had so excited the last session of Congress, relations with Britain and France. Joseph Fauchet was still a pleasant contrast to his predecessor, Genet, who was now living quietly on Long Island, having married a daughter of Governor George Clinton of New York. With Britain, there was little to report. Randolph had received several vague letters from Jay that indicated he was about to conclude a most unsatisfactory treaty. The secretary immediately sent correcting instructions, no matter how ineffectual they might be, and hoped they might arrive in time.[19]

Thus far, Washington had had to make only one major replacement in his cabinet, Randolph for Jefferson, and the new attorney general, Andrew Bradford, performed his duties adequately. Now within one year, Washington had to make three major appointments. After almost ten years of service, first for the old Congress, then for the new government, Henry Knox wanted to retire from his position as secretary of war, and the president could not resist the request. He appointed Timothy Pickering, a dour and opinionated New Englander then serving as postmaster general. Pickering had been an officer during the war, compiling the first drill manual used by the Continental forces and serving on Washington's staff during the siege of Yorktown. Hamilton, too, wanted to retire, and his successor was also close at hand. When the New Yorker left in January 1795, pleading the necessity of looking after his private finances instead of the nation's, he was replaced by the controller of the treasury, Oliver Wolcott Jr. Of a prominent Connecticut family, Wolcott promised competence but not much more in the performance of his duties. These men were all Federalists and were not likely to give Washington the differing advice he needed to serve effectively as the final arbiter of national questions. Of the original

[18] GW to Edmund Randolph, Oct. 16, 1794, to John Jay, Nov. 1, 1794, Sixth Annual Address to the Congress, Nov. 19, 1794, *Writings*, 34: 3–4, 17–18, 28–37.

[19] Reardon, *Randolph*, 280, 285–89.

1789 appointees, only Randolph was left, and only Randolph seemed to stand between the Federalists and the Republicans. Despised by the Federalists, who believed him to be yet another of the wild Republicans sent to the capital from Virginia, he was also distrusted by the Republicans, who saw him as either a crypto-Federalist or an indecisive neutral. Indeed, a neutral role was becoming increasingly more difficult to maintain as the parties rapidly crystallized, neither group trusting the uncommitted. Randolph was about to face the greatest crisis of his career lacking the support that a strong political base would have given him; without it, he was destroyed, and Washington lost the last non-Federalist voice in his cabinet. The conviction of a French conspiracy using disloyal Americans and putting at peril American freedom would be impressed firmly on the president.[20]

In February, Washington celebrated his sixty-third birthday, what the folk wisdom of the day styled his "grand climacteric." According to this wisdom, a special significance was attached to those ages whose numbers were multiples of seven by odd numbers; for example, at twenty-one, a youth became an adult, but at nine times seven, he crossed into old age. Having passed this mark, Washington felt certain he was exhibiting more and more signs of old age and probably wished that the remainder of the administration would be placid. In this wish, he would be disappointed.[21]

His disappointment originated in London, where Jay had been working to resolve the difficulties in Anglo-American relations. The treaty he negotiated did fulfill an essential point of his instructions, to keep the peace, but it did so only by compromising American interests and the French alliance. It may be true, as some historians have claimed, that Jay got the best possible treaty from the British; it is certainly true that the Republicans would have scathingly criticized any British treaty, but Jay's treaty appeared so one-sided that even the Federalist-controlled Senate could not accept it as it came to them.

---

[20] Carroll and Ashworth, 7: 228–33; see Reardon, *Randolph*, especially chaps. 16–19, for a more favorable view. The older study by Moncure D. Conway, *Omitted Chapters of History Disclosed in the Life and Papers of Edmund Randoph* (New York, 1888), has extensive quotations of relevant documents; hereafter, Conway, *Omitted Chapters*.

[21] Flexner, 4: 202.

Washington had waited in vain during the congressional session for a copy of the completed treaty. On March 3, shortly before the Senate's adjournment, he called for a special session on June 8 to deal with "certain matters touching the public good," trusting that by then the treaty would have arrived. The suspense and uncertainty ended four days later, on March 7, when a copy arrived at the State Department. A quick reading disclosed no material concessions by Britain to the United States but many concessions by the United States to Britain. By the treaty, Britain was generally permitted to treat neutral commerce as it had since the war's beginning, but in the past the United States had been able to protest these practices against a better day when the government might be able to prevent them by naval strength; this protest would no longer be possible. Article 18 permitted the British to purchase preemptively all provisions declared to be contraband; thus, they could keep the French from obtaining American wheat except at their sufferance. Article 12 permitted American vessels to trade with the British West Indies but under such restrictive conditions that the Senate rejected the article: ships could be no larger than seventy tons—"canoes," as Madison aptly called them—and the United States could not reexport certain tropical commodities, including cotton. This provision was designed to end the American reexport trade by which British restrictions had been avoided. The British also secured free-trade privileges in the Old Northwest, the use of the Mississippi, and an American promise to pay debts owed since before the War for Independence. On their part, the British promised to evacuate the military posts by July 1796; this promise was hardly much of a concession because it had initially been made in the Treaty of 1783, but not kept. Further, Britain agreed to submit the ship seizures of the previous winter to arbitration, but the United States agreed to do the same for the seizures made by Genet's privateers, agreements that, in principle if not in scope, canceled each other out. U.S. traders were admitted to the Canadian West, but the exclusion of the Hudson's Bay Company territory made this concession meaningless because it was the most lucrative area. Finally, it could be said that the very fact of Britain signing a treaty with the United States was a belated recognition of American nationality and independence from her former colonial overlord, but a patriot would have to be fainthearted indeed to take much cheer from that recognition. Washington and Randolph did not take any cheer at all from it.

The treaty was accompanied by a self-satisfied letter from Jay stating that his work "must speak for itself. . . . To do more was not possible." The president decided to keep the treaty secret between himself and Randolph until the Senate convened; by then Jay might be home with an explanation of some of the more exceptionable provisions. The secrecy fed press speculation, and Washington might have been amused as one ill-founded rumor after another chased the truth. When Jay arrived in late April, he landed in New York. In his absence, he had been elected governor of the state, and he resigned his Supreme Court seat by letter, explaining to Randolph that he was too tired to come to Philadelphia. His answers to a series of questions sent by the secretary were brief and uninformative. Because its negotiator would not, the treaty indeed would have to speak for itself.[22]

Certainly, Washington did not speak for it; the treaty was sent to the Senate with a formal and unrevealing letter of transmission, Jay's original instructions, and most of the correspondence between him and Randolph, nothing more. The Senate, during the three weeks it deliberated, kept its debates and the treaty secret, approving it by the barest margin possible, twenty to ten. In so doing, Washington was presented with two dilemmas: Now that the treaty was approved, should he go ahead and ratify it? And because the Senate had removed Article 12, should a new one be negotiated and resubmitted, or should it be inserted with no further action by the Senate? While the president pondered these problems, he directed Randolph to release the treaty to the gazettes. Unfortunately, while copies were being prepared, Senator Stevens Mason of Virginia took it upon himself to give a copy to Benjamin Franklin Bache, the fiercely Republican editor of the *Aurora,* who immediately published it in pamphlet form.

---

[22] The reception of the treaty and its subsequent consideration is described exhaustively in Carroll and Ashworth, 7: chaps. 8–9. See also Bemis, *Jay's Treaty;* Combs, *Jay Treaty;* Sharp, *American Politics;* and Elkins and McKitrick, *Age of Federalism.* Randolph's experience is treated in Reardon, *Randolph,* chaps. 20–22.

Thus, the administration looked as if it had tried to keep the treaty a secret until the president had ratified it.

The cabinet advised Washington to sign the treaty, but he delayed a bit, waiting for an opinion from Hamilton that he had requested. As he waited, he learned that the British had begun to confiscate—not purchase preemptively, but confiscate—provision cargoes destined for France. Were they intent on securing free what they would have to pay for after ratification? Or was this action an indication that the promises made in Jay's Treaty were no more reliable than those made in the 1783 treaty? Randolph suggested and Washington agreed that the secretary inform Hammond that the president would ratify the treaty, Article 12 excepted, just as soon as the order confiscating provisions was withdrawn. On July 13, he told Randolph he was irrevocably committed to this procedure.[23]

Two days later Washington took Martha south to Mount Vernon. Into that calm atmosphere, the fast-breaking controversy over the treaty penetrated. The president complained that party disputes were so muddying the waters that one could determine the truth only with difficulty; inferentially, Republican criticism of the treaty was the problem. He blamed its critics for the "most tortured interpretations and . . . the most abominable misrepresentations" of it and confided to Hamilton that some of their activity was certainly owing to French influence. He also commented favorably on the pro-treaty "Camillus" essays that had started to appear. He may have realized he was writing to their author, for he contrasted the author's activity with the usual inactivity of the "friends of order and good government." The intense and bitter controversy over the treaty was affecting Washington, and his latent sympathy for the political values of Federalism was surfacing.[24]

Reading the political billingsgate being published against the treaty convinced the president that he should return to Philadel-

---

[23] Samuel Flagg Bemis, *John Quincy Adams and the Foundations of American Foreign Policy* (New York, 1949), 74–75; Worthington C. Ford, ed., "Edmund Randolph on the British Treaty, 1795," *American Historical Review* 12 (Apr. 1907): 587–99; GW's reaction is in [Edmund Randolph], *A Vindication of Mr. Randolph's Resignation* (Philadelphia, 1795), 30–32.

[24] GW to Alexander Hamilton, July 29, 1795, *Writings*, 34: 262–64.

phia and prepare a special message to the British to be carried back by Hammond, who was being replaced. As he was preparing to return to Philadelphia, he received a request from Randolph that he come back as soon as possible; the cabinet had decided he was needed there. Accompanying this request was a mysterious note from Pickering marked "for your eyes alone" and confiding that "on the subject of the treaty I confess that I feel extreme solicitude, and for a *special reason*" (emphasis in original), which could be given to the president only in person. Washington must often have wondered what could have gotten the dour Yankee into such a fret until he reached the capital on August 11. Pickering came that afternoon and found Washington and Randolph at table; excusing himself, the president took Pickering into another room. As soon as the door closed, the secretary melodramatically pointed toward the dining room and flatly stated: "That man is a traitor!"[25]

He explained briefly that the British had turned over a captured French diplomatic dispatch to Wolcott, who had handed it on to him. According to Pickering's translation, the dispatch stated that Randolph had approached Minister Fauchét with an offer to influence American foreign policy in return for money. Randolph's well-known financial difficulties made the charge credible, and Washington was probably able only to nod dumbly as he was told that Wolcott would bring the relevant documents that evening. Later, after Washington had read them over, he saw that Fauchét's statements could support Pickering's charge. His closest associate and the only member of the 1789 cabinet to stay the distance had possibly betrayed the country.

The effect of this news on Washington can hardly be overestimated. He had befriended Randolph early in the war when he was politically orphaned by the departure of his loyalist father for Britain; during the 1780s, the young lawyer had performed many legal tasks for the retired general, never charging a fee. Lacking a son of his own, the older man often solicitously domi-

---

[25] What follows is treated fully in Reardon, *Randolph*, chaps. 21–22; Conway, *Omitted Chapters*, 290 ff.; Carroll and Ashworth, 7: chaps. 10–11; Irving Brant, "Edmund Randolph, Not Guilty!" *William and Mary Quarterly* 7 (Apr. 1950): 174–98; and Mary K. Bonsteel Tachau, "George Washington and the Reputation of Edmund Randolph," *Journal of American History* 73 (June 1986): 15–34.

nated the younger men around him. There is nothing to show that Randolph resented this domination. Indeed, in July, he had told the president that he could not foresee staying on in any successor's administration; his only purpose was to serve Washington, and he could not work so closely with anyone else. In turn, the president had recognized the services Randolph was performing and had increasingly relied on him as an advisor. Now he discovered that there was apparently a good reason to distrust that advice. If he could not trust Randolph, whom could he trust?

On August 12, Washington called the cabinet together and suggested that the treaty be ratified immediately and unconditionally. Randolph had ready a memorial defending a delayed and conditional ratification and, despite his surprise at Washington's unexplained about-face, defended it against a united opposition. When he had finished, the president, with no further comment, declared, "I will ratify the treaty," and ordered Randolph to prepare the necessary papers. Thus, the British had succeeded in one of their major purposes in turning over the dispatch: to remove Washington's respect for Randolph, whom they had tabbed as the only hostile member of the cabinet. For the next week, the two men met frequently, going over the anti-confiscation memorial and the draft ratification certificates. In none of these meetings did Washington give Randolph any hint that he distrusted him, and if he gave any explanation for his sudden reversal, it was probably that only an immediate ratification would end the harsh public controversy that now focused on Washington. By August 18, all the necessary documents had been prepared and the president ratified the treaty. Under the circumstances, it is clear that he signed it when he did only because of the allegations that had been made against Randolph on the basis of the captured dispatch. The secretary of state had been the only one in the cabinet arguing against immediate ratification; if Washington's independence of judgment had not disappeared, it had certainly been seriously compromised.

The next day, in the presence of Wolcott and Pickering, Washington confronted Randolph with the captured dispatch: "Mr. Randolph, here is a letter which I desire you to read, and make such explanations as you choose." After he had finished, Randolph offered to make as good an explanation as he could from memory only. After he had given what Wolcott called a "desultory" answer, an apparently unflustered Randolph was asked to leave the room while the other three talked it over. When he came back, his calmness was gone, and he answered sharply some perfunctory questions before interrupting with a statement that he could no longer remain in office. He left immediately, went first to the State Department, where he locked his room, leaving the key with the clerk, and then home, where he wrote his formal letter of resignation. In it, he denied ever asking for or receiving any money from Fauchét and gave what seems to be the most likely explanation for his resignation: "Your confidence, in me, Sir, has been unlimited and, I can truly affirm, unabused. My sensations, then, cannot be concealed when I find that confidence so immediately withdrawn without a word or distant hint being previously dropped to me! This, Sir, as I mentioned in your room, is a situation in which I cannot hold my present office, and therefore I hereby resign it."

In his acknowledgment, Washington expressed no regret for what had happened, simply explaining to Randolph how the document had come to him and agreeing to the latter's request that the affair be kept confidential until he could prepare a vindication. Now Washington was left with an exclusively Federalist corps of advisors. In the past, he had confided to Tobias Lear his concern that he was too "stationary" and did not hear enough different opinions; now even Lear was gone (he had resigned in 1793 to go into business), and Washington no longer seemed concerned that he was "stationary."

Randolph's *Vindication* appeared in December; a solid presentation of the evidence, it nevertheless failed to change his enemies' minds or even to reassure his friends as to his innocence. His major mistake was to concentrate on proving himself the victim of a British plot—he was, but neither he nor anyone else in America had the evidence to prove that—instead of explaining exactly what Fauchét had meant by the incriminating phrases in the captured dispatch. In a sense, perhaps, his fall was inevitable in that circumstances had raised him to a position to which his talents gave him only a tenuous claim. Presently Randolph fell into obscurity, an obscurity from which he emerged from time to time as an embarrassing reminder to the Federalists and Republicans of the casualties of their party warfare.

Washington asked Pickering to take over the State Department while he searched for a permanent successor to Randolph. Then, somewhat in the fashion of the bridegroom's father in the New Testament parable, he heard excuses, some real, some invented, from five men as to why they could not take the position. Finally, probably in desperation, he offered it to Pickering, who had to be talked into accepting it by Wolcott. This left only the vacancy in the War Department because Charles Lee of Virginia had just agreed to replace Attorney General Bradford, who had died. A letter from James McHenry recommending a fellow Marylander, Samuel Chase, for a Supreme Court vacancy, elicited not only Washington's acceptance of Chase but also an offer of the War Department to McHenry. McHenry's acceptance along with Oliver Ellsworth's of the chief justiceship meant that Washington began the last full year of his presidency with no major offices unfilled, but John Adams's comment on this situation was very much to the point: "The offices are once more filled, but how differently than when Jefferson, Hamilton, Jay, etc., were here." How differently indeed. None of the new appointees was a first-rate man, all were firm Federalists.[26]

Shortly after Randolph left office, Washington clearly signaled that he had no regrets about the treaty, whatever emotions he might have left unvoiced about his former secretary of state. Answering a memorial against the treaty from some Savannah citizens in mid-September, he assured them that in considering the treaty he was guided "by the great principle which has governed all my public conduct: a sincere desire to promote and secure the true interests of my country." In other words, he would do his duty as he saw it, regardless of public opinion. A few weeks later, he told Knox that because he had found no better "guide than upright intentions and close investigation, I shall adhere to these maxims while I keep the watch." The point might well be made as to how clearly he was seeing the interests of the country

---

[26] Carroll and Ashworth, 7: 300–340; John Adams to Abigail Adams, Feb. 8, 1796, in Charles Francis Adams, ed., *Letters of John Adams Addressed to His Wife* (Boston, [1841]), 1: 50–51.

and how much close investigation public matters were receiving. But the watch was certainly drawing to a close.[27]

Washington returned to Philadelphia on October 20 from a visit to Mount Vernon; in the capital, he felt the full blast of the uproar over his signing of the treaty, without any of the filtering effect that the calmness and serenity of his Virginia home gave. For example, on October 21, "Valerius" in the *Aurora* gave him no credit for any act of his public life and concluded that the American people well knew that "nature had played the miser when she gave you birth" and "education had not been lavish in her favours." Slurs of this sort could be, but probably were not, laughed off. After the treaty had been approved, Republican criticism of the administration was directed much more toward Washington than it had ever been before; it was now designed to make certain that Washington did not stand for election in 1796, a decision that his critics never imagined he had made in 1792. Republican criticism hit very close to home on October 23, when "A Calm Observer" alleged that Washington had overdrawn his salary account; unfortunately for Washington's composure and his concern about his reputation, the charges were true. There were several mitigating factors, carefully explained by Secretary Wolcott and his predecessor, not the least of which was that the president had never been aware of the advances. Republican editors brushed aside the explanations and delightedly repeated their basic point: Washington had overdrawn his salary. Yet this accusation was a kind of postscript to the treaty controversy, which had been going on since spring and was visibly winding down.[28]

Washington may have realized this when he gave his Annual Message to Congress on December 8. He began on a high note of congratulation and celebration, and with rare exceptions maintained it. A peace with the northern native tribes had recently been concluded, and negotiations with the southern tribes

---

[27] GW to the Republicans of Savannah (Noble Wymberly Jones), Aug. 31, 1795, to Henry Knox, Sep. 20, 1795, *Writings,* 34: 294–95, 310.

[28] Quoted from Donald R. Stewart, *The Opposition Press of the Federalist Period* (Albany, 1969), 526, 528–31, and see 520 ff. for discussion of the change in emphasis of the Republican press criticism of GW; hereafter, Stewart, *Opposition Press.*

were going well; a satisfactory treaty with the Barbary states was expected soon, and Thomas Pinckney, treating with the Spanish in Madrid, had reported substantial progress. The message only glanced at Jay's Treaty with the assurance that when British ratification was known, Congress would be immediately notified. Then, speaking generally of foreign and American Indian affairs, Washington said: "If by prudence and moderation on every side, the extinguishment of all the causes of external discord, which have heretofore menaced our tranquility, on terms compatible with our national rights and honor, shall be the happy result; how firm and how precious a foundation will have been laid for accelerating, maturing, and establishing the prosperity of our country!"

The balance of the address dealt with domestic affairs and in much the same tone. He was simply reiterating a theme he had used frequently when he was trying to keep the peace between Jefferson and Hamilton: if Americans would only compose their differences, the future alone guaranteed the greatness and strength of their republic. In the partisan atmosphere of 1795, this reassurance impressed relatively few Americans of either party, but for a time there was political peace.[29]

In this mood, Washington accepted from the new French minister, Pierre Adet, a richly ornamented tricolor flag, a return for an American flag that Monroe had given to the French Assembly and that hung in their chamber. The president thanked Adet and noted that "to call your nation brave, were to pronounce but common praise. Wonderful people! Ages to come will read with astonishment the history of your brilliant exploits," and informed the minister that the banner would be put in the "archives" of the United States—in other words, in a dusty corner of the State Department, not the hall of the House of Representatives. Adet may have noticed and resented this placement, but Congress did not.

The mood was maintained a while longer by receipt of a draft treaty with Spain from Thomas Pinckney. During Jay's stay in London, Pinckney had been relieved of his duties there and sent

---

[29] Seventh Annual Address to the Congress, Dec. 8, 1795, *Writings*, 34: 386–93.

to Madrid to seek a settlement of several outstanding matters. In part because of European conditions, in part because of fear that Jay's Treaty might hide an Anglo-American alliance, the Spanish gave the Americans a very generous settlement that the Senate unanimously approved on March 3. This act marked the end of the cheer and good fellowship.[30]

Washington had been waiting impatiently for receipt of the certificates of ratification from London, but they had been delayed by the inexperience of the American chargé there. On the strength of private reports that the treaty had been ratified in London, Washington declared it in effect on February 29, 1796. Because the treaty provided for several arbitration commissions whose expenses were to be shared by the signatories, Congress now had to appropriate money to carry it into effect. Appropriation bills customarily originated in the House, and that is where the fun started on March 2.

Washington predicted that now that the Republicans had a second chance at the treaty, "an attempt . . . will be made to censure it in several points"—but it was more than several points. Edward Livingston of New York immediately asked the House to request delivery of all documents relevant to the negotiations because the treaty raised "important constitutional questions." The implications here were obvious and significant; only the president and the Senate made treaties; the House had no role. Although in the past Washington had implicitly recognized that the House's assent was sometimes necessary in practice, this recognition was far different from permitting it to set aside a ratified treaty. The House debated the motion to request the documents for almost three weeks before passing it, softened somewhat, sixty-two to thirty-seven. Anticipating the action, Washington had already asked for advice. He had previously honored some calls for papers, but treaties had never been involved. The cabinet and Hamilton advised him not to comply with the call, and he readily agreed. Basing his refusal on expediency and the Constitution, he wrote: "The nature of foreign negotiations requires caution and their success must often depend on secrecy . . . a full

---

[30] Samuel Flagg Bemis's *Pinckney's Treaty: America's Advantage from Europe's Distress, 1783–1800*, rev. ed. (New Haven, 1960), treats the subject fully.

disclosure of all the measures, demands or eventual concessions
. . . would be extremely impolitic. . . . It does not occur that the
inspection of the papers . . . can be relative to any purpose under
the [constitutional] cognizance of the House. . . . It is perfectly
clear to my understanding that the assent of the House . . . is not
necessary to the validity of the treaty."

Many Republicans had expected the president's partial compliance in keeping with the now vanished mood of political reconciliation and were shocked by his complete refusal. No one
expected the Republicans to fold their tents and slink away, but
Washington now challenged them by sending nominations for
the arbitration commissions to the Senate for confirmation.
Against the president's firm determination to execute the treaty,
the House had a weapon of unsurpassing effectiveness: inaction.
If it did not vote the appropriations, the commissioners would
not be paid, and at least part of the treaty would be voided. Both
the House and the public debated the question for all of April;
contrary to the previous summer, this time there seemed to be a
popular majority in favor of execution. Public opinion, the difficulties that would come from repudiating the treaty, the likelihood that Britain would refuse to hand over the posts scheduled
to be surrendered in June, talk of war with Britain just when
France was said to be mistreating American commerce, and Britain's improving treatment of American commerce—all combined to break down the Republican majority, and the House
voted on April 29 to accept the president's reply to Livingston's
resolution. In several more close votes, the appropriations were
passed.[31]

In retrospect, Washington decided that the Republicans were
not questioning the value of Jay's Treaty as much as they were
trying to increase the power of the House with its Republican

---

[31] GW to Gouverneur Morris, Mar. 4, 1796, to the House of Representatives,
Mar. 30, 1796, *Writings*, 34: 483, 35: 2–5. Carroll and Ashworth, 7: 348–75,
give a reasonably complete reading of the House debate. See Noble E. Cunningham Jr., *The Jeffersonian Republicans: The Formation of Party Organization,
1789–1801* (Chapel Hill, N.C., 1957), 78–95, for the Republicans' actions during the debate. The subsequent history of Jay's Treaty is interesting: see Elkins
and McKitrick, *Age of Federalism*, 431–50, and Bradford Perkins, *The First Rapprochement: England and the United States, 1795–1805* (Berkeley, 1955), chaps.
2–4.

majority. Why they had to do so also interested him. "Charity would lead one to hope that the motives to it have been pure. Suspicions, however, speak a different language; and my tongue, for present, shall be silent." The people could decide correctly if only certain leaders "adverse to the Government" would stop bending all their efforts to mislead them. "To this source all our discontents may be traced, and from it our embarrassments proceed." No credit was given to the treaty's opponents for acting, however mistakenly, in good faith. Washington was now one with Hamilton and with other leaders of Federalism in suspecting the Republicans of playing the French game. The president went so far as to credit a fantastic rumor sent home by Gouverneur Morris that the French were sending a new envoy accompanied by a battle fleet and a demand that Jay's Treaty be repudiated within fifteen days, although he did wonder that "folly and madness would hardly go such lengths."[32]

Whatever his thoughts on the perfidy of the French, he could easily distract himself with a more pleasant prospect, his retirement in less than a year. Even before the question of the Jay's Treaty appropriations had been decided, he had discussed with Hamilton, who had become his principal political advisor, how best his decision not to accept reelection might be announced. Hamilton had offered his editorial assistance in preparing a letter to the people, and they spent most of the summer passing drafts and revisions back and forth between Philadelphia and New York. The first draft, which Washington himself prepared entirely, was a revealing document that showed how much the party animosities and newspaper attacks had injured his feelings and his need to be seen as the universally accepted leader of the people. For example, he mentioned his refusal to accept a salary during the war as well as his unwillingness to take it during the presidency and that his service had actually cost him money. He further commented that he had never sought office nor had he accepted it out of personal ambition or ignorance of its responsibilities. After a paragraph complaining of newspaper attacks, he

---

[32] GW to Charles Carroll of Carrollton, May 1, 1796, to Edward Carrington, May 1, 1796, to John Jay, May 8, 1796, to Alexander Hamilton, May 8, 1796, *Writings*, 35: 29–31, 32–39.

wrote: "It might be expected at the parting scene of my public life that I should take some notice of such virulent abuse. But, as heretofore, I shall pass them over in utter silence," having written almost ninety words about them. His own good sense must have told him that this approach would not do because he asked Hamilton to prune the draft of any "egotism's" it might contain. In the joint work of composition and revision, the message was changed and lengthened considerably, but it remained Washington's. Where Hamilton tried to slip something in that the president did not approve, Washington noticed and threw it out; for instance, where Hamilton prophesied that if the government fell, it would be because of excessive weakness, Washington crossed the lines out. The finished product does help to show how much of a Federalist Washington was; although Hamilton wrote most of the Farewell Address, Washington accepted it and put it out as his own.[33]

Generations of Americans have been accustomed to reading or thinking of Washington's Farewell Address as the first chapter of a kind of catechism of American politics and foreign policy. Read outside the time in which it was written, that is understandable. But if one recalls the circumstances of the summer of 1796, the address becomes a Federalist campaign speech, putting the stamp of Washington's approval on Federalist ideas and policies. The address began with sentiments suitable for a leave-taking, but then, where it could end, the president remarked: "Here, perhaps, I ought to stop." However, his concern for the welfare of the country led him to offer "some sentiments . . . which appear to me all important to the permanency of your felicity as a People." He then proceeded to dwell on the importance of the Union, religion and morality as props of society, the value of true neutrality, and the necessity of a proper regard for the public credit. Many of these comments are unexceptionable and some of timeless importance. But the best-remembered injunctions are the ones that were the most partisan in their implications. When Washington cautioned Americans to avoid "permanent alli-

---

[33] Victor H. Paltsits's *Washington's Farewell Address* (New York, 1935) describes and documents the process of composition; hereafter, Paltsits, *Farewell Address.* GW's first draft, GW to Alexander Hamilton, May 15, 1796, *Writings,* 35: 51–61, 48–51; Flexner, 4: 307.

ances," he was talking to a nation that had had only one such alliance in its short life, with France, a power that was showing scant regard for the interests of its supposed ally. When he urged his fellow citizens to avoid extreme and fixed feelings about a foreign country, he was talking to a people who during the Jay's Treaty controversy had heard frequent warnings from the Federalists that Republican opposition to the treaty was a product of their unreasoning antipathy to Britain and their uncritical attachment to France. When he warned that political parties brought foreign influences to bear on domestic questions, he was warning a people who well remembered Citizen Genet and who had recently seen the French minister send his government's messages (in French) to the U.S. secretary of state on the same day they were published in the *Aurora*. Thus, the address can be seen as the opening gun of a campaign to elect a Federalist president in 1796. That the gun was fired by a man who sincerely felt himself above parties adds to the irony of the situation; politicians do not always see themselves clearly.

Washington had originally hoped to see the valedictory in print shortly after Congress adjourned in the spring, but other matters intruded, and early fall, at least two months before the electors met, was set as the target. On September 16, the president called in David Claypoole of the *American Daily Advertiser* and asked him to "usher it to the world and suffer it to work its way afterwards." The address was published on September 19, the same day Washington left for Mount Vernon, where Bartholomew Dandridge wrote his uncle from Philadelphia "that not a single instance of disapprobation of any part has been found. . . . All seem to agree in the solid truths which the address contains." Either Dandridge was sparing his uncle's feelings, or he was not looking very hard. The *Boston Gazette* rejoiced that now Americans could look forward to a time when political "Principles will be investigated *unclouded by Names*" (emphasis in original)—in other words, free of Washington's influence. Actually, reaction divided pretty much along party lines, although most Republicans at least paid lip service to Washington's contributions.[34]

---

[34] GW to the People of the United States, Sep. 19, 1796, *Writings*, 35: 214–38; Bartholomew Dandridge to GW, Sep. 26, 1796, in Carroll and Ashworth, 7: 409; the *Boston Gazette* in Paltsits, *Farewell Address*, 63, 59–74, which contains

The president returned to Philadelphia at the end of October to find a complaint from the French on his desk (and in the pages of the *Aurora*). They complained that their observance of the 1778 treaties placed them at a disadvantage to the British because of the latter's special privileges under Jay's Treaty. There was some justice to the complaint, but Washington and Pickering would hear none of it. In his reply, Pickering informed the French that there were two kinds of international law, the standard variety and that which resulted from treaties. Only the former bound the United States and Britain, whereas the latter bound France and the United States. Simply because France's obligations were inconvenient did not mean that they could be set aside. Washington himself observed that there was "in the conduct of the French government . . . an inconsistency, a duplicity, a delay or something else which is unaccountable upon honorable ground." This from a man who had observed in 1791 that nations would obey treaties only as long as it was in their interest to do so.[35]

Washington probably was not blaming the French entirely for the trouble. James Monroe had become, in the eyes of the administration, more and more partisan in the conduct of his ministry in Paris. Recently Pickering had intercepted a letter (how is not clear) from Monroe to a Philadelphia friend giving the "real" news from the French capital, not the distorted version copied out of English newspapers by the Federalist press. The letter was obviously destined for the pages of the *Aurora,* and there was a promise of more to follow. The conviction had been growing in the administration that Monroe was representing the Republican Party, not the United States, in Paris and that he had been giving

favorable and unfavorable reactions. Historians' comments are sampled in Burton Ira Kaufman, ed., *Washington's Farewell Address: The View from the 20th Century* (1969, repr., Chicago, 1974). The analysis of the address here owes much to Alexander DeConde, *Entangling Alliance: Politics and Diplomacy under George Washington* (Durham, N.C., 1958), 464–71. See Joseph Ellis, *Founding Brothers: The Revolutionary Generation* (New York, 2000), chap. 4, esp. 148–61, for an analysis that removes the address from the politics of that time.

[35] Gerard H.Clarfield, *Timothy Pickering and American Diplomacy, 1795–1800* (Columbia, Mo., 1969), 61–65; GW to Alexander Hamilton, Nov. 2, 1796, *Writings,* 35: 255. For the earlier comment, see GW to Gouverneur Morris, July 5, 1791, *Writings,* 31: 327–28.

the French the mistaken impression that American foreign policy was the creation of a small and unrepresentative clique. This
letter seemed to confirm that suspicion, precipitating Monroe's
recall. Thomas Pinckney's brother, Charles Cotesworth Pinckney, agreed to take up the post. In truth, Monroe had been doing
a good job of representing the United States to a government
that felt itself injured by Jay's Treaty. Pinckney would now set the
French straight.[36]

As the Farewell Address was being allowed to "work its way,"
Washington turned to the preparation of his eighth and last Annual Message to Congress. The farewell had deliberately been
kept general because of its audience. As he was now, in effect,
saying good-bye to Congress, he took the occasion to remind
them of a number of items he had previously presented that he
still thought important and to add several new topics for legislation. When he came to foreign relations, however, his treatment
contrasted strongly with earlier messages. Where he had previously always tried to be evenhanded, he now permitted to show
an obvious displeasure with the French treatment of American
commerce in the West Indies, although he said little for fear of a
charge of trying to influence the election. A special message, to
be given at a later time, would treat the topic in detail. Relations
with Britain received a very different treatment; he depicted
even that power's lateness in handing over the military posts as
necessary and excusable. But Washington's treatment of domestic topics showed some of his anxieties about the durability of the
peace; he urged immediate planning for the construction of a
strong navy and for government aid or direct manufacture of
items necessary for defense that could not be supplied domesti-
cally. He also urged government sponsorship of boards charged
with the support and improvement of agriculture, an object of
"primary importance" to the nation's welfare, and the payment
of higher salaries to government officials: "it would be repugnant
to the vital principles of our Government, virtually to exclude
from public trusts, talents and virtues, unless accompanied by
wealth."

---

[36] Carroll and Ashworth, 7: 393–94; Harry Ammon, *James Monroe and the
Quest for National Identity* (New York, 1971), chaps. 7 and 8, for Monroe's work
in Paris.

A much larger than usual audience attended when Washington delivered the message on December 7 because it was the last time most could reasonably expect to see the man already generally referred to as the "Father of His Country." Henrietta Liston, the perceptive wife of the new British minister, Robert Liston, noticed "the extreme agitation he [Washington] felt when he mentioned the *French*. He is, I believe, very much inraged" (emphasis in original). Mrs. Liston would presently write of the only vain remark she ever heard Washington make, that his face never betrayed his emotions—vain and incorrect. The audience's emotion was apparent as the president concluded his talk:

> The situation in which I now stand, for the last time, in the midst of the Representatives of the People of the United States, naturally recalls the period when the Administration of the present form of Government commenced; and I cannot omit the occasion, to congratulate you and my Country, on the success of the experiment; nor to repeat my fervent supplications to the Supreme Ruler of the Universe, and Sovereign Arbiter of Nations, that his Providential care may still be extended to the United States; that the virtue and happiness of the people may be preserved; and that the Government, which they have instituted for the protection of their liberties, may be perpetual.

His last major public appearance as president behind him, Washington was free to concentrate on the election; although he wrote nothing to betray his interest, it can be assumed that he was gratified to see Adams squeak out a three-vote victory in the Electoral College over Jefferson, who thus became vice president. Recently Washington had seen a good bit more of his vice president than earlier, when Adams had suffered a kind of semi-exile because of his presumed championing of the form and substance of monarchy. Adams was pleased to note the similarity of views between himself and the president, a similarity the latter must also have noted. But Washington probably did not see Adams's independence, an independence that would not permit him to ask more of the French than of the British and that gave him a tumultuous and ultimately frustrating administration.[37]

---

[37] Eighth Annual Address to the Congress, Dec. 7, 1796, *Writings*, 35: 310–20. Henrietta Liston to James Jackson, Dec. 9, 1796, in Bradford Perkins, ed., "A

Rules of Civility & Decent Behaviour In Company and Conversation

1 Every Action done in Company, ought to be with Some Sign of Respect, to those that are present.

2 When in Company, put not your Hands to any Part of the Body, not usualy Discovered.

3 Shew nothing to your Friend that may affright him.

4 In the presence of Others Sing not to yourself with a humming Noise, nor Drum with your Fingers or Feet.

5 If you Cough, Sneeze, Sigh, or Yawn, do it not Loud but Privately; and Speak not in your Yawning, but put Your handkerchief or Hand before your face and turn aside.

6 Sleep not when others Speak, Sit not when others stand, Speak not when you Should hold your Peace, walk not on when others Stop.

7 Put not off your Cloths in the presence of Others, nor go out your Chamber half Drest.

8 At Play and at Fire its Good manners to Give Place to the last Commer, and affect not to Speak Louder than Ordinary.

9 Spit not in the Fire, nor Stoop low before it neither Put your Hands into the Flames to warm them, nor Set your Feet upon the Fire especially if there be meat before it.

10 When you Sit down, Keep your Feet firm and Even; without putting one on the other or Crossing them.

11 Shift not yourself in the Sight of others nor Gnaw your nails.

12 Shake not the head, Feet, or Legs rowl not the Eys lift not one eyebrow higher than the other wry not the mouth, and bedew no mans face with your Spittle; by approaching too near him when you Speak.

Rules of Civility and Decent Behaviour in Company and Conversation, as copied by George Washington, ca. 1744. (Library of Congress)

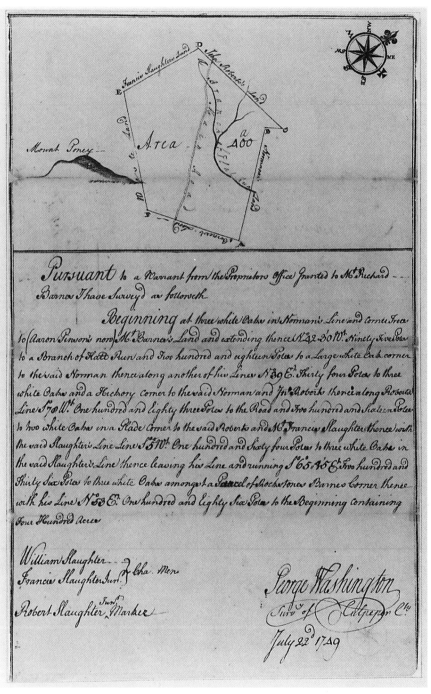

Survey for Richard Barnes, 1749. This survey, done for a Virginia neighbor by the seventeen-year-old Washington, was probably one of the first commissions he discharged. (The Virginia Historical Society, Richmond)

Virginia, ſ.

By the Hon. *ROBERT DINWIDDIE*, Eſq; His Majeſty's Lieutenant-Governor, and Commander in Chief of this Dominion.

A PROCLAMATION,

For Encouraging M E N to enliſt in his Majeſty's Service for the Defence and Security of this Colony.

WHEREAS it is determined that a Fort be immediately built on the River *Ohio*, at the Fork of *Monongahela*, to oppoſe any further Encroachments, or hoſtile Attempts of the *French*, and the *Indians* in their Intereſt, and for the Security and Protection of his Majeſty's Subjects in this Colony ; and as it is abſolutely neceſſary that a ſufficient Force ſhould be raiſed to erect and ſupport the ſame : For an Encouragement to all who ſhall voluntarily enter into the ſaid Service, I do hereby notify and promiſe, by and with the Advice and Conſent of his Majeſty's Council of this Colony, that over and above their Pay, Two Hundred Thouſand Acres, of his Majeſty the King of *Great-Britain's* Lands, on the Eaſt Side of the River *Ohio*, within this Dominion, (One Hundred Thouſand Acres whereof to be contiguous to the ſaid Fort, and the other Hundred Thouſand Acres to be on, or near the River *Ohio*) ſhall be laid off and granted to ſuch Perſons, who by their voluntary Engagement, and good Behaviour in the ſaid Service, ſhall deſerve the ſame. And I further promiſe, that the ſaid Lands ſhall be divided amongſt them immediately after the Performance of the ſaid Service, in a Proportion due to their reſpective Merit, as ſhall be repreſented to me by their Officers, and held and enjoyed by them without paying any Rights, and alſo free from the Payment of Quit-rents, for the Term of Fifteen Years. And I do appoint this Proclamation to be read and publiſhed at the Court-Houſes, Churches and Chapels in each County within this Colony, and that the Sheriffs take Care the ſame be done accordingly.

Given at the Council-Chamber in *Williamsburg*, on the 19th Day of *February*, in the 27th Year of his Majeſty's Reign, *Annoque Domini* 1754.

ROBERT DINWIDDIE.

G O D Save the K I N G.

Robert Dinwiddie, A Proclamation . . . February 1754. Authorization of the land bounty for the Virginia Regiment. Washington acquired a large tract on the Ohio River as a consequence of this proclamation. (Reproduced by permission of The Huntington Library, San Marino, California)

George Washington in the Uniform of a British Colonial Colonel, 1772, by Charles Willson Peale. The earliest portrait of Washington. (Washington-Custis-Lee Collection, Washington and Lee University, Lexington, Virginia)

George Washington, by Joseph Wright, 1783. This portrait, done as the war was ending, clearly depicts the extent to which Washington aged during the conflict. The painter prepared an altered version the following year which played down this aspect. (Historical Society of Pennsylvania [1972.9])

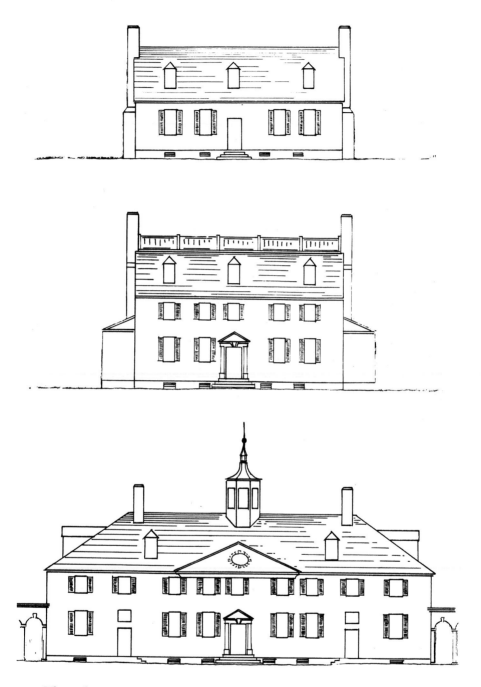

The enlargement of the mansion at Mount Vernon. The top sketch shows the house before Washington's marriage in 1759; the middle shows the enlargement at that time; the bottom shows the additions made between 1754 and the 1780s. (Courtesy of the Mount Vernon Ladies Association)

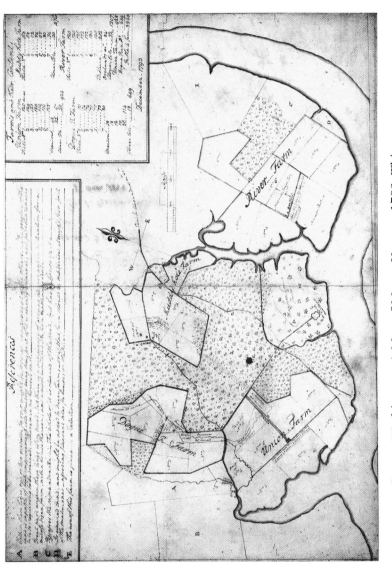

George Washington, A Map of Mount Vernon, 1793. This map, depicting the Mount Vernon farms at their fullest extent, shows that Washington had not lost his surveying skills. (Reproduced by permission of The Huntington Library, San Marino, California)

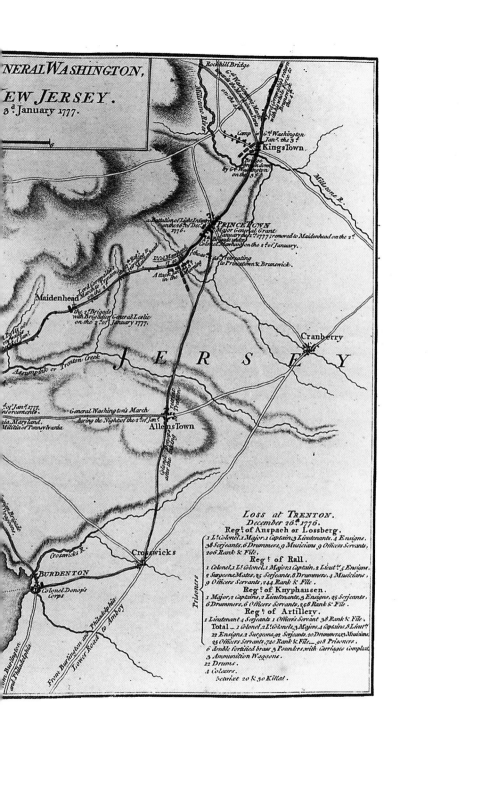

George Washington, ca. 1812–1815, by Gilbert Stuart. Originally painted in 1795, this portrait, one of the most widely known of Washington's portraits, was repainted many times by the artist. It is also known as the "Athenaeum" portrait. (Courtesy of Washington and Lee University, Lexington, Virginia)

Martha Washington, by Charles Willson Peale, 1795. This portrait, painted rather late in her life, is probably the best known depiction of the first "First Lady." (The Virginia Historical Society, Richmond)

"The Home of Washington," Thomas Barlow Oldham, 1860. Life at Mount Vernon as it was depicted, somewhat idealistically, in the nineteenth century. (Courtesy of the Mount Vernon Ladies Association)

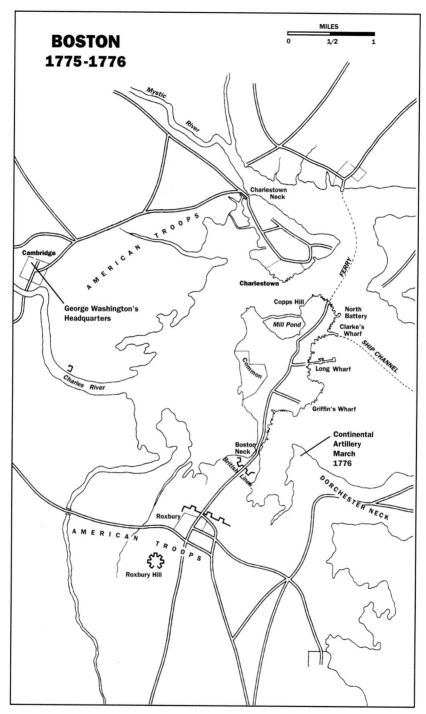

Boston, 1775–1776, illustrating the topography of the area during the siege by the Continental forces. (Maps by beerinc.com)

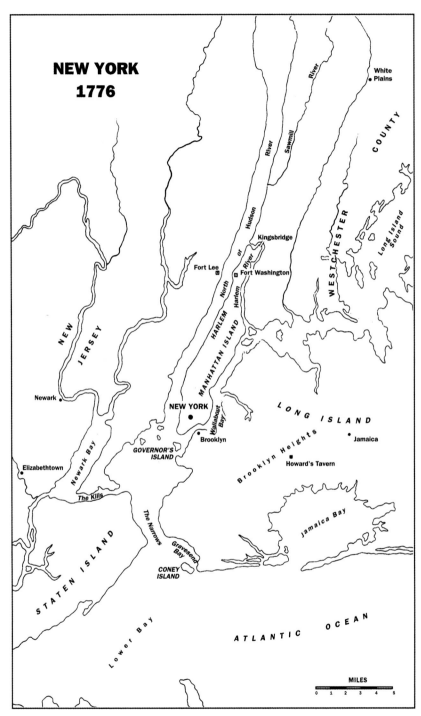

New York, northern New Jersey, 1776, the theater of operations during
the war's lowests point for the Continental army. (Maps by
beerinc.com)

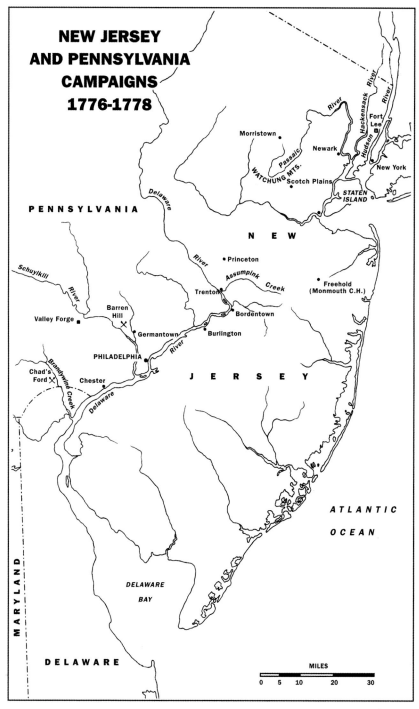

New Jersey and the Philadelphia area, 1776–1778, where the War for Independence was rescued and maintained. (Maps by beerinc.com)

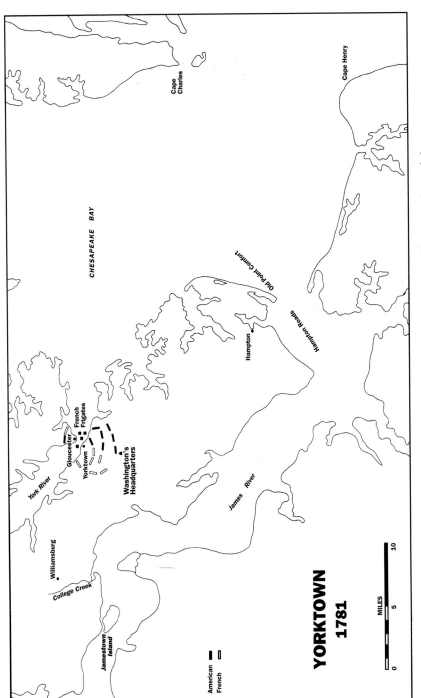

Yorktown, Virginia, 1781, the site of the last significant action of the war, where victory was ensured by French sea power and artillery. (Maps by beerinc.com)

Washington was not ready to be so evenhanded. In preparing the special message on relations with France, the secretary of state was instructed to point to the U.S. policy of "fair dealing towards all the Belligerent Powers" and to say further that, "wrapt up in its own integrity," the United States had not anticipated the ill treatment it had received from France. The administration was certain, Washington went on, that France would realize this also and offer compensation for vessels recently seized in the West Indies. But whether France realized it or not, there would be no change of U.S. policy. The message took the form of instructions to Minister Pinckney. In his dealings with the French, who considered themselves the injured party, Pinckney was charged to ask for more and offer nothing, not even consoling phrases.[38]

As the last days of his administration wound themselves down, Washington became more and more an object of scorn in the Republican press, which seemed determined to outdo itself in libeling him. Bache published an open letter from Tom Paine, who felt for various reasons that the president had wronged him. Speaking out of his hurt and his disappointment at affairs in both of his adopted countries, America and France, Paine questioned whether Washington had ever had "good principles" or had recently abandoned even the pretense of them. Bache eagerly joined in the chorus and on the day of Adams's inauguration rejoiced that "the man who is the source of all the misfortunes of our country is this day reduced to a level with his fellow citizens, and is no longer possessed of power to multiply evils upon the United States. . . . The name of Washington ceases from this day to give currency to political iniquity and to legalize corruption."

Within Bache's hyperbole, there nevertheless was a grudging and implicit acceptance of a point Mrs. Liston had made earlier when she learned of Washington's decision to retire: "There is a

---

Diplomat's Wife in Philadelphia: Letters of Henrietta Liston, 1796–1800," *William and Mary Quarterly* 11 (Oct. 1954), 606; hereafter, Perkins, "Diplomat's Wife." See also James C. Nicholls, ed., "Lady Henrietta Liston's Journal of Washington's 'Resignation,' Retirement, and Death," *Pennsylvania Magazine of History and Biography* 95 (Oct. 1971), 516.

[38] GW to Timothy Pickering, Jan. 9, 1797, *Writings*, 35: 360–61.

Magic in his name more powerful than the Abilities of any other man can ever acquire." The violence of Bache's language testified more convincingly to this "Magic" than could any of the hymns of praise being turned out by the Federalists.[39]

The inauguration of the second president of the United States took place on Saturday, March 4, 1797, in Congress Hall. The first president, dressed in a simple black suit, walked alone to the hall while a splendidly dressed Adams rode over in a new carriage. At the conclusion of the brief ceremony, Washington stepped forward and congratulated Adams, who probably came closer than anyone else to capturing his predecessor's feelings when he wrote: "He seemed to enjoy a triumph over me. Methought I heard him say, 'Ay! I am fairly out and you fairly in! See which of us will be happiest!" Washington emphasized his new status by refusing to walk out ahead of the new vice president but instead standing aside until Jefferson reluctantly went ahead of his former chief. Then, George Washington, private citizen, left the hall.[40]

---

[39] "Letter to George Washington, Jul. 30, 1796," in Philip S. Foner, ed., *The Complete Writings of Thomas Paine*, 2 vols. (New York, 1945), 2: 723; the *Aurora*, Mar. 5, 1797, in Stewart, *Opposition Press*, 533–34; Henrietta Liston to James Jackson, Oct. 15, 1796, in Perkins, "Diplomat's Wife," 604.

[40] Carroll and Ashworth, 7: 437.

7

The Final Commission, 1797–1799

> I see, as you do, that clouds are gathering and that a storm may ensue. . . . [It will be both painful and necessary] to quit the tranquil walks of retirement and enter the boundless field of responsibility and trouble.
>
> GW to James McHenry, July 4, 1798

WITH ADAMS'S INAUGURATION, Washington might have ceased being a public servant, but he was still very much a public person, and that night a farewell banquet was held in a hall decorated by a transparency depicting Washington being crowned by "Fame." A round of farewell visits and the necessary packing then took almost a week before the family was ready to leave. Tobias Lear, who had returned to Washington's employ, assumed the last-minute moving chores. Even with his help, items were forgotten or misplaced, not all to Washington's displeasure, for as he confided to Lear: "On one side I am called upon to remember the Parrot, on the other to remember the dog. For my own part I should not pine much if both were forgot." No matter how different the conditions or eminent the persons, moving a family (Martha's grandchildren, adopted by the Washingtons when their mother remarried, owned the pets) always seems to have been a bothersome chore. Dog, parrot, furniture, and people eventually all arrived safely on the Potomac, with the people getting there first, on March 14.[1]

As in 1783, Washington settled back quickly into the routine of the plantation, and again he discovered much to be done. Despite his visits and the services of a series of managers—James

---

[1] GW to Tobias Lear, Mar. 9, 1797, *Papers/Ret,* 1: 24–25; Carroll and Ashworth, 7: 438–39, for the festivities in Philadelphia.

Anderson, a Scot, was the incumbent—the lands and the buildings showed the absence of their owner's care. Soon the mansion
house began to resound with the bang of hammers while the
odor of paint overbore all the pleasant smells of a burgeoning
Virginia spring. The only new construction ordered was a small
outbuilding to house Washington's official papers, which, their
owner explained with characteristic understatement, "are volu-
minous, and may be interesting." (It was never built.) He described his daily routine to James McHenry, who had promised
to keep him informed on national affairs:

> I begin my diurnal course with the sun; that if my hirelings are
> not in their places at that time I send them messages expressive of
> my sorrow for their indisposition; then having put these wheels in
> motion, I examine the state of things further; and the more they
> are probed, the deeper I find the wounds are which my buildings
> have sustained by an absence and neglect of eight years; by the
> time I have accomplished these matters, breakfast—a little after
> seven o'clock . . . is ready. This over, I mount my horse and ride
> around the farms, which employs me until it is time to dress for
> dinner. . . . The usual time of sitting at Table, a walk, and Tea,
> brings me within the dawn of Candlelight; previous to which, if
> not prevented by company, I resolve that, as soon as the glimmer-
> ing taper, supplies the place of the great luminary, I will retire to
> my writing Table and acknowledge the letters I have received; but
> when the lights are brought, I feel tired, and disinclined to engage
> in this work, conceiving that the next night will do as well; the
> next night comes and with it the same causes for postponement
> . . . and so on.[2]

This passage, apparently expressive of the contentment Washington found at Mount Vernon, may not have told the whole
story. There is certainly a possibility that he missed the excitement and challenge of public office, although there is little doubt
he did not miss the wearying paperwork that went with it. For
now, however, he had to tend not only to his buildings, but also
to his fortunes.

His finances were in almost as much disarray as his buildings.

---

[2] GW to James McHenry, May 29, 1797, *Papers/Ret,* 1: 159–60.

During the presidential years, he had spent his salary and more maintaining the house in Philadelphia, with the income from Mount Vernon sufficient to pay its expenses. Confronting the cost of the Mount Vernon repairs as well as entertaining the increased number of visitors come to pay their respects (at one point, he wondered: "Pray, would not the word curiosity answer as well?"), Washington accepted the offer of a glib-talking land speculator, James Welch, for a long-term lease of some twenty-three thousand acres of his Kanawha lands. The rent, computed as 6 percent interest on $200,000, would be a welcome supplement to the income that the improved management of Mount Vernon might yield. Unfortunately Welch's words were more impressive than his accomplishment, and the rent never materialized. Other transactions had been more successful, though, and in 1799 he estimated that he had realized approximately $50,000 during the last five years. Except for this income, he would have been in serious debt; as it was, even with the land sales, he never solved what modern accountants would call a "cash-flow" problem. He was partially responsible for this problem because he could never bring himself to sue his creditors for repayment or even press them hard. His letters requesting payment almost always contained an extensive description of his own sad financial condition and sometimes sounded like those he had written to the old Congress during the war. Nor did he find it easy to cut down on expenditures. Indeed, he even increased them and in 1798 began the construction of a double house near the site of the Capitol in Washington. To complete the project, he was driven, for the first time in his life, to borrow $2,500 from an Alexandria bank at what he thought was "a ruinous interest." (The houses were a strong indication of the interest he took in the capital and of his anxiety about its being ready for the government in 1800; they were destroyed by the British in 1814.) Despite his shortage of ready cash, Washington was a successful land speculator. Anyone who could realize $50,000 and still have thousands of acres left had not done badly at all. At his death, his real-estate holdings were valued at almost half a million dollars. A major reason for his success was that he had been able to avoid going into debt to acquire his lands; with low or nonexistent taxes, he was easily able to hold on to them while they appreciated.[3]

His money troubles may have been partially responsible for his plans to lease his Mount Vernon farms and to free his slaves, plans that also came from an increasing repugnance for the institution. Approximately half of the slaves at Mount Vernon belonged to Washington; the remainder were "dower slaves" in whom Martha had a life interest. At her death, they went to her grandchildren, the children of John Parke Custis, who had died in 1781. Fortunately Washington had kept his antislavery sentiments to himself because these feelings would have antagonized the South and prevented him from leading the nation as its first president, but he could not stop thinking about how to deal with the problem. In 1793, he had proposed to lease the farms to British farmers (American farmers were too wasteful and tied up with slavery) and to use the income to support himself and those slaves who were unable to care for themselves; the rest would be freed. The two parts of the plan depended on each other, and the project fell through when no prospective lessors presented themselves. Except for some house servants who were allowed to stay behind in Philadelphia, Washington kept his slaves until he died. His will provided that they would be freed at Martha's death because their labor was needed to work the farms and support her. This plan proved impracticable because the slaves soon learned of the proviso, and Washington's nephew, Bushrod, who was to inherit the house and mansion farm at her death, feared what might happen with more than a hundred slaves waiting for her to die. In January 1801, they were, if they chose, freed along with several who belonged to Martha, except for those who were too old to work. Washington's will records only the necessary details relating to the upkeep of those who chose to stay and of the old and infirm at Mount Vernon. James McHenry recorded Washington's best explanation, other than a slowly developing repugnance for the institution, in the notebooks he kept while living at Mount Vernon, 1787–89: "The unfortunate condition

---

[3] Flexner, 4: 373–74; W. B. Bryan, *A History of the National Capital* (New York, 1914–16), 1: 312, 343, 627; GW to Samuel M. Fox, June 26, 1799, to William Herbert, Sep. 1, 1799, to Alexander Addison, Nov. 24, 1799, *Papers/Ret*, 4: 159, 298, 423.

of the persons, whose labour in part I employed, has been the only unavoidable subject of regret. To make the Adults among them as easy & comfortable as their actual state of ignorance & improvidence would admit; & to lay a foundation to prepare the rising generation for a destiny different from that in which they were born; afforded some satisfaction to my mind, & could not I hoped be displeasing to the justice of the Creator." Thus, because he could do nothing about the slaves without impoverishing himself and Martha, he resolved to live with the problem.[4]

Problems or no, Washington still found retirement to be gratifying. Mrs. Liston had commented earlier that he should not be acclaimed for stepping down because he was only satisfying his deepest desire. Thus, when the Listons visited Mount Vernon in December 1797, she was not surprised to find him "improved by retirement like a Man relieved from a heavy burthen. He has thrown off a little that prudence which formerly guarded his every word . . . he converses with the more ease and cheerfulness." Others noted the same change; now that he no longer spoke for the nation, he was freer in speaking for himself. When the shifting tides of the French Revolution put his wartime aide, the Marquis de Lafayette, in prison, the president had done all he could privately—for example, sending a sum of money to Madame de Lafayette—but doing nothing publicly that might offend the French. Near the end of his term, however, he brought the marquis's son, George Washington Lafayette, and his tutor, who had come to the United States some time earlier, to live with his family, his first public kindness to the young man. As soon as the young George had learned of his father's release from prison in October 1797, he left Mount Vernon, carrying an invitation to visit the plantation where Washington could receive the marquis as his private feelings and not his public position dictated.[5]

Adding to the pleasure of retirement was the generally good health Washington enjoyed. This was not something at which he

---

[4] Zagarri, *Humphreys' "Life,"* 78; Flexner, 4: chap. 12, treats the topic of slavery, as does Hirschfeld, *Slavery,* esp. chap. 7; GW's Last Will and Testament, Schedule of Property, July 9, 1799, and Slave List [June 1799] are in *Papers/Ret,* 4: 477–542; see also Twohig, " 'That Species of Property,' "114–38.

[5] Henrietta Liston to James Jackson, Dec. 8, 1797, in Perkins, "Diplomat's Wife," 614; Carroll and Ashworth, 7: 360, 482.

worked, other than getting enough exercise, chiefly by horseback riding. In October 1798, he answered Landon Carter, who had sent some personal prescriptions for keeping well, by saying, in effect, no thank you: "Having, through life, been blessed with a competent share of [good health], without using preventatives against sickness, and as little medicine as possible when sick; I can have no inducement now to change my practice, against the effect of time and age, no remedy has ever yet been discovered."

He hoped he would submit gracefully to the inevitable effects of old age. He did not assume the same for Martha and hired a housekeeper to ease the burden of heavy entertaining that seemed to be the Washingtons' lot in life, in or out of office. By this act of kindness and others, Washington showed his high regard for the woman who had given him comfort and encouragement during the difficult years of the war and the presidency without ever embarrassing him by the betrayal of a husbandly confidence or even simply by an imprudent statement of a personal opinion that could be taken as reflecting his feelings. Only those close associates who were contrasts to Washington seem to have survived his tendency to dominate those around him, James Madison and Alexander Hamilton, for example. Martha was so complementary to her husband that her attractiveness, intelligence, and skill at her tasks as the general's wife and as the first "First Lady" have not been sufficiently appreciated. Their relationship was not the material for high romance or for a novel of romantic love, and Washington confessed as much to Eliza Powel, a close friend of the couple in Philadelphia. When they moved in 1791, she had purchased a desk from them and found in it a packet of letters from Martha to him. Although she returned it unopened, she could not resist teasing him by suggesting the letters contained such torrid passion that they might burst into flame. He assured her that if she had read them, she would have found them to be "more fraught with expressions of friendship, than of *enamoured* love" (emphasis in original). They would have to be burnt to give any warmth. Great romance, no, but a quiet, kindly love, yes.[6]

---

[6] GW to Landon Carter, Oct. 5, 1798, to Tobias Lear, July 31, 1797, *Papers/ Ret*, 3: 79, 1: 281; *Diaries*, Dec. 6, 1797, 6: 271; GW to Elizabeth Powel, Mar. 26, 1797, *Papers/Ret*, 1: 51–52. See Joseph E. Fields, comp., *"Worthy Partner:" The Papers of Martha Washington* (Westport, Conn., 1994), for what letters sur-

The reader of several newspapers and, despite his disclaimer to McHenry, an active correspondent with friends throughout the country, Washington knew sooner than most of the French decision not to receive Charles Cotesworth Pinckney. This news moved him to confess that French policy was "so much beyond calculation, and so unaccountable upon any principle of justice or even . . . of plain understanding" that he would not even try to understand it. He approved of President Adams's urging of unity against the French at a special session of Congress in May 1797, commenting that "the idea that the Government and People have different views [should not] be suffered any longer to prevail, at home or abroad." The French needed to see "an unequivocal expression of the public mind," an expression, Washington was certain, that would support his policies—policies he saw President Adams continuing. He thought well of Adams's sending John Marshall, a Virginia Federalist, and Elbridge Gerry, whose political affiliation was uncertain (possibly even to Gerry himself) to Paris to help Pinckney convince the French of their errors. Gerry, whom Adams knew to be honest and well-meaning, was a kind of good faith token to the Republicans. The new envoys carried instructions little changed from Pinckney's; the United States still asked for much and offered little. Washington saw the problem as stemming from a French misconception of American politics; the French still believed they could make the United States do their will by swaying the interests and allegiance of the Republicans. But they were mistaken; "the *Mass* of our Citizens require no more than to understand a question to decide it properly, and an adverse conclusion of the negotiation will effect this" (emphasis in original). Taking away the value judgment implicit in "properly," this assessment rather closely fitted what was to happen.[7]

Washington showed how strongly he felt about Republican Francophilia in foreign affairs when he reacted angrily to Mon-

vive from and to Martha, along with a sensitive biographical sketch by Ellen McCallister Clark. See Higginbotham, "Three Women," for a more complete discussion of Martha's character and her role in GW's life.

[7] GW to James McHenry, Apr. 3, 1797, to Thomas Pinckney, May 28, 1797, to Oliver Wolcott Jr., May 29, 1797, to John Marshall, Dec. 4, 1797, *Papers/Ret,* 1: 71, 157–58, 161–62, 499–502.

roe's defense of his Paris ministry, contained in *View of the Conduct of the Executive . . . 1794, 5 & 6*. Some of the former minister's criticisms were valid, but mostly they worked out to a disapproval of Jay's Treaty. Uncharacteristically, Washington wrote comments in the margin of his copy, holding an angry debate with the author. When Monroe alleged that if the United States had not abandoned France, the latter would have denied America nothing, Washington retorted: "That is to say, if we w[ould] not press them to do us Justice, but had yielded to *their* violations, they would have aided us in every measure which would have cost them: *Nothing*" (emphasis in original). Washington met most of Monroe's other contentions with the same untypical spirit of angry sarcasm as he filled margin after margin with angry rejoinders. He took every care to note Monroe's mistakes but gave him no credit at all for his accomplishments. Increasingly, in Washington's view, criticism of the administration's actions and policies was an unallowable criticism of the government. With the prospect of even more difficult relations with France, such an attitude did not indicate that Washington would take kindly to attempts to explain or justify French policy. His mind was made up.[8]

Nor did his comments regarding the ultimate correctness of the people reflect optimism about the immediate future; there were too many obstacles to a "proper" understanding. The Republicans were using "cowardly, illiberal and assasin like" weapons to "subvert [the government's policy and] to destroy all confidence in those who are entrusted with the Administration" of that policy. Washington was afraid that "Misrepresentation and party feuds" might well end in "confusion and anarchy." What had seemed about to occur ten years earlier, contentions ending in disunion, again seemed to be in prospect. As he celebrated his sixty-sixth birthday, all he could see was "internal dissentions and political hostilities in the councils" of the republic. Although retired, "I cannot but view these things with deep con-

---

[8] GW's comments along with the relevant passages from Monroe are in *Papers/Ret*, 2: 169–217; the quotation is on 205; see also James Monroe, *View of the Conduct of the Executive in the Foreign Affairs of the United States Connected with the Mission to the French Republic, during the Years 1794, 5 & 6* (Philadelphia, 1797).

cern." Much, if not all, depended on what was happening in Paris, but no one on this side of the Atlantic had heard anything about the progress of the mission. By early March, Washington felt that only the guillotine could explain the silence of the American delegates in Paris.[9]

But the reason for lack of news was much more prosaic. To avoid capture by the British, the commissioners' dispatches had been sent by a roundabout route that caused them to be bunched up. Just as Washington was worrying about the commissioners, their reports were being read in Philadelphia. However, the story they contained was anything but prosaic. On their arrival in Paris the previous October, the emissaries had been greeted with delaying tactics by the custodian of French foreign policy, Charles Maurice de Talleyrand-Perigord, the former bishop of Autun, who had already adapted from the Old Regime to the new and would continue adapting until he was serving the restored Bourbon monarchy at the end of the Napoleonic Era. Talleyrand let the Americans know that they would have to wait for a report on Franco-American relations then being prepared for the Directory, the executive body of the French Republic. He did tell them that the directors were angry about Jay's Treaty and about the subsequent attitude of the United States toward France. Soon, the emissaries discovered just how angry the directors were. Persons claiming to be agents for unnamed individuals within the French government approached them and demanded a combination of bribes and forced loans to the French government before their credentials would be received and negotiations begin. The Americans had recognized the likely necessity of paying bribes in the shifting, corrupt atmosphere that pervaded the French capital at this time, but they would pay only for results, not opportunities, and certainly not the several million dollars demanded. As one of the French agents put it, "You do not speak to the point, it is money; it is expected that you will offer money." At this outburst of Gallic avarice, Pinckney thundered: "It is no, no; not a sixpence." By January 1798, the Americans' patience was worn thin, and they presented Talleyrand with a near ultima-

---

[9] GW to Timothy Pickering, Feb. 6, 1798, to Alexander White, Feb. 22, Mar. 1, 1798, to James McHenry, Mar. 4, 1798, *Papers/Ret*, 2: 76–77, 113–14, 117.

tum to come to the point, accept their credentials, and begin negotiating. He did not reply to this ultimatum for six weeks. His reply made clear that the French were not ready to treat the United States with anything other than thinly veiled contempt. Convinced their mission had failed, Marshall and Pinckney left. Talleyrand convinced Gerry that war would certainly come if all negotiations ceased, and Gerry agreed to stay, but by July he too had left without any result.[10]

The dispatches President Adams received in March told enough of the story to convince him the mission was a failure; this failure, combined with the news of increased French seizures in the West Indies, led him to realize he was sitting on a volcano. He tried to buy time by reporting to Congress only that dispatches had been received and revealed no hope "that their mission can be accomplished on terms compatible with the safety, the honor, or the essential interests of the nation." But he recommended only defensive measures, possibly expecting the French presently to furnish grounds for war.

Both Republicans, who believed that Adams's vague language concealed a moderate response by the French, and extreme Federalists, who wanted what they were confident was a sordid tale revealed for all to see, passed a congressional resolution calling for the dispatches. For once, the Federalists' hopes were gratified, and the Republicans could not defeat a joint resolution for publication. In releasing the dispatches to Congress, President Adams had replaced the French agents' names with initial letters (to protect the guilty?), and so by mid-April the public was able to read the whole story of the "X,Y,Z Affair." The immediate result was a strong outburst of anti-French feeling that brought the Republican party temporarily to its knees, the nation into an undeclared naval war with France and a virtual alliance with Britain, and Congress to the enactment of strong defensive mea-

---

[10] This paragraph and those following it, dealing with the XYZ mission and its aftermath, are based on Alexander DeConde, *The Quasi War: The Politics and Diplomacy of the Undeclared Naval War with France, 1798–1801* (New York, 1966), chaps. 2 and 3 (hereafter, DeConde, *Quasi War*); Stephen Kurtz, *The Presidency of John Adams* (Philadelphia, 1966), chaps. 12–17 (hereafter, Kurtz, *Adams Presidency*); Page Smith, *John Adams*, 2 vols. (Garden City, N.Y., 1962), 2: chaps. 73–75 (hereafter, Smith, *John Adams*); and Elkins and McKitrick, *Age of Federalism*, chaps. 12–14.

sures and domestic legislation that had for its aim the extinction of the opposition party. President Adams became the hero of the moment and the recipient of hundreds of addresses pledging loyalty and aid in the crisis. Washington shared fully in the anger and could only wonder how, after seeing "that the measure of infamy was filled" and the extent of the "profligacy" and "corruption" of the French government, some Americans could still hold back from condemning it. He believed the leaders of the "Demos" would change their opinions only if a "manifest desertion" from their ranks occurred. Just that seemed to be happening, and in May Hamilton wrote the general, asking if he could not help it along by travelling, ostensibly for his health, through Virginia and North Carolina, and speaking discreetly about the crisis. He also hinted that, if war should break out, Washington was the only possible choice to command the army. The general ingenuously replied that his health had never been better but, more to the point, that his presence would not be very persuasive. Politicking was for others, not for him. Soldiering was quite another thing. Although he doubted it would come to that, "if a crisis should arrive when a sense of duty, or a call from my Country, should become so imperious as to leave me no choice," he would go, albeit "with as much reluctance from my present peaceful abode, as I should do to the tombs of my Ancestors." Reluctantly, perhaps, but he would accept, and the reluctance may have been more apparent than real considering that he also chose at that time to write President Adams and Secretary McHenry about unrelated matters, almost as if he wanted to call attention to himself. He need not have bothered; as Mrs. Liston noted, "this Man from the mere Magic of his name is, as has been often repeated, a Host of himself," a point in which President Adams concurred.[11]

In addition to other defensive measures, such as the establishment of a separate navy department, Congress had increased the authorized strength of the army by twelve regiments, the "New

[11] GW to Timothy Pickering, Apr. 16, 1798 (two letters), to James McHenry, May 6, 1798, Alexander Hamilton to GW, May 19, 1798, GW to Alexander Hamilton, May 27, 1798, Papers/Ret, 2: 242–43, 253–54, 279–81, 297–99; Henrietta Liston to James Jackson, July 12, 1798, in Perkins, "Diplomat's Wife," 618.

Army," and the organization of a "Provisional Army," to be called out only in anticipation of an immediate French invasion. (The feared invasion was of a small force from the French West Indies, carrying weapons, which would attempt to raise a rebellion among the slaves of the lower South.) It was to the command of the Provisional Army that Washington was likely to be called. Both McHenry and Adams hinted at this possibility, although the president wrote asking only for the use of the general's name. In answering McHenry, Washington made clear that he would have to be able to appoint his officers, regardless of the seniority list of the last war. This conflict, if it came, would bring new conditions, and Washington doubted that, among the veteran officers, one could find "men of sufficient activity, energy and health, and of *sound politics*" (emphasis added) to meet the new requirements. The military considerations were understandable; suppressing rebellious slaves led by French officers would be quite different from the War for Independence, and Washington surely recalled the difficulties he had in securing and keeping competent officers during the conflict. But the reference to "sound politics" revealed his fears about the ultimate loyalty of some Republicans. In a conflict with the French, perhaps a new type of loyalist would appear, and the army could not tolerate any of those in the ranks.[12]

Before Washington could be certain his stipulations had been received in Philadelphia, President Adams found it necessary to appoint him to the command without consultation. Washington was not the unanimous choice; many Federalists, especially the extremists who would welcome a war with France, wanted Hamilton to head the proposed force. In Philadelphia, everywhere Adams turned, Hamilton was put forward. Probably reflecting her husband's fears, Abigail Adams asked her son-in-law if any New Englanders were speaking up for the New Yorker; if they were, they clearly did not know him. She was certain he would be a "second Buonaparty." Just about the last thing the president wanted was to see Hamilton controlling a real army. Further, Adams saw a navy as the only effective measure against a French

---

[12] Kohn, *Eagle and Sword,* 229 n; GW to John Adams, July 4, 1798, *Papers/Ret,* 2: 369–71.

invasion; the proposed army was important mainly as a negotiating tool, a sign the United States meant business. In order to cut short the pro-Hamilton sentiment, Adams sent Washington's name to the Senate for final approval as lieutenant general and commander in chief of the army; on July 2, the Senate approved the nomination unanimously.[13]

The appointment did not surprise Washington. What concerned him was his inability to set prior conditions; now the conditions would have to be negotiated before acceptance. Hamilton underscored the necessity of doing so when he warned the general that Adams's military ideas were "of the wrong sort." If Washington accepted the president's appointees for his subordinates, "it will be conceived that the arrangement is yours, and you will be responsible for it in reputation." The fact that Hamilton was playing on the older man's concern for his reputation shows not only his knowledge of what arguments carried weight with Washington, but also his eagerness to win his point. His comments were probably unnecessary because Washington already agreed with him, and when McHenry visited Mount Vernon to inform the general of his appointment, he was instructed to write Adams that he would bring back a list of those whom Washington wanted on his staff "and without whom, I think, he would not serve." What followed during the next two months is a sequence of events so confusing that it is impossible to describe here in detail. Washington made it clear that he would not take the field unless an invasion occurred, so the second in command would be in effective charge of the army until then. Under these circumstances, Adams wanted someone he could trust in the second spot and suggested, in order of seniority, Henry Knox, Charles Cotesworth Pinckney (not yet back from France), and, perhaps, Hamilton. Washington's original choice had been Charles Cotesworth Pinckney, whose residence in South Carolina was advantageous because a French invasion, if it came, was expected in the South, and Washington believed Knox was too old

---

[13] Abigail Adams to William Smith, July 7, 1798, in Mitchell, *New Letters*, 201. The brief account of the complex chain of events that follows is based on the relevant pages in Carroll and Ashworth, vol. 7; Flexner, vol. 4; Kurtz, *Adams Presidency;* DeConde, *Quasi War;* Kohn, *Eagle and Sword*, part 3; and the correspondence in *Papers/Ret*, vol. 6.

for an active command. After his visit from McHenry and letters from prominent Federalists, he moved Hamilton forward, placing him immediately under him as inspector general. Adams resisted this choice as long as he decently could, but all the advantages lay with Washington and his awesome popular standing. Had the conflict turned into a public confrontation, Washington would probably have resigned in protest and American resistance to the French would have been weakened along with confidence in the president. Adams, knowing he would lose anyway, dated the commissions for the top three generals— Hamilton, Pinckney, and Knox (who angrily declined to serve under Hamilton, very much his junior in the War for Independence)—on the same day, leaving to Washington to arrange them as he chose and preserving at least a semblance of presidential authority. During the quarrel, Washington used Adams's cabinet as if it were his own, listened to the advice of extreme Federalists only, was conveniently forgetful of statements that could have embarrassed him, and in the showdown threatened to take the issue to the public. The affair ended without serious repercussions only because John Adams was moderate and George Washington was not. It was one of the sorriest episodes of his adult life.

In late fall, Washington went to the capital to confer with Hamilton and Pinckney on choices from among the flood of applicants for commissions. One of the criteria they used turned out to be loyalty to the Federalist Party. When Adams tried to appoint two Republicans, Aaron Burr and Frederick Augustus Muhlenberg, as brigadier generals to help the administration in the key states of New York and Pennsylvania respectively, the generals would not hear of it. Washington had already warned McHenry that the "Brawlers against government measures" were eager for commissions. "The motives ascribed to them are, that in such a situation they would endeavor to divide, and contaminate the Army, by artful and seditious discourses, and perhaps at a critical moment, bring on confusion." None but the politically pure were to command this army. Washington and Hamilton were also concerned about McHenry's presumed administrative ineptitude, so, being unable to remove him, they drew up infinitely detailed regulations and procedures to reduce the likelihood of error. All this procedure delayed the organization and enlistment of the New Army past the point where, as will be seen, it was needed. Because President Adams was content to have merely the appearance of additional troops being readied, he ignored military affairs except when he was not himself throwing in a monkey wrench of his own.[14]

Although Washington believed himself to be overworked while in the capital, his diary records many more evenings when he was out socially than in his lodgings, presumably working. The most bizarre of these outings must have been November 27, 1798, when he dined "in a family" with Robert Morris; tactfully omitted from his diary was the place, debtor's prison, where Morris's land speculations had landed him. On another occasion, Washington was not tactful at all when George Logan called, accompanied by a local clergyman, whose card was the only one sent up to the general's room. Normally the prominent physician and agricultural reformer would have been a welcome guest, but Dr. Logan was also a Republican who had just returned from a one-man peacemaking effort in France. (His excursion so frightened the Federalists in Congress that they passed a law making such activities illegal; if peacemakers were to be called the children of God, they might also be called felons, at least in the Federalist United States.) Despite the physician's persistent attempts to get Washington's attention, the general spoke only to the clergyman until the latter left. Then Logan tried to assure Washington that the French had already begun to change their policy, and if the United States refrained from antagonizing them, peace would not be broken. Washington shot back that everything America had done was in self-defense. Did the French look "upon us as worms; not even allowed to turn when tread upon? for it was evident to all the world that we had borne and forborne beyond what even common respect for ourselves required and I hoped that the spirit of this Country would never suffer itself to be injured with impunity by any nation under the Sun." After replying, the unchastened Logan left. So far had pol-

---

[14] See Marshall Smelser's "George Washington and the Alien and Sedition Acts," *American Historical Review* 59 (1954): 322–34, for the context of GW's partisanship on this occasion; hereafter, Smelser, "Alien and Sedition Acts."

itics taken the man who considered himself above them that he could not listen courteously and dismiss politely a perhaps mistaken but certainly sincere Quaker physician.[15]

At the end of their work, the generals reported on the preparedness of the forces; in Hamilton's lawyerlike prose, the statement examined the provisions of the law, the existing situation, even the availability of money, and concluded by urging that the force be brought to full strength as soon as possible. All that Washington apparently contributed to the report was his signature. During the War for Independence, he had developed the knack of making others' prose his own and had continued this practice in the presidency; now he was content to let Hamilton speak for him and to urge an unwanted army on an unwilling president.[16]

By early December, Washington, Hamilton, and Pinckney had returned to their homes, leaving McHenry to wrestle as well as he could with the tasks of organizing the army and answering respectfully the sometimes raspy letters of inquiry from his generals. Away from the frenetic atmosphere of the capital, war seemed much less likely, and Washington soon slackened his demands on McHenry. He was even able to consider calmly, something few other Federalists were able to do, the news that President Adams was sending yet another mission to France. In late fall, the president had begun to receive, by a variety of channels, signals that the French might be ready to treat. Talleyrand had been brought to the decision to change France's American policy by the remarkable success the new American navy had had against French commerce raiders in the Caribbean, the close cooperation between American and British forces, and the political successes the undeclared war had given the Federalists. Because the last thing the French wanted was to cement the Federalists in power as they worked in a near alliance with the British, a change of policy was in order. Late in 1798, Talleyrand began indirectly (he never did anything directly) to signal Adams of this change; by February 1799, the president was sufficiently convinced of a

---

[15] *Diaries*, 6: 322–26, for GW's entire stay in the capital, Nov. 5–Dec. 19; "Memorandum of an Interview [with George Logan]," Nov. 13, 1798, *Papers/Ret*, 3: 200–202.

[16] Kohn, *Eagle and Sword*, chap. 12.

French willingness to treat that he nominated William Vans Murray, already minister to Holland, as minister plenipotentiary to France. Talleyrand's signals had been subtle and private, so the nation was naturally astonished at the president's action, with one Federalist, Harrison Grey Otis, putting the point succinctly: "Is the man mad?" Washington's initial reaction was also strong; he would have made the French put all their cards on the table before responding formally, for as he saw it, the French were "playing the same loose, and roundabout game" as before, but he then admitted that he might not be seeing everything, that "not being acquainted with all the information, and the motives which induced the measure, I may have taken a wrong impression, and therefore shall say nothing further on the subject." As president he had sometimes based decisions on information he could not share with Congress or with the people, and now he was giving Adams the same leniency he had asked for himself. This attitude may have been induced in part by the fact that Washington himself was one of the channels through which Adams had received his information. Joel Barlow, an American living in Paris, had written of the pacific intentions of the French; the general had sent the letter on to Philadelphia with the wish that the country might "pass this critical period in an honorable and dignified manner, without being involved in the horrors and calamities of War." Both he and the nation were recovering from the war fever that had infected them since the previous spring.[17]

In addition to defensive measures, Congress had reacted to the XYZ dispatches by passing domestic legislation lumped together as the Alien and Sedition Acts. Even before the news had come from Paris, the Federalists had been upset over the presence of large numbers of French refugees from the rebellion of blacks on the island of Santo Domingo, smaller groups of émigrés from metropolitan France, and some Irish political refugees fleeing the abortive 1798 revolt. These refugees, mixing with American Republicans, seemed to the Federalists to be a direct threat to the integrity of the country. Congress dealt with the alien problem by making naturalization a lengthier process, giv-

---

[17] GW to Timothy Pickering, Mar. 3, 1799, *Papers/Ret,* 4: 405–6; Carroll and Ashworth, 7: 368–70.

ing the president the authority to expel any alien he deemed dangerous and providing a procedure by which enemy aliens might be removed in event of war. The most important of these acts, and the only one to be enforced, was the Sedition Act, which made the common-law crime of seditious libel a matter for prosecution in federal courts. It protected the president, cabinet, and Congress from criticism and imposed penalties for resisting or opposing the laws of Congress or the acts of the president. Taken broadly—and it was—it made any criticism of the government a crime. The political intent of the act was obvious from its studied exclusion of the vice president, Thomas Jefferson, from its protection and in its length, to March 3, 1801—the end of Adams's administration—and no longer. The Sedition Act was a tool to crush the Republican Party and to ensure the election of a Federalist (not necessarily Adams) as president in 1800. It resulted in seventeen convictions of Republicans, although the level of Federalist political invective was no higher or more factual than that of their opponents. The act was also enforced through prejudiced and partial means—improper procedures, packed juries, and partisan judges being common. It brought about a reign of legal terror and, while it lasted, put every Republican editor under the threat of fine and imprisonment. Paradoxically, the effect of the act was to increase substantially the number of Republican newspapers in the country.[18]

Although Washington never explicitly approved of the Sedition Act and its companions by name, there is little doubt that he believed them to be necessary and even wholesome pieces of legislation. As early as 1793 he had suggested to Henry Lee that Freneau's and Bache's journals had the tendency to bring the government into disrepute, and it was "difficult to prescribe bounds to the effect." In 1794, he had linked both the Whiskey Rebellion and the sudden growth of the Democratic-Republican Societies to foreign agitation. That same year he vetoed Jefferson's suggestion that the president's project of a national university could be easily accomplished by importing the faculty of the University of Geneva, then in danger of being banished by

---

[18] James Morton Smith, *Freedom's Fetters: The Alien and Sedition Laws and American Civil Liberties* (Ithaca, 1956); Stewart, *Opposition Press*, chap. 15.

French-inspired revolutionaries. The only immigrants Washington wanted were useful mechanics and farmers, and even then he did not want them to settle in groups where they would "retain the Language, habits and principles (good and bad) which they bring." After the controversy over Jay's Treaty, the incident that most influenced him toward Federalism, he distrusted immigrants who came here "full of prejudice against their own government, some against all government." And, repeating a favorite Federalist charge, he linked the agitation over the treaty with the activities of French ministers and Republican editors.

Shortly after Washington had left the presidency, he commented to Rufus King that nothing would "change the sentiments, or (which perhaps would be more correct) the conduct of some characters amongst us." By the end of 1797, he feared that conduct could include placing the affairs of America under the influence and control of a foreign nation. During the uproar following the publication of the XYZ dispatches, he never expressed any disapproval of any of the government's actions, telling Charles Carroll of Carrollton that "I even wish they had been *more energetic*" (emphasis in original). When Alexander Spotswood doubted the constitutionality and policy of the acts, Washington defended them, although he only argued about the danger of aliens, not dissident citizens. He also defended the acts from John Marshall's criticism of them, commenting that if the Republicans did not have them to criticize, they would find something else. Thus, the general tenor of Washington's remarks, at least from the time of the Whiskey Rebellion, shows him gradually adopting the Federalist theory of a Republican plot, possibly initiated but certainly aided by the French, aiming to bring down the government and to place the United States under French tutelage. While he was president, his comments were guarded and indirect, and he never proposed any checks on freedom of the press or on any other civil liberties, but in retirement he gave full vent, albeit privately, to his fears and suspicions about the Republicans and resident aliens.[19]

As noted, the Federalists had hotly resented Adams's decision

---

[19] Smelser, "Alien and Sedition Acts," 322–34, describes GW's sentiments on this topic.

to send yet another mission to France, and some tried to replace him as candidate in 1800. Washington was naturally high on any list of this kind, and Governor Jonathan Trumbull of Connecticut posed the question forthrightly in July 1799; equally forthrightly, Washington refused. He first suggested that he no longer could give fair value to the public; although he was in good health, "I am not insensitive to my declination in other respects." The other reasons showed a grudging recognition of the damage his Federalist politics had done to his reputation; he doubted he would receive one vote from the "anti-Federal" side. Thus, any other Federalist could run and do as well as he could, perhaps better. Further, he would be charged "not only with irresolution, but with concealed ambition . . . in short, with dotage and imbecility." When Trumbull persisted, Washington sternly advised him that "principles, instead of men" should be "the steady pursuit of the Federalists." "No eye, no tongue, or thought" should be turned toward his possible candidacy. The governor and his brother, Colonel John Trumbull, also failed to enlist him in one of Francisco de Miranda's efforts (through Rufus King in London) for the liberation of Latin America.[20]

Although the general refused to take any active part in politics, he showed a lively interest in national affairs, fretting, for example, at the silence of the French, despite Adams's peace overture. Federalist resistance to Adams's policy had succeeded only in adding two others to serve along with Murray on the mission to France. When the additional representatives left the United States in November 1799, Washington had little faith in their mission: "This business seems to have commenced in an evil hour, and under unfavorable auspices; and I wish mischief may not tread in all its steps, and be the final result of the measure." But because there was nothing he could do about the situation, he accepted it; as men viewed the same measure differently, he could only hope the president's decision was the correct one.[21]

Although Washington did not consider himself to be near

[20] GW to Jonathan Trumbull, July 21, Aug. 30, 1799, *Paper/Ret,* 4: 202–3, 275–76; Marshall Smelser, "George Washington Declines the Part of *El Libertador,*" *William and Mary Quarterly* 11 (Jan. 1954): 42–51.

[21] GW to Alexander Hamilton, Oct. 27, 1799, "Private" to Timothy Pickering, Oct. 20, 1799, *Papers/Ret,* 4: 373, 355.

death—his constant planning for the future of Mount Vernon shows that—in July 1799 he took out his best watermarked paper and in a bold, clear hand, with the utmost attention to neatness and legibility, filled twenty-seven pages with his will. Except for some small bequests, Martha was to have all his property for her lifetime, with the household furnishings, supplies, and so on given outright to her. The Mount Vernon farms were carefully divided, with the larger part and the mansion going to his brother John Augustine's son, Bushrod, and another part to the sons of his late nephew George Augustine. Both his brother and his nephew had managed the estate for him, John during the Virginia Regiment years, George during the years of the presidency; so, in a sense, these bequests were deferred salary payments. Thus, the estate that Washington had carefully assembled and assiduously cultivated was broken up, and a good portion of its labor force dispersed. It had been a kind of monument to his independence and power; now, it would be allowed to decay slowly, in time to be rescued for posterity. Other tracts went to other Washington nephews. The western lands were to be sold, the proceeds divided as prescribed among nephews, nieces, and Martha's grandson, George Washington Parke Custis. All specific bequests of land kept it within the Washington family. Any family debts outstanding at his death were forgiven. Money bequests and gifts of mementos, swords, and the like were made to relatives and friends. His secretary, Tobias Lear, received the free life lease of a Mount Vernon farm he was currently renting. The provisions freeing those Mount Vernon slaves whom Washington owned have already been noted. He also made provision to take care of those older slaves who chose to remain at Mount Vernon. In conclusion, he directed his heirs to settle any disputes regarding the will by arbitration rather than by legal process. In his death, as in his life, all was to be arranged as much as possible with order and regularity.[22]

Almost as though Providence was compelling the general to contemplate death, news came in September of the final illness

---

[22] The will and GW's "Schedule of Property" are in *Papers/Ret*, 4: 477–542. See Dalzells, *Mount Vernon*, 217–22, for a description of the will and comment on the breakup of the estate.

of his brother Charles, moving him to muse: "I was the *first,* and am now the *last* of my father's children by the second marriage who remain, when I shall be called to follow them, is known only to the giver of life" (emphasis in original). But the "giver" was keeping those intentions to himself, for Washington felt himself to be in good health as he followed his busy schedule about the farms. One of the few signs of age that showed came when he declined an invitation for himself and Martha to a dancing assembly in Alexandria: "But alas! Our dancing days are no more."[23]

On Thursday, December 12, a day marked by rain, sleet, and finally snow, Washington made his usual round of the farms on horseback; when he came in, Lear remarked on the snowflakes in his hair, but he brushed them off, saying his greatcoat had kept him dry, and went into dinner immediately, without changing as he usually did. The next day, Washington noted the weather in his diary: "morning snowing and ab[ou]t. 3 inches deep. Wind at the No[rth] E[ast], and Mer[cury] at 30. Cont[inuin]g Snowing until 1 O'clock, and Ab[ou]t 4 it became perfectly clear." Despite the cold and snow, as soon as it cleared, he went out on the lawn and marked some trees he wanted taken down, more for the exercise and an opportunity to get out of the house than for any necessity. That evening, although he complained of a sore throat and sounded hoarse, he sat with Martha and Lear, reading newspapers and frequently commenting on interesting or humorous items with no serious discomfort apparent.[24]

---

[23] GW to Burgess Ball, Sep. 22, 1799, *Papers/Ret,* 4: 318; to Jonathan Swift et al., Nov. 17, 1799, *Writings,* 37: 425 n.

[24] *Diaries,* Dec. 12, 13, 1799, 6: 378–79. Washington's last illness and death are described in all biographies; the most recent and authoritative account is Peter R. Henriques, "The Final Struggle between George Washington and the Grim King: Washington's Attitude toward Death and an Afterlife," *Virginia Magazine of History and Biography* 107, no. 1 (winter 1999): 74–97.Henriques has expanded this account into *He Died As He Lived: The Death of George Washington* (Mount Vernon, Va., 2000); it includes Tobias Lear's account, the only complete and contemporary account in writing. A diagnosis given by W. McK. Wallenborn, M.D., "George Washington's Terminal Illness: A Modern Medical Analysis of the Last Illness and Death of George Washington," is also available at www.virginia.edu/gwpapers/articles/wallenborn. Dr. Wallenborn diagnoses the illness as *epiglottitis,* an infection of the epilglottis that swells that organ and the surrounding tissue and blocks the airway. In effect, GW smothered to death, a long and painful trial.

In the middle of the night, however, he woke Martha, complaining of an extremely sore throat and difficulty in breathing. With the dawn of December 14, Lear and one of the overseers were sent for—the overseer to bleed the general at his own insistence, for he believed it to be the sovereign remedy for all ills. Lear tried to get him to swallow a soothing mixture, but he could not get it down, and the secretary contented himself with bathing Washington's throat externally. Despite Lear's gentleness, Washington complained, "'Tis very sore." During the morning, Dr. Craik, his friend since the days of the Virginia Regiment, came to bleed him again and tried without success to get him to swallow a palliative. Craik noted he was having increasing trouble breathing. That afternoon Craik was joined by Doctors Elisha Cullen Dick and Gustavus Richard Brown. Nothing they prescribed, which included doses of emetics and laxatives, blisters, and two more bleedings, eased Washington's breathing or lessened the pain. Dr. Dick, the youngest of the physicians, proposed a novel treatment, a tracheotomy, to permit the general to breathe, but this procedure was vetoed by the older men as too untried and drastic for someone of Washington's age.

Washington bore with the various treatments patiently until early evening, when he whispered to the physicians: "I feel myself going, I thank you for your attentions; but I pray you to take no more trouble about me, let me go off quietly, I can not last long." Earlier he had made certain Martha had destroyed an old will and put the new one in a safe place; he had also given Lear some brief directions about his papers, confided to him his belief that he would not survive this illness, and thanked him for his attempts to make him comfortable. After his directions to the physicians, he did not speak again until about ten o'clock, when he motioned Lear close to him. Lear reported that "He made several attempts to speak to me before he could effect it, at length he said,—'I am just going. Have me decently buried; and do not let my body be put into the Vault in less than three days after I am dead.' I bowed assent, for I could not speak. He then looked at me again and said, 'Do you understand me?' I replied 'Yes.' ' 'Tis well,' said he."

Washington spoke no other words; twenty minutes later he died. Lear wrote that throughout the long and painful day Wash-

ington had borne his illness with "patience, fortitude, & resignation . . . always endeavoring (from a sense of duty as it appeared)
to take what was offered him, and to do as he was desired by
the Physicians." His sense of duty, hard earned but well learned,
stayed with him to the last.

8

Ordinary Man, Extraordinary Leader

> Simple truth is his best, his greatest Eulogy.
> She alone can render his Fame immortal.
>
> Abigail Adams to Mary Cranch, January 28, 1800

MRS. ADAMS'S INJUNCTION is well worth pondering by anyone who is attempting to arrive at a proper appreciation of a great character in history, but especially so in the case of George Washington, about whom the words were written. That perceptive woman may have realized the extent to which Americans would obscure the simple truth with both adoring myth and debunking billingsgate until the historical Washington was obscured, perhaps irretrievably lost. Not that the mythologizing and its almost inevitable sequel, debunking, are alone responsible for making Washington a difficult person to understand. Any one of us is sufficiently complex to challenge the skills of the biographer, and that complexity is magnified when a person is a significant actor in times as consequential as the American Revolution and the founding of the republic. All the misrepresentation of Washington has done is to increase the difficulties of an already formidable undertaking: the writing of another's life. What follows is my personal distillation of George Washington's character and most significant accomplishments.

W. E. Woodward has commented that Washington was an ordinary man raised to the highest levels; although he meant that comment to be disparaging, it has always struck me as one of the most telling compliments anyone could have paid the "Father of His Country."[1] Washington's talents in most fields were relatively

---

[1] William E. Woodward, *George Washington: The Image and the Man* (London, 1928), 361.

commonplace; what he did was to raise those talents to the level of superlative accomplishment by self-discipline, a character trait in which he was certainly extraordinary. This trait enabled him, in turn, to pay unremitting attention to details, essential to coordinating all the disparate parts of an organization so they worked together toward the accomplishment of a goal, whether it be the lands and slaves of Mount Vernon toward the attaining of personal wealth or the resources of the states and the soldiers of the Continental army toward a victory over the British. Helping him in these tasks was an innate liking for symmetry and order, as well as an aptitude—more exactly, perhaps, a fascination—for counting and computation. But these gifts, like those of truly ordinary people, would have been ineffectual without his self-discipline and devotion to duty. How many of us ordinary folk make such effective use of our natural talents? Few, because few of us are willing to work as hard as Washington did.

Aside from his discipline and devotion to duty—which, with Washington, were two sides of the same coin, practically speaking—it is difficult to single out any commanding characteristics; a nineteenth-century British writer put it well: "the imposing effect [of Washington] is more dependent upon the nice balance and exact symmetry of parts, than upon the commanding stature of any of his faculties, if estimated singly."[2] But those nicely balanced components can be commented on separately.

One of the first things to be noted is that as an adult Washington was very different from what he was as a youth; he underwent a steady maturing that refined much that was gross and unpleasant, leaving behind a highly controlled personality that constantly disciplined the very strong feelings and almost uncontrollable impulses of the young Washington—what Paul K. Longmore has referred to as the "invention" of George Washington. Because the early death of his father deprived him of the inheritance and help necessary to place him securely in Virginia society, he looked to his stepbrothers for the "interest" he needed and that his mother could not supply. His brother Lawrence did what he could and introduced him to the Fairfaxes. Before and after his

---

[2] Cyrus Edwards in W. S. Baker, ed., *Character Portraits of Washington* (Philadelphia, 1887), 192.

marriage, Washington learned much from the only family of the top rank of Virginia gentry to which he had easy access. The early commissions from Governor Dinwiddie owed a good bit to Fairfax friendship. His association with the Fairfaxes also acquainted him with the manners of the class to which he aspired. The Fairfaxes were a significant aid for a social climber, and Washington wanted to climb. But they also gave him an important check to his ambition, the Stoic values stressing service to the state as one of the major aspirations of the virtuous person. These values may have been the most significant influence on the development of the mature Washington.

As a young man, he was also strongly acquisitive; witness his concern over his salary and his efforts to get Dinwiddie to increase it. In his attempt to obtain a royal commission, he curried favor with both Braddock and Forbes as well as Lord Loudoun; commissions were commonly given only to favorites, and he did much to be a favorite. Yet he was also a most difficult subordinate for Governor Dinwiddie, constantly demanding more of everything with no realization of the difficulties under which the older man was working. Although Washington could occasionally forget his own concerns, as when he antagonized Forbes by his relentless championing of Virginia's interest in Braddock's road, he generally kept them prominently in mind, as when he pushed through the redemption of the 1754 land bounty, thus securing more than thirty thousand acres on the Ohio, although the bonus was probably meant only for the enlisted men. The bounty lands also awakened or strengthened an interest in the West as an area of boundless opportunity. In time, this interest would become blended with the conviction that the future of the United States lay in the exploitation of its resources. Only in this way would it become the great country he was certain it was destined to be.

As Washington established himself at Mount Vernon, he became more relaxed about acquiring land, although he never lost interest in what he saw as the most secure of all assets. It ought to be noted that his personal honesty was never questioned, and he had a reputation for integrity as good as any man's. But the most significant development in his personality was one that was not obvious until he assumed command of the Continental army in 1775, and that was the iron self-control he had succeeded in imposing on himself. General Washington could not be said to be a perfect example of calmness and serenity; he gave way to fits of temper, and he often tended to view his immediate situation in the gloomiest way possible, yet the contrast between the colonel and the general is striking and unmistakable. He immersed himself in the cause of American independence with a singular lack of regard for his person and fortune, becoming a symbol of America's unswerving desire to be free of British rule. He remained throughout the war the servant of Congress, helping to establish civilian control of the military as one of the most important features of the new republic's polity. His actions at New Windsor in March 1783 are simply one conspicuous (and significant) example of his contribution.

What also came to the fore noticeably during the war was Washington's practice of the Stoic ideal that the favor of a free people was the highest reward a citizen could receive. Thus, his service for expenses only was not a theatrical gesture but rather a practical example of his belief that public approval was the only proper coin for public service. This coin was not an unalloyed benefit. Although it permitted him to act unselfishly with regard to money, it also made him very sensitive of his reputation and difficult for him to accept criticism. Washington often professed a willingness to listen to serious, fair criticism, but he saw comment by anyone outside the army as a plot to unseat him: for example, the Conway Cabal.

His sensitivity about his reputation sometimes made it difficult for him to make up his mind as he tried to puzzle out the effect different steps might have on his standing with the people. This practice is difficult to assess separately, for he was always slow in coming to a conclusion—in part because he realized that many of his actions might have long-term significance, something he frequently stated explicitly, even when he was in the army, but especially when he was serving as president. Thomas Jefferson once wrote that Washington's mind was "slow in operation, being little aided by invention or imagination, but sure in conclusion."[3]

---

[3] Thomas Jefferson to Walter Jones, Jan. 2, 1814, in Peterson, *Jefferson: Writings*, 1318.

At Washington's appointment as commander in chief, Congress urged him to use the "council of war," a practice common in the British army of bringing the officers together to ponder possible courses of action. His use of this practice developed into the habit of asking anyone suitable for advice, considering the advice, then making up his mind, and giving his decision at the last minute. Slow in coming to a decision, he was quick and unrelenting in execution. As president, this trait worked admirably, for most problems were long term, and in that more leisurely age crises took their time in developing. This slow deliberation also held back Washington's tendency to move quickly, an impetuosity more characteristic of the gambler than of the statesman, but a characteristic he did possess. Asking everyone for advice, however, helped to lead to frequent charges that he was unduly influenced by those around him, such charges usually coming from those whose advice he had not followed.

One aspect of Washington's personality that impressed contemporaries was his silence, which, the more perceptive noted, concealed his control of strong feelings. As John Adams commented, perhaps enviously, Washington possessed the "gift of silence. . . . He had great self command. It cost him a great exertion sometimes, and a constant constraint; but to preserve so much equanimity as he did required a great capacity." Washington himself realized this, for he once said he had tried to do his duty "as far as human frailties and perhaps strong passions" allowed him.[4]

The strong feelings to which both Washington and Adams referred included a sense of pessimism lying just below the surface of an apparently calm exterior. The need to keep this feeling and others under control helps to explain the almost ceaseless activity in which Washington immersed himself: work, exercise— either horseback riding or, in the worst weather, pacing the Mount Vernon veranda—the preoccupation with detail, even to the point of calculating the number of seeds in a pound of timothy or rye seed and counting the number of panes in the mansion house windows. As long as he had something to do, he could keep the Furies at bay.

---

[4] John Adams to Benjamin Rush, Apr. 15, 1808, in Smith, *John Adams*, 2: 1084; GW to Burgess Ball, Sep. 22, 1799, *Papers/Ret*, 4: 318.

Despite his silence and gravity, he was able to capture and hold the affections of those near him, especially the younger men who served on his staff during the war. This was true from the days of the Virginia Regiment, as his officers testified in a moving statement when he resigned his commission in December 1758. But he was respected, not loved, by the enlisted men, and his general orders to them were rigid and admonishing; in Marcus Cunliffe's words, "They do not *give* praise; they *bestow* it" (emphasis in original).[5]

I have already discussed Washington's generalship, his role in the formation of the Constitution, and his conduct of the presidency. Here I would simply underline the symbolic role he played in each of these areas; this is not to denigrate his general accomplishment and his specific contributions. Although other men could have been adequate generals, presided over the Convention, and seen the new government into being, it is difficult to see anyone other than Washington holding the army and then the states together as he did. In becoming the symbol of the unity of the colonies by serving as commander in chief of the army, he assumed a role that he thereafter found impossible to forsake. He remained the symbolic focus of the unity of the republic throughout his life. His lapse into partisanship in the last years of his presidency did not seriously tarnish his image with other than partisan Republicans in Congress, for once Jay's Treaty was ratified, his other actions could be explained by the necessity of executing the treaty. France's subsequent negative reaction to the treaty was laid at John Adams's door. Furthermore, most Americans were not yet involved in the discord between Federalists and Republicans and so ignored the allegations of the latter regarding Washington's activities. The partisan selection of the officer corps of the Provisional Army during the undeclared war with France did not become generally known and, because the army was not actually raised, was of little practical significance. Thus, for most Americans, Washington was never identified with either political party. He remained, in Henry Lee's now hackneyed but still accurate

[5] Cunliffe, *Man and Monument*, 109.

phrase, "First in war, first in peace, first in the hearts of his countrymen." The Federalist sympathies so apparent in his second term were the surfacing of basic sympathies he had held all along. He had expected the government to be a cooperative enterprise of gentlemen discussing with other gentlemen the problems of government and devising remedies in a calm, orderly manner. The division between the pro- and anti-administration groups apparent by the end of the first term disconcerted and disappointed him. The messiness of what might be called democratic discourse was not at all to his liking, and he gradually moved away from those who seemed able only to criticize. It might be pertinent to point out Washington's frequent use of theatrical metaphors and his lifelong interest in the theater. Most men of the time used military metaphors in speaking of public affairs—a battle ending in victory for one side, defeat for the other. Washington referred instead to the theater, where the play ends with all concerned holding hands and taking the presumably merited applause together. This was his model of what the new government was to be—consensus, not controversy. When it did not turn out that way, he was deeply disappointed.[6]

Washington gave the United States what history has demonstrated every new nation needs, a leader who stands above the contention of the moment and ties the disparate parts of the country together until a national spirit has developed; but he did this, as few others have, without giving serious ground for fearing the introduction of monarchical or authoritarian rule. No one has said it quite as well as Thomas Jefferson: "His was the singular destiny and merit of leading the armies of his country successfully through an arduous war for the establishment of its independence, of conducting its councils through the birth of a government, new in its forms and principles, until it settled down into a quiet and orderly train; and of scrupulously obeying the laws through the whole of his career, civil

---

[6] Personal Observation of Jack D. Warren Jr. to the author, May 2001; Dr. Warren was an assistant editor of *The Papers of George Washington* at the University of Virginia. He is also the author of *The Presidency of George Washington* (Mount Vernon, Va., 2000).

and military, of which the history of the world furnishes no other example."[7]

This leadership was Washington's most significant contribution to the success of the American Revolution and to the great experiment in republican government that came from that revolution.

---

[7] Thomas Jefferson to Walter Jones, Jan. 2, 1814, in Peterson, *Jefferson: Writings*, 1319.

WORKS CITED

Adams, Charles Francis, ed. *Letters of John Adams Addressed to His Wife.* 2 vols. Boston: Little Brown, [1841].

Alden, John R. *General Charles Lee: Traitor or Patriot?* Baton Rouge: Louisiana State University Press, 1951.

Ammon, Harry. *The Genêt Mission.* New York: Norton, 1973.

———. *James Monroe and the Quest for a National Identity.* New York: McGraw–Hill, 1971.

Anderson, Fred. *Crucible of War: The Seven Years War and the Fate of Empire in British North America.* New York: Alfred A. Knopf, 2000.

Anderson, Niles. "The General Chooses a Road—The Forbes Campaign of 1758 to Capture Fort Duquesne." *Western Pennsylvania Historical Magazine* 42 (1959): 109–38, 241–58, 383–401.

Baker, William S., ed. *Character Portraits of Washington.* Philadelphia: Robert M. Lindsay, 1887.

———, ed. *Early Sketches of George Washington.* Philadelphia: Lippincott, 1894.

Baldwin, Leland D. *Whiskey Rebels: The Story of a Frontier Uprising.* Rev. ed. Pittsburgh: University of Pittsburgh Press, 1968.

Bemis, Samuel Flagg. *Jay's Treaty: A Study in Commerce and Diplomacy.* New rev. ed. New Haven: Yale University Press, 1962.

———. *John Quincy Adams and the Foundations of American Foreign Policy.* New York: Alfred A. Knopf, 1949.

———. *Pinckney's Treaty: America's Advantage from Europe's Distress, 1783–1800.* New rev. ed. New Haven: Yale University Press, 1960.

Bernath, Stuart L. "George Washington and the Genesis of American Military Discipline." *Mid–America* 49 (1967): 83–100.

Bickford, Charlene Bangs, and Kenneth R. Bowling, *Birth of the*

Nation: The First Federal Congress, 1789–1791. Madison, Wis.: Madison House, 1989.

Billias, George A. *George Washington's Generals.* New York: William Morrow, 1964.

——. *George Washington's Opponents.* New York: William Morrow, 1969.

Bliven, Bruce. *Battle for Manhattan.* 1956, repr., Baltimore: Pelican, 1964.

Boller, Paul F., Jr. *George Washington and Religion.* Dallas: Southern Methodist University Press, 1963.

Bowling, Kenneth R. *The Creation of Washington, D.C.* Fairfax, Va.: George Mason University Press, 1991.

Bowling, Kenneth R., and Helen E. Veit, eds. *The Diary of William Maclay and Other Notes on Senate Debates.* Vol. 9 of *The Documentary History of the First Federal Congress.* Baltimore: Johns Hopkins University Press, 1988.

Bowman, Allen. *The Morale of the American Revolutionary Army.* Washington, D.C.: American Council on Public Affairs, 1943.

Bradley, Harold W. "The Political Thinking of George Washington." *Journal of Southern History* 11 (Nov. 1945): 469–86.

Brant, Irving. "Edmund Randolph, Not Guilty!" *William and Mary Quarterly* 7 (Apr. 1950): 174–88.

Bryan, W. B. *A History of the National Capital.* 2 vols. New York: Macmillan, 1914–16.

Burnett, Edmund C. *The Continental Congress.* 1941, repr., New York: Norton, 1964.

——, ed. *Letters of Members of the Continental Congress.* 7 vols. 1921, repr., Gloucester, Mass.: Peter Smith, 1963.

Butterfield, Lyman H., ed. *The Adams Papers, Series II: Adams Family Correspondence.* Vol. 2. Cambridge, Mass.: Harvard University Press, 1963.

Carp, E. Wayne. *To Starve the Army at Pleasure: Continental Army Administration and American Political Culture, 1775–1783.* Chapel Hill: University of North Carolina Press, 1984.

Chase, Philander D. "A Stake in the West: George Washington as Backcountry Surveyor and Landholder." In Warren R. Hofstra, ed., *George Washington and the Virginia Backcountry,* 159–94. Madison, Wis.: Madison House, 1998.

Clarfield, Gerard H. *Timothy Pickering and American Diplomacy, 1795–1800.* Columbia: University of Missouri Press, 1969.

Combs, Jerald A. *The Jay Treaty: Political Battleground of the Founding Fathers.* Berkeley: University of California Press, 1970.

Conway, Moncure Daniel. *Omitted Chapters of History Disclosed in the Life and Papers of Edmund Randolph.* New York: G. P. Putnam's, 1888.

Cook, Ray B. *Washington's Western Lands.* Strasburg, Va.: Shenandoah, 1930.

Cunliffe, Marcus. *George Washington: Man and Monument.* 1958, repr., New York: New American Library, n.d.

Cunningham, Noble E., Jr. *The Jeffersonian Republicans: The Formation of Party Organization, 1789–1801.* Chapel Hill: University of North Carolina Press, 1957.

Currie, David P. *The Constitution in Congress: The Federalist Period, 1789–1801.* Chicago: University of Chicago Press, 1997.

Dalzell, Robert F., Jr., and Lee Baldwin Dalzell. *George Washington's Mount Vernon: At Home in Revolutionary America.* New York: Oxford University Press, 1998.

Darlington, William M., ed. *Christopher Gist's Journals.* Pittsburgh: J. R. Weldin and Co., 1893.

Decatur, Stephen, Jr. *The Private Affairs of George Washington: From the Records and Accounts of Tobias Lear, Esq., His Secretary.* Boston: Houghton Mifflin, 1933.

DeConde, Alexander. *Entangling Alliance: Politics and Diplomacy under George Washington.* Durham, N.C.: Duke University Press, 1958.

———. *The Quasi War: The Politics and Diplomacy of the Undeclared Naval War with France, 1798–1801.* New York: Scribner's, 1966.

Elkins, Stanley, and Eric McKitrick. *The Age of Federalism: The Early American Republic, 1788–1800.* 1993, repr., New York: Oxford University Press, 1995.

Ellis, Joseph. *Founding Brothers: The Revolutionary Generation.* New York: Alfred A. Knopf, 2000.

Farrand, Max, ed. *The Records of the Federal Convention of 1787.* Rev. ed. 4 vols. New Haven: Yale University Press, 1966.

Fields, Joseph E., comp. *"Worthy Partner": The Papers of Martha Washington.* Westport, Conn.: Greenwood Press, 1994.

Fleming, Thomas. *Beat the Last Drum.* New York: St. Martin's, 1963.

Flexner, James Thomas. *The Traitor and the Spy: Benedict Arnold and John André.* New York: Harcourt Brace, 1953.

Foner, Philip S., ed. *The Complete Writings of Thomas Paine.* 2 vols. New York: Citadel Press, 1945.

Ford, Paul Leicester, ed. *The Writings of Thomas Jefferson.* Vol. 8. New York: G. P. Putnam's Sons, 1897.

Ford, Worthington C., ed. "Edmund Randolph on the British Treaty, 1795." *American Historical Review* 12 (Apr. 1907): 587–99.

————, ed. *Journals of the Continental Congress.* Vol. 5. Washington, D.C.: Government Printing Office, 1906.

Greenberg, Allan. *George Washington, Architect.* London: Andreas Papadaikis, 1999.

Griswold, Rufus W. *The Republican Court; or American Society in the Days of Washington.* New Additions. New York: D. Appleton, 1863.

Hamilton, Charles, ed. *Braddock's Defeat.* Norman: University of Oklahoma Press, 1959.

Harris, C. M. "Washington's Gamble, L'Enfant's Dream: Politics, Design, and the Foundation of the National Capital." *William and Mary Quarterly* 56 (July 1999): 527–64.

Haworth, Paul L. *George Washington: Country Gentleman.* Indianapolis: Bobbs, Merrill, 1925.

Henriques, Peter R. "The Final Struggle between George Washington and the Grim King: Washington's Attitude toward Death and an Afterlife." *Virginia Magazine of History and Biography* 107, no. 1 (winter 1999): 74–97.

————. *He Died as He Lived: The Death of George Washington.* Mount Vernon, Va.: Ladies of Mount Vernon, 2000.

Hirschfeld, Fritz. *George Washington and Slavery: A Documentary Portrayal.* Columbia: University of Missouri Press, 1997.

Higginbotham, Don. *George Washington and the American Military Tradition.* Athens: University of Georgia Press, 1985.

————. "George Washington and Three Women." In *George Washington and Conceptions of the Eighteenth Century South,* edited by Greg O'Brien and Tamara Harvey. Gainesville: University of Florida Press, forthcoming.

———. *The War of American Independence: Military Attitude, Policies, and Practice, 1763–1789*. New York: Macmillan, 1971.

Hofstra, Warren R., ed., *George Washington and the Virginia Backcountry*. Madison, Wis.: Madison House, 1998.

Holcombe, Arthur N. "The Role of Washington in the Framing of the Constitution." *Huntington Library Quarterly* 19, no. 4 (Aug. 1956): 317–34.

Hughes, Sarah S. *Surveyors and Statesmen: Land Measuring in Colonial Virginia*. Richmond: Virginia Association of Surveyors, 1979.

Johnson, Samuel. *A Dictionary of the English Language*. 1755, repr., New York: AMS Press, 1967.

Kaufman, Burton Ira, ed. *Washington's Farewell Address: The View from the 20th Century*. 1969, repr., Chicago: Quadrangle Press, 1975.

Ketcham, Ralph. *Presidents above Party: The First American Presidency, 1789–1829*. Chapel Hill: University of North Carolina Press, 1984.

Knollenberg, Bernhard. *George Washington and the Revolution, A Reappraisal: Gates, Conway, and the Continental Congress*. 1940, repr., Hamden, Conn.: Archon Books, 1968.

———. *George Washington: The Virginia Period, 1732–1775*. Durham, N.C.: Duke University Press, 1964.

Kohn, Richard H. *Eagle and Sword: The Beginnings of the Military Establishment in America, 1783–1802*. New York: Free Press, 1975.

Kolp, John G. *Gentlemen and Freeholders: Electoral Politics in Colonial Virginia*. Baltimore: Johns Hopkins University Press, 1998.

Kurtz, Stephen. *The Presidency of John Adams*. Philadelphia: University of Pennsylvania Press, 1966.

Kwasny, Mark V. *Washington's Partisan War, 1775–1783* . Kent, Ohio: Kent State University Press, 1996.

Labaree, Benjamin W. *The Boston Tea Party*. New York: Oxford University Press, 1964.

Lee, Charles. *The Lee Papers*. 4 vols. Vols. 4–7 of *Collections of the New-York Historical Society*. New York: New-York Historical Society, 1871–74.

Leibiger, Stuart. *Founding Friendship: George Washington, James*

Madison, and the Creation of the American Republic. Charlottesville: University Press of Virginia, 1999.

Link, Eugene Perry. *The Democratic-Republican Societies, 1790–
1800.* 1942, repr., New York: Octogon Books, 1965.

Longmore, Paul K. *The Invention of George Washington.* Berkeley:
University of California Press, 1988.

Louthan, H. T. "The Estate of J. P. Custis." *William and Mary
Quarterly,* 2d series, 23 (April 1943): 209–11.

Lundin, Leonard. *Cockpit of the Revolution: The War for Independence in New Jersey.* Princeton: Princeton University Press,
1940.

Mackesy, Piers. *The War for America, 1775–1783.* Cambridge,
Mass.: Harvard University Press, 1964.

Martin, James Kirby. *Benedict Arnold, Revolutionary Hero: An American Warrior Reconsidered.* New York: New York University
Press, 1997.

Maurer, Maurer. "Military Justice under General Washington."
Military Affairs 28 (1964): 8–16.

McDermott, John F., ed. *The Spanish in the Mississippi Valley,
1762–1804.* Urbana: University of Illinois Press, 1974.

Mitchell, Stewart, ed. *New Letters of Abigail Adams, 1788–1801.*
Boston: Houghton Mifflin, 1947.

Monroe, James. *View of the Conduct of the Executive in the Foreign
Affairs of the United States Connected with the Mission to the French
Republic, during the Years 1794, 5 & 6.* Philadelphia: B. F.
Bache, 1797.

Moore, Charles, ed. *George Washington's Rules of Civility and Decent
Behaviour in Company and Conversation.* Boston: Houghton
Mifflin, 1936.

Morison, Samuel Eliot. "Young Man Washington." In *By Land
and by Sea,* 168–72. New York: Alfred A. Knopf, 1953.

Nettels, Curtis. *George Washington and American Independence.* Boston: Little Brown, 1951.

Nicholls, James C., ed. "Lady Henrietta Liston's Journal of Washington's 'Resignation,' Retirement, and Death." *Pennsylvania
Magazine of History and Biography* 95 (Oct. 1971): 511–20.

Palmer, John M. *General von Steuben.* New Haven: Yale University
Press, 1937.

Paltsits, Victor H. *Washington's Farewell Address*. New York: New York Public Library, 1935.

Pancake, John S. *1777: The Year of the Hangman*. Tuscaloosa: University of Alabama Press, 1977.

Perkins, Bradford. *The First Rapprochement: England and the United States, 1795–1805*. Berkeley: University of California Press, 1955.

———, ed. "A Diplomat's Wife in Philadelphia: Letters of Henrietta Liston, 1796–1800." *William and Mary Quarterly* 11 (1954): 592–632.

Peterson, Merrill, ed. *Thomas Jefferson: Writings*. New York: Library of America, 1984.

Phelps, Glenn A. *George Washington and American Constitutionalism*. Lawrence: University Press of Kansas, 1993.

Quarles, Benjamin. *The Negro in the American Revolution*. Chapel Hill: University of North Carolina Press, 1961.

Quitt, Martin H. "The English Cleric and the Virginia Adventurer: The Washingtons, Father and Son." In Don Higginbotham, ed., *George Washington Reconsidered*, 15–37. Charlottesville: University Press of Virginia, 2001.

Ragsdale, Bruce. "George Washington, the British Tobacco Trade, and Economic Opportunity in Prerevolutionary Virginia." *Virginia Magazine of History and Biography* 97, no. 2 (Apr. 1989): 133–62. Also in Don Higginbotham, ed., *George Washington Reconsidered*, 67–93. Charlottesville: University Press of Virginia, 2001.

———. *A Planters' Republic: The Search for Economic Independence in Revolutionary Virginia*. Madison, Wis.: Madison House, 1996.

[Randolph, Edmund]. *A Vindication of Mr. Randolph's Resignation*. Philadelphia: n. p., 1795.

Reardon, John J. *Edmund Randolph: A Biography*. New York: Macmillan, 1974.

Reuter, Frank T. *Trials and Triumphs: George Washington's Foreign Policy*. Fort Worth: Texas Christian University Press, 1983.

Rhodehamel, Edward, ed. *Writings of the American Revolution: Writings from the War of Independence*. New York: Library of America, 2001.

Ritcheson, Charles R. *Aftermath of Revolution: British Policy toward the United States, 1783–1795.* 1969, repr., New York: Norton, 1971.

Ritchie, Carson I. A., ed. *General Braddock's Expedition.* London: n.p., 1962.

Roche, John F. *Joseph Reed.* 1957, repr., New York: AMS Press, 1968.

Rossie, John G. *The Politics of Command in the American Revolution.* Syracuse, N.Y.: Syracuse University Press, 1975.

Rossiter, Clinton. *1787, The Grand Convention.* 1966, repr., New York: Macmillan, 1968.

Royster, Charles. *The Fabulous Story of the Dismal Swamp Company: A Story of George Washington's Times.* New York: Alfred A. Knopf, 1999.

Satzmary, David. *Shays' Rebellion: The Making of an Agrarian Insurrection.* Amherst: University of Massachusetts Press, 1980.

Sayen, (William) Guthrie. "George Washington's 'Unmannerly' Behavior: The Clash between Civility and Honor." *Virginia Magazine of History and Biography* 107, no. 1 (winter 1999): 5–36.

Scheer, George F., and Hugh F. Rankin. *Rebels and Redcoats.* 1957, repr., New York: Mentor, 1959.

Schlesinger, A. M. *The Colonial Merchants and the American Revolution.* 1917, repr., New York: Ungar, 1957.

Scribner, Robert L., ed. *Revolutionary Virginia: The Road to Independence.* Vol. 1. Charlottesville: University Press of Virginia, 1973.

Sears, Louis M. *George Washington and the French Revolution.* Detroit: Wayne State University Press, 1960.

Sharp, James Roger. *American Politics in the Early Republic: The New Nation in Crisis.* New Haven: Yale University Press, 1993.

Slaughter, Thomas P. *The Whiskey Rebellion: Frontier Epilogue to the American Revolution.* New York: Oxford University Press, 1986.

Smelser, Marshall. "George Washington and the Alien and Sedition Acts." *American Historical Review* 59 (1954): 322–34.

———. "George Washington Declines the Part of *El Libertador.*" *William and Mary Quarterly* 11 (Jan. 1954): 42–51.

Smith, James Morton. *Freedom's Fetters: The Alien and Sedition Laws and American Civil Liberties.* Ithaca: Cornell University Press, 1956.

Smith, Page. *John Adams.* 2 vols. Garden City, N.Y.: Doubleday, 1962.

Smith, Thomas E. V. *The City of New York in the Year of Washington's Inauguration, 1789.* New York: Randolph, 1889.

Stewart, Donald R. *The Opposition Press of the Federalist Period.* Albany: State University of New York Press, 1969.

Stryker, W. S. *The Battle of Monmouth.* Princeton: Princeton University Press, 1927.

———. *The Battles of Trenton and Princeton.* Boston: Houghton Mifflin, 1898.

Sydnor, Charles S. *Gentlemen Freeholders: Political Practices in Washington's Virginia.* Chapel Hill: University of North Carolina Press, 1952.

Syrett, Harold C., ed. *The Papers of Alexander Hamilton.* Vol. 5. New York: Columbia University Press, 1966.

Tachau, Mary K. Bonsteel. "George Washington and the Reputation of Edmund Randolph." *Journal of American History* 73 (June 1986): 15–34.

———. "The Whiskey Rebellion in Kentucky: A Forgotten Episode of Civil Disobedience." *Journal of the Early Republic* 2 (fall 1982): 239–59.

Tansill, Charles C., ed. *Documents Illustrative of the Formation of the Union.* 1926, repr., Washington, D.C.: Government Printing Office, 1965.

Thomas, Charles M. *American Neutrality in 1793: A Study in Cabinet Government.* New York: Columbia University Press, 1931.

Thompson, Mary. "George Washington and Religion." Unpublished essay.

Tilberg, Frederick. "Washington's Stockade at Fort Necessity." *Pennsylvania History* 20 (1953): 240–57.

Titus, James. *The Old Dominion at War: Society, Politics, and Warfare in Late Colonial Virginia.* Columbia: University of South Carolina Press, 1991.

Twohig, Dorothy. " 'That Species of Property': Washington's Role in the Controversy over Slavery." In Don Higginbotham, ed., *George Washington Reconsidered,* 114–38. Charlottesville: University Press of Virginia, 2001.

VanDoren, Carl. *Mutiny in January.* New York: Viking, 1948.

————. *The Secret History of the American Revolution*. New York: Viking, 1941.

Wallenborn, W. McK., M.D. "George Washington's Terminal Illness: A Modern Medical Analysis of the Last Illness and Death of George Washington." Available online at www.virginia.edu/gwpapers/articles/wallenborn.

Ward, Christopher. *The War of the Revolution*. John R. Alden, ed. 2 vols. New York: Macmillan, 1952.

Warren, Jack D., Jr. *The Presidency of George Washington*. Mount Vernon, Va.: Ladies of Mount Vernon, 2000.

Whitaker, Arthur P. *The Mississippi Question, 1795–1803*. 1927, repr., Gloucester, Mass.: Peter Smith, 1962.

White, Leonard. *The Federalists: A Study in Administrative History*. 1948, repr., New York: Free Press, 1965.

Wills, Gary. *Cincinnatus: George Washington and the Enlightenment*. Garden City, N.Y.: Doubleday, 1984.

Wilstach, Paul. *Mount Vernon: George Washington's Home and the Nation's Shrine*.

Garden City, N.Y.: Doubleday and Sons, 1925.

Woodward, W. E. *George Washington: The Image and the Man*. London: Jonathan Cape, 1928.

Zagarri, Rosemarie, ed. *David Humphreys' "Life of General Washington" with George Washington's "Remarks."* Athens: University of Georgia Press, 1991.

GUIDE TO FURTHER READING

THIS GUIDE SHOULD BE understood as an extension of the works cited list that precedes it. Although there is some duplication, I have made an effort to keep it as concise as possible. By and large, I mention only items referring to Washington directly, nor have I tried to include everything or even most of everything written on Washington during the relatively recent past. The renewed interest in the "Father of His Country" has made that an impossible task.

As noted in the preface, anyone wanting to know more about Washington has a valuable resource in *The Papers of George Washington* project, currently under way at the University of Virginia. The volumes already published are described in the list of abbreviations. Dorothy Twohig has edited *George Washington's Diaries: An Abridgement** (Charlottesville: University Press of Virginia, 1999), which contains a representative sample of the six-volume original.[1] Ms. Twohig also edited *The Journal of the Proceedings of the President, 1793–1797* (Charlottesville: University Press of Virginia, 1980), from a record kept by Tobias Lear. Useful one-volume collections of Washington's letters and speeches are John Rhodehamel, ed., *George Washington: Writings* (New York: Library of America, 1997), and W. B. Allen, ed., *George Washington: A Collection** (Indianapolis: Liberty Fund, 1988). Rhodehamel also edited *The American Revolution: Writings from the War of Independence* (New York: Library of America, 2001). Joseph E. Fields has compiled *"Worthy Partner": The Papers of Martha Washington* (Westport, Conn.: Greenwood Press, 1994). Contemporary impressions of Washington can be gathered from John P. Kaminski and Jill Adair McCaughan, eds., *A Great and Good Man: George Washington in the Eyes of His Contemporaries* (Madison, Wis.: Madison House, 1989). On another level entirely, Marvin Kitman has

---

[1] An asterisk (*) indicates that a paperback edition of the work is available.

edited (and embellished) *George Washington's Expense Account* (New York: Simon and Schuster, 1970); the value of the work lies not in the editorial comments, but in the facsimile reproduction of the accounts in Washington's hand, submitted to the Register of the Treasury in June 1783.

The multivolume biographies by Douglas Southall Freeman and James T. Flexner, especially the former, contain all the average student would want (see the list of abbreviations). John E. Ferling's *The First of Men: A Life of George Washington* (Knoxville: University of Tennessee Press, 1988) is a solid, informative, one-volume biography. John R. Alden's *George Washington, A Biography* (Baton Rouge: Louisiana State University Press, 1984) emphasizes the War for Independence; Esmond Wright, a British scholar of American history, has written *Washington and the American Revolution** (New York: Collier, 1962). Older works that retain value are by William R. Thayer, Louis M. Sears, John C. Fitzpatrick (the first modern editor of George Washington's writings), and Nathaniel W. Stephenson and Waldo H. Dunn. Marcus Cunliffe's *George Washington: Man and Monument** (1958, repr., New York: New American Library, n.d.) is the best brief interpretation of Washington. Also valuable are Edmund S. Morgan's *The Genius of George Washington** (New York: Norton, 1980), Bernard Mayo's *Myths and Men: Patrick Henry, George Washington, and Thomas Jefferson** (Athens: University of Georgia Press, 1959), and Samuel Eliot Morison's "Young Man Washington," in *By Land and By Sea* (New York: Alfred A. Knopf, 1953).

In commemoration of the two hundredth anniversary of Washington's death, numerous exhibitions were held. The catalogs for two of them combine an excellent text with reproductions of documents and paintings, along with site photographs: John Rhodehamel, *The Great Experiment: George Washington and the American Republic* (New Haven: Yale University Press, 1998), and William S. Rasmussen and Robert S. Tilton, *George Washington: The Man behind the Myths** (Charlottesville: University Press of Virginia, 1999). An older, somewhat more limited work is Wendy C. Wick's *George Washington, An American Icon: The Eighteenth Century Portraits* (Washington, D.C.: Smithsonian Institution, 1982). *George Washington: American Symbol* (New York: Hudson Hills Press, 1999), edited by Barbara Mitnick, has essays and depictions of the later uses that artists, illustrators, advertisers, and others made of Washington.

A number of recent anthologies bring together varied interpretations of particular aspects of Washington's career and character. They include Don Higginbotham's *George Washington Reconsidered** (Charlottesville: University Press of Virginia, 2001) and Warren R. Hofstra's *George Washington and the Virginia Backcountry* (Madison, Wis.: Madison House, 1998). Doron Ben-Atar and Barbara B. Oberg's *Federalists Reconsidered** (Charlottesville: University Press of Virginia, 1998) has essays on various aspects of the 1790s.

Various authors have examined the symbolic uses to which contemporaries and succeeding generations have put the "Father of His Country": Daniel J. Boorstin, "The Mythologizing of George Washington," in his *The Americans: The National Experience** (New York: Random House, 1965); Jay Fliegelman, "George Washington and the Reconstituted Family," in his *Prodigals and Pilgrims: The American Revolution against Patriarchal Authority* (New York: Cambridge University Press, 1982); and Barry Schwartz, *George Washington: The Making of an American Symbol* (New York: Free Press, 1987). In *Cincinnatus: George Washington and the Enlightenment** (Garden City, N.Y.: Doubleday, 1984), Garry Wills examines the uses Washington made of various symbols.

Numerous students have examined Washington's conduct of the War for American Independence. Don Higginbotham's *The War of American Independence: Military Attitude, Policies, and Practice, 1763–1789* (New York: Macmillan, 1971) is a clear, balanced examination of the entire war; his *George Washington and the American Military Tradition* (Athens: University of Georgia Press, 1985) is a thoughtful commentary on Washington's entire military career, from Fort Necessity to his surrender of his commission to Congress. John Shy's "General Washington Reconsidered," in *The John Biggs Cincinnati Lectures in History and Command,* edited by Henry S. Bauman (Lexington, Va.: VMI Foundation, 1986), is a critical examination of Washington as tactician and strategist. Bernhard Knollenberg's *George Washington and the Revolution, A Reappraisal: Gates, Conway, and the Continental Congress* (1940, repr., Hamden, Conn.: Archon Books,

1968) concentrates on Washington's relations with those entities mentioned in the subtitle. In *President Washington's Indian War: The Struggle for the Old Northwest* (Norman: University of Oklahoma Press, 1985), Wiley Sword describes a generally neglected topic.

Curiously, President Washington has not received as much attention as that part of his career would seem to deserve. Forrest McDonald's *The Presidency of George Washington** (Lawrence: University Press of Kansas, 1974) overemphasizes Alexander Hamilton's role, making him something of a gray eminence ultimately responsible for just about everything. In *George Washington and American Constitutionalism** (Lawrence: University Press of Kansas, 1993), Glenn A. Phelps presents a more balanced picture, with a plausible interpretation of Washington as a "hidden hand" president; it is useful throughout Washington's public career. *Inventing the American Presidency,** edited by Thomas E. Cronin (Lawrence: University Press of Kansas, 1989), and *George Washington and the Origins of the American Presidency*, edited by Mark J. Rozell, William D. Pedersen, and Frank J. Williams (Westport, Conn.: Praeger, 2000), contain political scientists' essays on the topic. Simon P. Newman has interesting comments on Washington's image as a national leader in "Principles or Men? George Washington and the Political Culture of National Leadership, 1776–1801," *Journal of the Early Republic* 12 (1992): 475–507. Chapter 5 of Ralph Ketcham's *Presidents above Party: The First American Presidency, 1789–1829** (Chapel Hill: University of North Carolina Press, 1984) describes Washington's adherence to a nonpartisan, consensual ideal of the presidency. Richard Norton Smith has written what might be called a presidential biography of Washington in *Patriarch: George Washington and the New American Nation* (Boston: Houghton Mifflin, 1993), covering the period from March 1790 to December 1799.

The University of Virginia maintains a website for *The Papers of George Washington* at www.virginia.edu/gwpapers; the site contains transcripts or digital images of many Washington letters and documents, as well as illustrations and articles on various aspects of Washington's career and life or death—for example, the essay on the cause of his death by Dr. W. Wallenborn,

"George Washington's Terminal Illness: A Modern Medical Analysis of the Last Illness and Death of George Washington." The Library of Congress "American Memory" is an online resource that includes that institution's holdings of the George Washington Papers; it can be reached at www.loc.gov.americanmemory.

Index